Parental Rights in Peril

Parental

Rights

in Peril

EDITED BY STEPHEN M. KRASON

✟ Franciscan University Press

Franciscan University Press
1235 University Boulevard
Steubenville, OH 43952
740-283-3771

Distributed by:
The Catholic University of America Press
c/o HFS
P.O. Box 50370
Baltimore, MD 21211
800-537-5487

Library of Congress Cataloging-in-Publication Data
Names: Krason, Stephen M., editor.
Title: Parental rights in peril / edited by Stephen M. Krason.
Description: Steubenville, OH : Franciscan University Press, 2022. |
Includes bibliographical references and index.
Identifiers: LCCN 2022026067 | ISBN 9781736656143 (hardcover)
Subjects: LCSH: Parent and child (Law)—United States. | Children—
Legal status, laws, etc.—United States. | Home schooling—Law and
legislation—United States. | Education—parent participation—
United States. | Parent and child (Law)
Classification: LCC KF540 .P35 2022 | DDC 346.7301/7—dc23/eng/20220924
LC record available at https://lccn.loc.gov/2022026067

Design and composition by Kachergis Book Design
Printed in the United States of America.

Contents

8. The Assault on Parental Rights by Sex Education
   in the Schools   132
   CATHY RUSE

9. In Defense of Homeschooling: A Response to Critics
   of Parents' Rights to Educate Their Children   161
   JAMES R. MASON

10. The Weakening of the American Family and How It
    Has Undermined Parental Rights   177
    ALLAN C. CARLSON

11. Immutable Traits: Blackness, Poverty, and Child
    Protective Services   191
    ALLISON FOLMAR

12. False Child Abuse Allegations, the Child Protective
    System, and the Threat to Parental Rights   200
    STEPHEN M. KRASON

13. Parental Rights in the United States and Internationally:
    The Right to Determine the Values Taught to One's Child   233
    MICHAEL FARRIS

List of Contributors   247
Index   249

Preface

Parental rights have been a significant issue in American life and law for decades. To a significant degree, the undermining of and attacks on parental rights have been the result of the weakening of the family for numerous reasons and indeed the attempt to undercut the family's character and authority—even to the point of trying to change the meaning of what is a family—in American thinking, public policy, and law. While the assault on parental rights has been persistent and pronounced for some time now, it often goes unnoticed for these very reasons of the marginalization and undermining of the family, and also because there is more public and scholarly attention to other rights, such as those explicitly spelled out in the Bill of Rights. It was the crucial nature of parental rights and awareness of the serious attempts to undermine them in various arenas and ways in contemporary American life that motivated the organizing of the major conference on Parental Rights at Franciscan University in, Steubenville, Ohio, on October 15–16, 2021. Certain of the cosponsoring entities of the conference have as their purpose or one of their purposes protecting parental rights and ensuring that they are upheld. Besides the Department of Political Science and Veritas Center for Ethics in Public Life at the University, the other cosponsors were the Society of Catholic Social Scientists, which is headquartered at the university; the Alliance Defending Freedom; the Home School Legal Defense Association; and the Parental Rights Foundation. The conference speakers—whose conference presentations comprise the chapters this book—are noted authorities in the areas of parental rights that they address. This book is comprehensive in addressing many leading areas and topics in parental rights, beginning with the philosophical, historical, and legal background and then examining the nature of the multifaceted assault on parental rights in our time.

∽

Many thanks go to Franciscan University of Steubenville for hosting the conference this book emerged from and for its commitment, in line with the Catholic teaching it so firmly and avowedly embraces, to upholding the dignity of the family, of which the respect for parental rights is part. Thanks are also due to Sarah Wear and Franciscan University Press for their interest in publishing this book from the conference; to Anne Hendershott, director of the Veritas Center for her support; and to the heads of the various cosponsoring organizations: James Mason of the Parental Rights Foundation (where a conference like this was first discussed, which led to its becoming a reality), Michael Farris of the Alliance Defending Freedom, and J. Michael Smith of the Home School Legal Defense Association.

Parental Rights in Peril

1

Who Has Primary Responsibility for Rearing and Educating Children?

PATRICK LEE

Who has primary responsibility in the upbringing, direction, and education of children? What is the basis of, and what are the limits to, that primary responsibility? Some have argued that while parents should have some say in their children's education, parental authority needs frequently to be overridden for the interests of the child and for the interests of society.

For example, Elizabeth Bartholet—the Morris Wasserstein Professor of Law and faculty director of the Law School's Child Advocacy Program at Harvard Law School—argues that homeschooling is dangerous for children and recommends that states have a presumptive ban on the practice. According to Bartholet, homeschooling violates children's right to a "meaningful education," and so she believes the government should step in to override and correct widespread parental shortcomings. Speaking with obvious disapproval, Bartholet says, "We have an essentially unregulated regime in the area of home-schooling."[1]

Amy Gutman, president of the University of Pennsylvania, argues that the authority for the education of the child does not belong chiefly to parents but is shared by the parents and the state on an equal plane, and that parental judgment should frequently be overridden for the sake of ensuring and protecting a democratic, pluralistic, and tolerant society.[2]

I argue that the primary and direct responsibility for the nurturing, upbringing, and education of children belongs to the parents, and that the normal role of the state is subsidiary rather than overriding or substitutional. The state may override the immediate authority of the parents only in cases of severe neglect, abuse, or, if necessary, to protect public health and safety. And the basis of parental authority is the biological relationship itself of the parents to their children, or, in the case of adoptive parents, the lawful assumption of the parental role.

My overall argument for this position is as follows. First, the relationship between the parents and their children is a pre-political relationship, and the family is a pre-political community. These realities are not constructs of the state. Second, the nature of the family is such that the primary and immediate responsibility and authority for the love, care, and direction of children belongs to the parents. Third, the political community's—that is, the state's—rightful authority is limited by the nature of its common good, that is, the public good. Fourth, the public good does not include taking over functions that belong to smaller communities, especially natural communities, such as marriage and the family. Therefore the state acts beyond its rightful authority if it usurps the natural authority of parents—as opposed to acting with delegated authority and in an assisting or subsidiary function in the direction and education of the child.

That's the outline of the overall argument. Now to provide support and explanation of the steps in that argument.

1. Erin O'Donnell, "The Risks of Homeschooling," *Harvard Magazine* (May–June 2020): https://www.harvardmagazine.com/2020/05/right-now-risks-homeschooling. Also, see Elizabeth Bartholet, "Homeschooling: Parent Rights Absolutism vs. Child Rights to Education and Protection," *Arizona Law Review* 62, no. 1 (2020): 1–80.

2. Amy Gutman, *Democratic Education* (Princeton, NJ: Princeton University Press, 1999).

The first point is that the natural and biological relationship of a parent to his or her child grounds a special responsibility to love and care for that child. The tendency among many philosophers and our culture as a whole is to deny this point, because they tend to deny the inherent significance of any biological aspects of the human person.

Now, most of us—even those who believe the state has primary or equal responsibility for the well-being of children—still say that a parent usually has in some sense greater responsibility to his or her own children than to other people. But what is the source of this greater responsibility? To see who has primary responsibility for the care and education of children, we must see what the source of parental responsibility is and how parental responsibility compares to that of the state.

In general, a personal relationship to someone gives rise to special responsibilities—different types of responsibilities that correspond to different personal relationships. For example, a generic friendship grounds certain responsibilities to one's friend, a teacher-student relationship generates responsibilities to a student, a doctor-patient relationship to a patient, and so on.[3]

Some philosophers argue that relationships give rise to special responsibilities only if those relationships have been voluntarily assumed, so that, in effect, special responsibilities exist only if they have been at least implicitly consented to. In a famous article on abortion, Judith Thomson argued that a mother does not acquire special responsibility toward her child unless and until she chooses to bring that child home from the hospital, whereby the mother has voluntarily assumed special responsibilities to that child.[4]

But not all special responsibilities arise from someone having voluntarily assumed them, or on the basis of someone's voluntarily entering a relationship that brings with it special responsibilities. Children have special responsibilities to their parents even though they did not voluntarily assume such responsibilities or voluntarily enter into that relationship. Suppose I'm watching television at home one night, and

3. Melissa Moschella, *To Whom Do Children Belong? Parental Rights, Civic Education, and Children's Autonomy* (New York: Cambridge University Press, 2016), chap. 1.

4. See, e.g., Judith Jarvis Thomson, "A Defense of Abortion," *Philosophy and Public Affairs* 1 (1971): 47–66; reprinted, among other places, in Joel Feinberg, ed., *The Problem of Abortion*, 2nd ed. (Belmont, CA: Wadsworth, 1984).

the doorbell rings. I answer it and find a baby on my doorstep, but no one in sight who might have left the baby. In that case, I find myself with a special responsibility—I might not have a responsibility to raise the child all the way to adulthood, but it seems clear that I now do have a special responsibility to this child. And that responsibility is based on my being in the right place at the right time—that is, on a specific connection to that child—though I did not voluntarily assume that connection.

The general reason behind this point can be partly understood as follows. Human persons are not mere isolated individuals whose fulfillment is merely individualistic. On the contrary, although I am a distinct individual with distinct interests and rights, at the same time, I am by nature a member of various communities. That is, being connected or united with others in various ways, being a member of various communities, is part of who I am. Thus my own well-being partly consists of the well-being of other persons with whom I am united. And so my general moral responsibilities become specified partly by voluntarily entering into communion with other people, but also by having or acquiring various types of real connections to or unions with other people, in ways that are anterior to my voluntarily assuming or consenting to such connections.[5]

Now, some of these connections or unities are biological in nature. Much of our culture denies the importance of the bodily part of human persons. Indeed, many in our culture view the body as a mere instrument, extrinsic to the self, or even as a kind of raw stuff that lacks any inherent meaning, upon which we can therefore impose any meaning we choose.

But the human body is an integral part of the human person, for the human person is a body-soul composite, the soul related to the body as its form or principle of unity. Therefore a bodily connection or union is personal. The person—what I refer to as "I" or you refer to as "you" or "he"—is not a soul that possesses or inhabits the body. Rath-

---

5. St. Thomas argued that one ought to love more intensely those with whom one is more closely united, even though the other persons not so closely united to one might be more excellent or virtuous in themselves. Thomas Aquinas, *Summa Theologiae* (*ST*) II-II, q. 26.

er, the person—the I or he or she—is the body and the soul together, those being parts of the one human person.

A brief argument for this point is as follows. Writing with a pencil is a bodily action, since it is done with hands and fingers, just as walking is a bodily act because it is done with legs and feet. Hence the agent that performs the act of moving a pencil across a piece of paper is a bodily being. Now, everyone—including those who deny that the person is a bodily being—refers to the entity that performs the act of understanding, and is self-conscious, as "I" or the ego. But it must be the same agent, the same I, that performs the act of writing on the one hand and performs the act of understanding, and is self-conscious, on the other hand. Since the agent that writes with the pencil is a bodily being, it follows that I—the one who understands and is self-conscious—am a bodily being.[6]

Because the body is an integral part of the person, bodily connections do have inherent significance. And we become aware of this point at least implicitly in many contexts. After the mother has given birth and she is getting ready to go home from the hospital, the nurses don't simply give her whatever baby happens to be nearest the door. Rather, extensive care is taken to ensure that the mother goes home with her own biological baby. The bodily connection *matters*.

Again, the fact that people are generally selective about who they will have sex with—requiring for example, that they at least know and like who they have sex with—is best explained by our awareness that bodily sexual activity carries with it, or demands, a personal connection to go with the close bodily union or connection realized in sexual activity.[7] Sexual intercourse involves a thoroughgoing bodily *union*. The man and the woman each has only part of a reproductive system; in sexual intercourse they complete each other, becoming a whole reproductive system and the single subject of a single biological function. The two become truly organically united—truly one body, or one

6. See Patrick Lee and Robert P. George, *Body-Self Dualism in Contemporary Ethics and Politics* (New York: Cambridge University Press, 2008), chap. 1; Michael Augros, *The Immortal in You* (San Francisco: Ignatius Press, 2017), 100–117.

7. Patrick Lee and Robert P. George, *Conjugal Union: What Marriage Is and Why It Matters* (New York: Cambridge University Press, 2014), chap. 3.

flesh. This fact, and our awareness of it, at least on some level, explains why sexual activity has an inherent personal significance: biology does matter.

So, a close union with another grounds a special responsibility to that person. Now it is clear that there is a close bodily union of the parents to their children. Radical feminists are wrong to say that the embryo or fetus is merely a part of the woman's body, for the child is a distinct, actively growing, individual human being. Nevertheless, their claim is not totally groundless. The relationship is one of physical continuity or prolongation. There is a unique biological unity or continuity of children to their parents. The parents become bodily one in their sexual act—it truly is a one-flesh union, a biological union. And from that biological union the child is generated. Thus the mother and the father, and their unity, are in a certain sense prolonged and continued in their offspring.

The child comes to be from the bodily parts—the sex cells, the gametes—that come from the mother and the father. That is, the body of the new child was just moments before parts of the mother and of the father—the child coming to be from union of the sex cells from the father and from the mother. The child also receives from the union of those sex cells a genetic code that provides the fundamental, individual blueprint for the active self-development of the child all the way to her mature stage. So, although the baby is not literally a part of the mother or of the father—or at least not a *mere* part—the baby has a strong and thoroughgoing biological union with both the mother and the father. Viewing this relationship from the standpoint of the new child, we can see that the baby's specific and individual identity—who she is as a body-soul person—is bound up with her connection to her mother and her father.

Children come into the world in a needy condition. They need nurturing, care, love, and direction. Moreover, given that who they are—their unique, personal identity—is in part constituted by their connection to their own biological parents, children have a need for the love and care of their parents. And not just some parents or other, but their own parents. If the parents—one or both of them—die or abandon the child, other individuals may step in and assume at least many of the parental responsibilities, becoming real, not substituted, parents. Nevertheless, the child would still be deprived of something important, namely, the love and care of his own biological parents.

In sum, we have a special responsibility to those people with whom we have a close personal union. But we do have an intimate and thoroughgoing union that is fully personal with our children. Therefore we have a special responsibility to our children.

Note that what the child needs, and so what the parent has a special responsibility to provide, is not just that the child be nurtured, cared for, and educated, but also that the parents themselves be the ones who provide this care. The parents' responsibilities to their child are not fully transferrable to someone else. For example, as a father, I ought, if possible, to attend my son's track meets, and I could not fulfill this responsibility by hiring someone else to go in my place.[8] Hence there are two parts to a parent's responsibilities: He or she has a duty to ensure that the child receive care and education—that's part of the special responsibility to the child—but also a duty to provide these *himself* or *herself*.

Of course, the parents may enlist the assistance of others in providing for care and education for their children. Because of the limitations of their knowledge and skill, the need for at least one of them to work outside the home, and their other responsibilities, the parents will inevitably need assistance from others—perhaps schools, tutors, other role models, and so on. How much of this relying on help from others is appropriate, and not a derogation of duty to provide personal care themselves, will be a prudential matter. In any case, this outsourcing of some care to others is *delegated* responsibility and remains subsidiary to the parents' authority, direction, and approval.

Generally, a parent does not fulfill his or her responsibilities to the child if he or she *completely* hands over those tasks to others. The child needs the personal relationship with his own mother and father. But in

8. Melissa Moschella, *To Whom Do Children Belong? Parental Rights, Civic Education, and Children's Autonomy* (New York: Cambridge University Press, 2017), 34–45; Alexander Pruss, *One Body: An Essay in Christian Sexual Ethics* (South Bend, IN: University of Notre Dame Press, 2012) 381–92.

some tragic circumstances, a parent may see that he or she is unable to fulfill the duties of a parent, and in that case, handing the child over for adoption could be right thing to do. But this is not a case of actually fulfilling one's parental responsibility through another; rather, it is a case of being unable to fulfill one's parental responsibilities completely, of doing the best one can to fulfill those responsibilities partially, to the extent one is able.[9]

It is worth noting also that adoptive parents are related to the child in the genuine parental role, and the child's character would be formed in union with these parents. Therefore adoptive parents are true parents, not just similar to parents. Still, if a child loses his parents or is given up for adoption, then, although his adoptive parents may be excellent, the absence of the love and care of the child's own biological parents is still a deprivation.

The special responsibility that one has to one's biological children is to be present as a mother or father who will provide the child with the nurturing and directing—the directing of the child to his or her mature, fulfilled, and virtuous state—that she specifically needs. In other words, the responsibility one has to one's children is a structured one and has definite content. It arises from the biological relationship to the child, and this responsibility is defined by the child's own good—his or her own full development, physically, emotionally, intellectually, morally, and religiously—to the stage where she can take on the task of the principal direction or government of her life herself.

If we add to these points what we will next see about the limits of the authority of the state, it will follow that for the state to override parental authority—as opposed to providing assistance or acting with delegated authority, except for cases of parental abuse or serious neglect, or when necessary for public safety and order—is a profound injustice. To support and explain this point, I turn now to a more detailed look at the limits of the state's authority.

The state's authority does not reach in every way into every aspect of a human being's fulfillment. Like any other community, the state's authority—the legitimate scope of its action—extends only as far as its

9. Pruss, *One Body*, 385*ff*.

specific common good. And since a community is simply a multitude of people agreeing to cooperate for the sake of a common purpose, the state's specific common good is defined by the need for this community.[10]

Now, some intrinsic human goods can be pursued only in cooperation with others, and so these goods naturally require the formation of smaller, pre-political communities—friendship and marriage. In addition, other basic goods, such as health, knowledge, and play, can be pursued by us as individuals but can also frequently be more effectively pursued in communion with others. And so pursuit of such goods leads us to form other pre-political communities such as hospitals, schools, study groups, and athletic communities. We ought to form various communities, at the pre-political level, because only thus can we pursue some goods at all, and we can more effectively pursue other goods by forming such communities.

But beyond these smaller communities there is need for a wider community, a state. By a political community—a state—is meant an overarching community within a region, a community that coordinates the actions of all the individuals and of other communities within that region—an overarching community in the sense that there is no higher or more extensive temporal authority in that region—what Aristotle and Thomas Aquinas referred to as a "complete community."[11]

Now, the following activities cannot be effectively or sufficiently performed at the pre-political level, and so the common good of the state will include them: protecting the individuals and families within a region against external attacks; protection from injustices committed by other members within the region and compensation or vindication for such injustices; the coordination of the actions of the residents in the region with respect to common interests such as the exchange of goods, transportation and travel, resolution of disputes; and, impor-

10. John Finnis, *Natural Law and Natural Rights*, 2nd ed. (New York: Oxford University Press, 2011), chap. 6; Germain Grisez, *The Way of the Lord Jesus*, vol. 2, *Living a Christian Life* (Quincy, IL: Franciscan Press, 1993), 846–58; Yves Simon, *Philosophy of Democratic Government* (South Bend, IN: University of Notre Dame Press, 1993), chaps. 1–2.

11. Aristotle, *Politics*, Book I; *ST* I-II, q. 90, a. 2. Also see Finnis, *Natural Law and Natural Rights*, 147–150.

tantly, assistance for those with basic needs owing to disability or disadvantage and who will not be sufficiently cared for by individuals or by pre-political communities.

The political community, the state, is needed because there are various important goods that we cannot effectively pursue without it. The state's common good is not an additional fundamental good not already pursued in some way at the pre-political level. Rather, it is the added effectiveness and harmony in our various pursuits, made possible by coordination and action at the higher or more extensive level of common action.

Interests that *can* be just as effectively—or, most often, more effectively—pursued by pre-political groups or individuals should be pursued by them, not directly by the state. Moreover, there are interests the state is not competent directly to pursue and are inappropriate (for various reasons) for the state to do so—such as, for example, the business of matchmaking or, more significantly, religion—and so the direct participation in these goods is not part of the state's common good and does not belong to its proper authority. In sum, the proper scope of the state's action—the *public good*—includes only what can be more effectively and appropriately pursued by the state; other interests and goods or aspects of goods belong to the *private good*. The state's legitimate authority is limited to the public good.[12]

Thus the state's common good does not include the provision for its members of all benefits or the direction of every aspect of their lives. Such is the totalitarian and socialist view of government, not the natural law view I am setting out here. Rather, the chief role of the government is *subsidiary:* not chiefly to provide people with goods—though in some cases we as a political community must do that—but to set the conditions for people and pre-political communities to facilitate their own realization of the various intrinsic goods. Vatican Council II expresses this point in its document *Gaudium et Spes* as follows: "The common good embraces the sum total of all those conditions of social

---

12. Germain Grisez and Joseph Boyle, *Life and Death with Liberty and Justice* (South Bend, IN: University of Notre Dame Press, 1979), 34–55; Robert P. George, "Ruling to Serve," *First Things Magazine* (April 2013): https://www.firstthings.com/article/2013/04/ruling-to-serve.

life which enable individuals, families, and organizations to achieve fulfillment more completely and more expeditiously."[13]

As indicated above, the family is a natural and pre-political community, and it has an objective structure consequent to the nature of its own specific common good. So, the state has a duty to respect the structure of the family. The state has the duty—except where abuse or public order or safety absolutely require—not to intrude into the interior direction of the family and a duty to respect the inherent authority of the parents in this community.

The state surely has a role in setting conditions that can facilitate families pursuing family life. But its authority with respect to children and the family is limited to setting those conditions. The state's common good does not include taking over that function, making the internal functioning of the family a direct part of its purpose. This fundamental moral truth has been called "the principle of subsidiarity." It has been a central point in the social teachings of the Catholic Church, first articulated clearly by Pope Leo XIII and then repeated by popes in several important encyclicals, by the Vatican Council II, and by the *Catechism of the Catholic Church*. In 1931, in the encyclical *Quadragesimo Anno*, Pope Pius XI expressed it as follows:

Just as it is gravely wrong to take from individuals what they can accomplish by their own initiative and industry and give it to the community, so also it is an injustice and at the same time a grave evil and disturbance of right order to assign to a greater and higher association what lesser and subordinate organizations can do. For every social activity ought of its very nature to furnish help to the members of the body social, and never destroy and absorb them.[14]

Now, in fact, the state acts beyond its authority whenever it substitutes its own judgment for that of the leaders in *any* pre-political

---

13. Vatican II, *Gaudium et Spes, Pastoral Constitution of the Church in the Modern World* (Vatican City: Vatican Press, 1965), 74. This same point—that the common good is limited, consisting primarily in providing conditions for individuals, families, and other groups for themselves to attain their real fulfillment and thus that the state exists for the sake of the persons within it, in whom the common is realized—has been expressed several times by popes in their teaching on the duties of and toward political society. See, e.g., Pope Pius XII, *Summi Pontificatus*, no. 59–60; Pope John XXIII, *Mater et Magistra* no. 65; Pope John Paul II, *Centesimun Annos*, no. 37.

14. Pope Pius XI, *Quadragesimo Anno*, no. 79.

community with respect to that community's proper end—even such a community as a chess club or a bakery. For example, a bakery's common good is to provide baked goods at a fair price, with friendly service and a profit for the bakery and wages for its employees. The state can of course regulate the activities of the bakery in many ways, but only with respect to how the bakery affects the public good. The state can properly make laws and regulations to ensure honesty, public accommodation for minors, and that the bakery not unduly pollute the atmosphere. But the state would act *ultra vires*—beyond its legitimate authority—if it substituted its judgment for that of the bakery's manager in an area that directly concerns the specific common good of the bakery, for example, by setting the bakery's prices or requiring a certain quota of rye bread or sourdough bread. These would not be merely unwise acts but injustices, for the state would be depriving the baker and his or her employees of self-direction in their work, detracting from an important human good—self-fulfillment in work.

Similarly, the state may at times rightly regulate the family's internal activities, but only when they involve a clear case of abuse of a child or if they affect the broader common good, for example, if the parents were training their children to be terrorists.

The relationship between the state and the family can also be compared to the state's relationship to religion. Religion is of course an important intrinsic good, integral to the flourishing of human individuals and families, and indeed for most religious people the most central aspect of their lives. The state need not—and should not—ignore or be indifferent to religion. It is proper for the state to try to set conditions that facilitate the religious practice of individuals, families, and churches—the individuals and communities who directly pursue this good.

But the state should not intervene in the choice itself to be religious, nor should it promote this or that specific religion, nor take over the governance of religious activities to their end, which transcends the common good of the state. This is true partly for the same reason that the state should not intrude into the inner workings of a bakery, but it is more clearly true, and more urgent, because the state is not *competent* in the area of religion, and its making the religious decisions for individuals and families is inappropriate. Religion is the harmony or friendship with God—a relationship that is by its nature voluntary. And so it is not appropriately directly pursued by the state, since membership in the state is not fully voluntary (which political community one can be a member of is usually largely determined by one's location).

By analogy, the raising and governance of a child are tasks for which the parents are especially suited, and the state especially *unsuit-*ed. The creation of a *home*—a place of love, care, warmth, discipline, focused on cultivating the interior as well as the external development of the person—is a voluntary and deeply personal task or mission that is not performed well by the larger and less personal political community. The duty or service to the child by the parent is irreplaceable, as the state simply cannot fulfill what the parent can and is obligated to do.

So, the state damages intrinsic goods if it acts beyond its legitimate authority in two different ways. First, it might harm the community by substituting unwise or inappropriate direction for the more reliable direction of those closer to and more personally related to the members of a pre-political community. The state could damage health by substituting its own more distant judgment for the more up-close judgments of a hospital or a gym, or by imposing misleading or false information about health.

Second, by intruding and substituting its own authority for the proper authority of the specific pre-political community, it undermines the rightful authority for that community and to that extent degrades that community. This is important with respect to any community, but it is crucial in regard to the family, where the community itself is a distinct type of intrinsic good and where the personal authority of the parents is vital for the well-being of children.

As the Second Vatican Council taught:

Since parents have given children their life, they are bound by the most serious obligation to educate their offspring and therefore must be recognized as the primary and principal educators. This role in education is so important that only with difficulty can it be supplied where it is lacking. Parents are the ones who must create a family atmosphere animated by love and respect for God and man, in which the well-rounded personal and social education of children is fostered.[15]

In sum, the legitimate authority of the state is limited. The proper role of the state is to set the conditions that facilitate individuals, families, and other pre-political communities to realize their own genuine fulfillment. The family is a natural and pre-political community and is itself a distinct form of intrinsic good. It has an objective structure consequent to the nature of its common good, which is the development and education of children to their true and mature fulfillment. So, the state has a duty to respect the structure of the family. The responsibility and authority of parents in relation to their children are grounded in the nature of the personal relationship itself of the parents to their children. So, the state has the duty—except where abuse or public order and safety absolutely require—not to intrude into the interior direction of the family, and to respect the inherent authority of the parents for this community.

15. Second Vatican Councli, *Gravissimum Educationis, Declaration on Christian Educations*, no. 3.

2

A Legal Overview and History of Parental Rights in the United States

MICHAEL P. DONNELLY

Among the most famous of phrases ever penned by a US court regarding family rights are the timeless words from *Pierce v. Society of Sisters* (1925), written by Justice McReynolds on behalf of a unanimous Supreme Court: "The child is not the mere creature of the State; those who nurture him and direct his destiny have the right, coupled with the high duty, to recognize and prepare him for additional obligations."

Although written in the context of education, *Pierce* was one of the first cases in which the Supreme Court employed what has become known as substantive due process, asserting itself into reviewing state laws in areas of governmental authority previously exercised exclusively by the states. Since *Pierce*, the court has recognized the role of parents in child-rearing as being "established beyond debate as an enduring American tradition," that there is a presumption that fit parents act in the "best interests of their children," and that there is "normally no reason for the State to inject itself into the private realm of the family to further question fit parents' ability to make the best decisions regarding their children."[1] Through the theory (or some would say doctrine) of substantive due process, the Supreme Court has determined that it will review situations in which society (acting through legislative, executive, and judicial branches) interferes with parental decisions.

The issue of parents' rights has become increasingly relevant as the modern state has increasingly intruded in family matters, passing laws at both the state and federal levels regarding children's matters in the areas of education, health, and welfare. Issues related to the composition of families have also morphed with the increase in divorce, cohabitation, and the redefinition of marriage. Increases in procreative-related procedures such as in vitro fertilization, surrogacy, abortion, and sex alteration protocols have added further complexity to the definition and interest of parental rights. In this limited space, we cannot delve into detail on any of these weighty and complex issues. Rather, we skim the surface of selected major issues and trends, primarily through the sharply focused lens of judicial conflict. We also focus on the modern history of parental rights beginning around the time of *Pierce*. We focus on federal court opinions (mostly at the Supreme Court level) because they have become definitive and, through the doctrine of substantive due process, authoritative.

The Modern Chapter

Through the court's creation and use of "substantive due process," the pronouncements of the US Supreme Court have become the weightiest authority in defining legal boundaries and principles when it comes to parental rights. This concept demands at least some introduction and discussion because the US Constitution makes no explicit mention of "parental rights" beyond the Ninth Amendment (which asserts that rights not enumerated in the Constitution are not "dispar-

---

1. See *Wisconsin v. Yoder*, 406 U.S. 205, 232; *Parham v. J. R.*, 442 U.S. 584, 602, and *Reno v. Flores*, 507 U.S. 292, 304.

aged" thereby) and the Tenth Amendment (which states that "powers" not delegated to the federal government nor prohibited thereto are reserved either to the states or the people). Although states exert primary influence over family law through the general police power, federal courts, because of Supreme Court jurisprudence, have taken a supreme supervisory role over adjudicating disputes whether government has interfered with parental rights.

Parental rights is only one area of law not explicitly mentioned in the US Constitution in which the Supreme Court has involved itself under the judicially invented doctrine of "substantive due process." The phrase derives from Section One of the Fourteenth Amendment, which states that "all persons born or naturalized in the United States, and subject to the jurisdiction thereof, are citizens of the United States and of the state wherein they reside. No state shall make or enforce any law which shall abridge the privileges or immunities of citizens of the United States; nor shall any state deprive any person of life, liberty, or property, without *due process* of law; nor deny to any person within its jurisdiction the equal protection of the laws" (emphasis added). Section Five of the Fourteenth Amendment grants Congress the power to enforce the amendment through legislation, although Congress has rarely referenced the section specifically in its lawmaking activities.[2]

The Fourteenth Amendment was passed shortly after the Civil War and was intended to protect freed slaves from being treated disparately (the Equal Protection Clause) and from being deprived of "life, liberty, or property without due process of law." Justice Stevens in *Daniels v. Williams* describes the function of this modern doctrine this way: "First, it incorporates [against the states] specific protections defined in the Bill of Rights ... Second, it contains a substantive component sometimes referred to as 'substantive due process' ... Third, it is a guarantee of fair procedure, sometimes referred to as 'procedural due process.'"

With the doctrine of incorporation, or, as some describe it, "selective incorporation," the court began to apply selected provisions of the

2. Ronald D. Rotunda, "The Powers of Congress under Section 5 of the Fourteenth Amendment after *City of Boerne v. Flores*," *Indiana Law Review* 32, no. 1 (1998).

Bill of Rights against state governments. This was an obvious change from the founding era because in 1833 the Supreme Court had affirmed that the Bill of Rights applied only to the federal government (see *Barron v. City of Baltimore*). Incorporation began thirty years *after* the ratification of the Fourteenth Amendment with *Chicago, Burlington and Quincey Railroad Co.* (1897). Here, the Supreme Court "incorporated" the requirements of the Fifth Amendment, holding that due process pursuant to the Fourteenth Amendment required a state government to provide just compensation when taking private property for public use. About twenty-five years later, in *Gitlow v. New York* (1925), the court "incorporated" the Free Speech Clause of the First Amendment to apply to the state of New York (and thereby all other states). In *Palko v. Connecticut* (1937) the court first used the term "selective incorporation." Since then, the court has continued to incorporate most of the substantive rights of the Bill of Rights. In 2010, in *MacDonald v. Chicago*, the court "incorporated" the Second Amendment to apply to the states.

Historically, "due process" had been defined by the court to be primarily "procedural." That is, states that exercise a general police power may interfere with a person's life (e.g., capital punishment), liberty (e.g., arrest and imprisonment), or property (e.g., confiscation of contraband or eminent domain) so long as the person received due process. Due process meant that a person essentially had a fair hearing, notice of the hearing, an opportunity to present witnesses, and in criminal cases was presumed innocent. Commentators and courts use the term "substantive" to distinguish certain court decisions from this more "procedural" due process. Essentially, the court's doctrine of "substantive due process" presumes it may interpret the term "liberty" in the Fourteenth Amendment to include substantive rights. This is distinct from procedural rights such as right to a speedy jury trial, right to have notice and opportunity to be heard, right to confront accusers, right to an attorney, and similar protections that relate to the procedures used by the government when interfering with a citizen's life, liberty, or property.

Among the first examples of the court's substantive use of the term liberty in the Fourteenth Amendment was the court's establishment of the "liberty to contract" in the 1905 case *Lochner v. New York*, where the court invalidated state labor laws on the grounds that individuals had a freedom to contract, with which the state was proscribed from interfering. *Lochner* was overruled by the 1937 case *West Coast Hotel v. Parrish*, where the court reacted to Franklin D. Roosevelt's proposed "court packing" plan to uphold the National Labor Relations Act. Recently, substantive due process has been used to define new rights in controversial areas of so-called abortion rights (*Roe v. Wade* and *Planned Parenthood v. Casey*), homosexual conduct (*Lawrence v. Texas*), and marriage (*Obergefell v. Hodges*). Conversely, in *Washington v. Glucksburg*, the court declined to find the right to assisted suicide under substantive due process.

The history of substantive due process is relevant to parental rights because the US Supreme Court exercises judicial review over cases or controversies arising under the US Constitution. This means that the court, having determined that parental rights are included in the doctrine of substantive due process, decides what parental rights are, when they count, and when any governmental act—whether state or federal, executive or legislative—that allegedly interferes with parental rights is valid. Prior to the development of these various doctrines, states exercised plenary power over this area of law without interference or "oversight" by the federal judiciary.

The Modern Administrative State

The rise of the modern administrative state helps to explain why the issue of parental rights has become more relevant. States continue to be the primary locus of legislative, regulatory, and judicial action related to the family, partly in response to federal action as described below and partly resulting from general government expansion in all areas. In response to the latter issue, state legislatures have become more active in recognizing and protecting parental rights. Eleven states have statutes that define and protect parental rights, and thirty state courts have applied strict scrutiny to parental rights claims.

Some legislatures, like those in Michigan and Arizona, have simply passed short statements recognizing that parental rights are fundamental and are due the highest judicial protection.[3] These statutes establish for their courts the Supreme Court's strict scrutiny formula. (The state must have a compelling interest, and the state's action must meet the least restrictive means test.) In other states such as Florida, lengthy descriptive statutes lay out specific protections to parents in the areas of education, health care decision-making, data collection, biometric data usage, and more. [4]

The federal government, through both legislation and administrative rulemaking, has gained dramatic power over parental rights. Although the Constitution does not give the federal government authority over parental rights, at least as an enumerated power subject to lawmaking by Congress, the courts have allowed Congress to spend money for virtually any purpose that "promotes the general welfare." Through funding initiatives, Congress incentivizes states to adopt desired policy measures in areas where it lacks legislative authority pursuant to its enumerated powers under the US Constitution. By conditioning the receipt of hundreds of millions of dollars of "grants" on states' passing laws, Congress is able to federalize large swaths of state power.

Some argue this strategy creates predictability and uniformity beneficial to the nation, while others object to it as an unconstitutional workaround that undermines state sovereignty and impedes the "laboratory of democracy" that dual federalism allows when states attempt different approaches. Theoretically, states could eschew the money, and in recent years some have attempted to refuse the grants, but most have been unable to just say no.

One such federal program that uses congressional spending power to give grants to states that comply with certain provisions is the Child Abuse Prevention and Treatment Act (CAPTA). Two of CAPTA's more significant provisions are the requirement that states create mandato-

3. Ariz. Rev. Stat. § 1–601; Mich. Comp. Laws Ann. § 380.10.
4. Florida Legislature, HB 241 Enrolled Bill, June 18, 2021, https://www.myfloridahouse .gov/Sections/Documents/loaddoc.aspx?FileName=_ho241er.docx&DocumentType=Bill& BillNumber=0241&Session=2021.

ry reporter laws and enable anonymous reporting of suspected child abuse and neglect. States must also report certain data to the federal government, which then keeps statistics about child abuse and neglect. For example, according to the 2019 child maltreatment report, 6 million children were the subject of reports of abuse or neglect.

The creation of large child protective agencies with swarms of social workers to investigate suspected abuse or neglect, along with the use of family courts with civil versus criminal law procedures, has contributed to increasing alarm of governmental overreach into families. Although states have their own definitions of abuse and neglect, the statistics show that 90 percent of reports relate to neglect, the definition of which can be vague, while only 10 percent of reports reflect abuse. The federal statistics also show that almost 90 percent of investigated allegations end up being classified as unfounded. What this means is that 90 percent of families are subjected to intrusive, scary—even sometimes traumatic—unwarranted state intrusions.

Although CAPTA does require that states train their workers on the constitutional rights of the people they investigate, most states do not effectively fulfill this requirement, nor does the federal government prioritize it for grant review. Therefore asserting one's constitutional rights in such circumstances sometimes results in harsher retaliatory responses from agencies, and many people are simply unaware of their constitutional rights.

The perception that child abuse is rampant and the publicizing of health providers' (and others') duty to report "suspected abuse" has resulted in high numbers of unfounded reports of child abuse. Now it is not unusual for routine trips to the doctor's office or a trip to an emergency room for a minor injury to result in a potentially traumatic conflict between state child protective service agents and families.[5]

The extent, frequency, and character of government intervention in family decision-making, to assert objections to certain parental behavior or to investigate suspected abuse or neglect, have increased as states and federal agencies have created laws, regulations, and pro-

5. Diane L. Redleaf, *They Took the Kids Last Night: How the Child Protection System Puts Families at Risk* (Santa Barbara, CA: ABC Clio, 2018).

grams targeted at serving what these agencies call vulnerable children. While government should protect children from harm at the hands of caregivers or others, the methods by which government agencies do this have been heavily criticized.

On the one hand are the interests of parents in the care, custody, and control of their minor children—as well as the interests of the children to be subject to the care, custody, and control of their parents. On the other hand are the interests of children to be protected when their parents or other caregivers inflict harm or create a serious risk of harm. The perceived authority of Child Protective Services (CPS) to take children whenever they want terrifies parents, and a visit by CPS can be a frightening encounter. Even when, as is often the case, CPS investigators are professional and assure subjects of an investigation that they do not intend to remove children, the specter of the government's power and the intrusive nature of the interaction are highly unsettling to virtually everyone.

I have personally assisted thousands of families facing CPS investigations and have been on the phone with them during tense moments of an investigation. Sometimes, CPS investigators alone can be highly intimidating, but when they bring police officers with them (even if police are there simply for the potential safety of the investigator), the pressure skyrockets and creates a stress- and fear-inducing situation for any normal person. During initial interactions the CPS investigator often shows up unannounced, and the parents have no idea why he is demanding they admit him into their home, answer numerous personal questions, produce their children for one-on-one interviews, or consent to a strip search (even if the allegations have nothing to do with physical abuse).[6]

This is just one area that reflects the conflict between parents and the state. But the wrongful removal of a child from the care and protection from his parents is any parent's worst nightmare. In the following sections we explore the development of the court's jurisprudence related to parental rights.

6. For a helpful treatment of this subject in more detail and discussion of the impact of CAPTA, see Stephen M. Krason, ed., *Child Abuse, Family Rights, and the Child Protective System: A Critical Analysis from Law, Ethics, and Catholic Social Teaching* (Lanham, MD: Scarecrow Press, 2013).

The Court's Opinions

Education

Government involvement in education dates to the very founding of the republic, although some states were more hands-on than others. For example, the Massachusetts Bay Colony passed several laws in 1642 and 1648[7] requiring that children be educated, primarily to ensure that children grew up able to read the Bible, a primary school text. In 1850, Massachusetts established the first compulsory school attendance law, and by 1918, all states had passed compulsory attendance laws. As of 2021, all states still have compulsory attendance laws, and many have ongoing efforts to expand the reach of these laws to younger ages and for longer periods.[8]

That education is not mentioned in the Constitution has not stopped Congress from passing all kinds of laws (mostly exercising its spending powers as liberally construed by the Supreme Court): free and reduced lunch programs; the Individuals with Disabilities Education Act (IDEA); and a series of elementary and secondary laws such as the serial reauthorization of the 1965 Elementary and Secondary Education Act (ESEA), No Child Left Behind Act, and its successor, the Every Student Succeeds Act. Federalization has extended to virtually every aspect of education through application of incorporation and substantive due process doctrine to cases relating to school funding, voucher and charter schools, graduation requirements, freedom of (or, as some might argue, freedom from) religion, college affirmative action, dress codes, sports participation by gender dysphoric children, and more.[9]

Since *Brown v. Board of Education* and Congress's increasing legislative activity in education, there have been thousands of federal cas-

---

7. Michael S. Katz, *A History of Compulsory Attendance Laws*, Fastback Series No. 75, Bicentennial Series. Bloomington, IL: Phi Delta Kappa, 1976. https://eric.ed.gov/?id=ED119389.

8. Cassidy Francis and Zeke Perez, "50-State Comparison: Free and Compulsory School Age Requirements," Education Commission of the States, August 19, 2020, https://www.ecs.org/50-state-comparison-free-and-compulsory-school-age-requirements/.

9. Carolyn Jefferson-Jenkins and Margaret Hawkins Hill, "Role of Federal Government in Public Education: Historical Perspectives," League of Women Voters, June 22, 2011, https://www.lwv.org/role-federal-government-public-education-historical-perspectives.

es involving education. Building on *Meyer v. Nebraska* (1923), which had invalidated a Nebraska prohibition on instruction in any language but English, the Supreme Court in *Pierce v. Society of Sisters* (1925) invalidated an Oregon voter initiative that prohibited the operation of private schools and mandated that virtually all children attend the state's public schools. In both cases the court applied the Fourteenth Amendment's Due Process Clause to hold that the right of parents to direct their children's education was fundamental and protected from state intrusion by a high standard of judicial scrutiny.

In *Wisconsin v. Yoder* (1972) the court further held that Amish parents who were religiously motivated to stop sending their children to public school after the eighth grade were exempt from the application of compulsory attendance laws. The majority reasoned that the parents' interest in the free exercise of their religion was stronger than the state's interest in the education of the Amish children. In *Yoder* the court asserted that "the history and culture of Western civilization reflect a strong tradition of parental concern for the nurture and upbringing of their children. This primary role of the parents in the upbringing of their children is now established beyond debate as an enduring American tradition."

This respect for the religious convictions of parents was undermined somewhat, however, in *Employment Division v. Smith* (1990). In *Smith*, Justice Scalia wrote for a majority that laws of general applicability that were neutral on their face (such as the compulsory attendance laws at issue in *Yoder*) would no longer be subject to strict scrutiny if challenged by a religious freedom claim. Scalia distinguished the outcome in *Yoder* without overruling *Yoder* because it was, he reasoned, a "hybrid" claim of religious freedom plus parental rights. The holding in *Smith* overturned decades of cases that had treated religious freedom claims as worthy of judicial examination. In response to the case, Congress passed (almost unanimously) the Religious Freedom Restoration Act (RFRA), which reinstated strict scrutiny of religious freedom claims even if laws are neutral on their face and apply to all.[10]

10. In *Boerne v. Flores* (1997) the court ruled that Congress exceeded its authority under federalism by applying RFRA to the states and had violated the court's supreme authority to

Smith has been criticized, and at least three of the conservative members of the court have signaled that they are ready to revisit its "severe" rule that "overturned forty years of precedent."[11]

But while parents might have the fundamental right to exempt their children from public education, once a child is enrolled in a public school, their rights have been increasingly subject to federal action as courts have permitted virtually unchecked federal intrusion into state education policy. Starting in the 1960s, Congress began passing laws under its spending clause powers to co-opt state policy either by conditioning grant eligibility on a state's passing certain laws or policies or by mandating certain rules for any institution receiving virtually any kind of federal funding. A cornerstone of President Lyndon B. Johnson's War on Poverty, the assault on federalism in education began with the first Elementary and Secondary Education Act, or ESEA, which has been expanded every time it is reauthorized. Through its rules, ESEA has given the federal government and the Department of Education virtually plenary power over vast swaths of education policy for every single school in the country.[12] The various "titles" of the law include funding for (and concomitantly regulations relating to) reading programs, bilingual education, privacy rights of students and parents' rights to access records (through the Family Educational Rights and Privacy Act, or FERPA), education for individuals with disabilities (IDEA, which prescribes due process protections for parents and children), school libraries, education for gifted and talented children, prohibition of sex-based discrimination in schools, testing and accountability (No Child Left Behind), and common core standards (Every Student Succeeds Act).

Title IX has become of concern to many parents because it poten-

---

determine the meaning of the Constitution's religious freedom protections, but RFRA would still apply to the federal government.

11. Andrea Picciotti-Bayer, "From the Court, a Vindication of Faith-Based Service. From Alito, a Blueprint for the Future," SCOTUS Blog, June 18, 2021, https://www.scotusblog.com/2021/06/from-the-court-a-vindication-of-faith-abaed-service-from-alito-a-bblueprint-for-the-future/.

12. For a helpful history of the ESEA and its various reauthorizations, see Catherine Paul, "Elementary and Secondary Education Act of 1965," VCU Libraries Social Welfare History Project, accessed June 21, 2021, https://socialwelfare.library.vcu.edu/programs/education/elementary-and-secondary-education-act-of-1965/.

tially exposes their children to situations where males and females will be permitted, or required, to mix in previously sex-segregated settings, such as locker rooms and bathrooms. The Civil Rights Division of the US Department of Justice (DOJ) issued a memorandum asserting that the Supreme Court's ruling in *Bostock v. Clayton County* (2020), which concluded that discrimination "because of sex" includes "gender identity," also "informs" the application of Title IX in schools. The DOJ points to appellate cases in Fourth, Sixth, Seventh, and Eleventh Circuit decisions supporting the general premise that Title IX applies to so-called transgender children being discriminated against on the basis of their "gender identity."[13]

Courts have generally found that parents do not have the right to interfere with the general operation of schools, including the selection of specific materials or content to be used for the education of their children. Over the years, however, parents have objected to a variety of content because it violates their religious convictions or those of their children, or because it interferes with their ability to raise their children in accordance with their convictions.

In response to parental concerns relating to the teaching of sensitive issues, twenty-five states have passed laws that require prior notice when sex education is being provided, five states require parental consent before children may receive instruction in sex education, and thirty-six states allow parents to opt out of the instruction for their children.[14] Other than state provisions for opting out, however, the courts have firmly insisted that parents' rights regarding input on content their children are exposed to are virtually nonexistent, primarily because parents can choose to send their children to private schools or to homeschool them.

In *Mozert v. Hawkins* (1987)[15] the Sixth Circuit ruled that students, whose parents brought the religious freedom claims on their behalf,

13. Pamela S. Karlan, "Memorandum for Federal Agency Civil Rights Directors and General Counsels, Application of Bostock v. Clayton County to Title IX of the Education Amendments of 1972," March 26, 2021, https://www.justice.gov/crt/page/file/1383026/download.

14. National Conference of State Legislators (NCSL), "State Policies on Sex Education in Schools," NCSL website, October 1, 2020, https://www.ncsl.org/research/health/state-policies-on-sex-education-in-schools.aspx.

15. 827 F.2d 1058.

exposed to reading materials that offended their religious beliefs were not entitled to prohibit the school from using the reading materials when parents had the legal option of either homeschooling or matriculating in a private school. The *Mozert* decision distinguished the rights at issue from those in *Yoder*:

> The parents in *Yoder* were required to send their children to some school that prepared them for life in the outside world or face official sanctions. The parents in the present case want their children to acquire all the skills required to live in modern society. They also want to have them excused from exposure to some ideas they find offensive. Tennessee offers two options to accommodate this latter desire. The plaintiff parents can either send their children to church schools or private schools, as many of them have done, or teach them at home. Tennessee law prohibits any state interference in the education process of church schools.[16]

In *Mozert* the court pointed out that the US Supreme Court, in *Bethel v. Fraser* (1986),[17] held that parents could not interfere with the experts operating the public schools because this would impede the purpose of teaching fundamental values "essential to a democratic society."[18] The court asserted that these values "include tolerance of divergent political and religious views" while taking into account "consideration of the sensibilities of others."[19] Previously, in *Ambach v. Norwick* (1979),[20] the court cited the works of J. Dewey, N. Edwards, and H. Richey for the proposition that schools are rightly viewed as an "assimilative force" that brings together "diverse and conflicting elements" in our society "on a broad but common ground."[21]

But citing Dewey for the proposition of advancing tolerance is like saying that foxes want chickens to be "tolerant" of their presence in the henhouse. John Dewey was an ardent proponent of secular humanism and viewed schools as a means to advance his pragmatic or instrumentalist philosophy that rejected "immutable truth." For Dewey, ed-

16. 827 F.2d, at 1067.
17. 478 U.S. 675.
18. 827 F.2d 1058, 1068.
19. Id., at 1068.
20. 441 U.S. 68.
21. Id., at 77.

ucation was all about the "regulation of the process of coming to share in the social consciousness; and that the adjustment of individual activity on the basis of this social consciousness is the only sure method of social reconstruction."[22]

This view that parents do not have a right to direct their children's education *in schools* was also affirmed by the First Circuit in *Parker v. Hurley* (2008).[23] The Parkers objected to their kindergarten-aged children being exposed to the reading of books that they argued sought to normalize homosexual "marriage." The court surveyed the circuits and found ample support for the position that parents do not have this right and stated that there was no Supreme Court jurisprudence to the contrary.

The right of parents to homeschool has never been presented to the Supreme Court but has been the subject of state-level judicial, legislative, and executive action. For a discussion of homeschooling and the parental rights issues implicated, see chapter 9, by James R. Mason, in this volume. Few debate the importance of the role of parents in the lives of their children. Although few object to parents' homeschooling, a small cadre of intellectuals do. They tend to see the state as preeminent in the lives of children and argue on ideological grounds primarily.[24]

Health Care

Generally, courts have recognized the need for parents to be involved in providing informed consent for medical care for minors. This is usually not disputed, except where abortion advocates have sought to aggressively shield minors from their parents' involvement. Since the Supreme Court's usurpation of states' authority to regulate abortion with the increasingly controversial decision in *Roe v. Wade*, abor-

22. Jo Ann Boydston, ed., *John Dewey: The Early Works, 1882–1898, 1895–1898. Early Essays* (Carbondale: Southern Illinois University Press, 2008), 93.

23. 514 F.3d 87.

24. James G. Dwyer and Shawn F. Peters, *Homeschooling: The History and Philosophy of a Controversial Practice* (Chicago: University of Chicago Press, 2019). See also Elizabeth Bartholet, "Homeschooling: Parent Rights Absolutism vs. Child Rights to Education and Protection," *Arizona Law Review* 62, no. 1 (2020).

tion has been among the most contentious and litigated issues on the court's docket. Although the court has invalidated laws it considers too restrictive, however, over time, it has acknowledged the importance of parental involvement in this area as well.

The idea that the taking of a human life is considered "health or medical care" is abhorrent to many. In 1973 the Supreme Court federalized the "right to an abortion" in *Roe v. Wade*, concluding it was part of a "zone of privacy" that the court created in *Griswold v. Connecticut* just eight years earlier. The court's federalization of this issue via its use of the Fourteenth Amendment's asserted substantive due process power subjects the states to ongoing supervision by the Supreme Court. This limitation on the states' sovereign police power to protect the lives of unborn human beings has been the subject of regular legislation and litigation ever since *Roe* was decided. Abortion continues to be challenged and litigated with increasing frequency. Justice Amy Coney Barrett declined to call *Roe* a "super precedent," unlike other cases she wrote about in a Texas law review article.[25] During her confirmation hearings, she said that *Roe* is not super precedent because "calls for it to be overturned have not ceased," unlike other cases such as *Brown v. Board of Education*.[26] In 2021, there were twenty-three cases pending in federal courts, mostly challenging states' continuing pressure to restrict abortion practices.

A 1979 plurality opinion in *Bellotti v. Baird*[27] held that a Massachusetts statute that required parental consent *or* judicial approval was an unreasonable constraint on the ability of underage girls who wanted to abort their unborn children:

As we held in *Planned Parenthood of Central Missouri v. Danforth*, "the State may not impose a blanket provision ... requiring the consent of a parent or person in loco parentis as a condition for abortion of an unmarried minor during the first 12 weeks of her pregnancy." Although ... such deference to

25. Amy Coney-Barret, "Precedent and Jurisprudential Disagreement," *Texas Law Review* 91, no. 1711 (2012–13).

26. Morgan Phillips, "Barrett Says *Roe v. Wade* Is Not a 'Super Precedent' That Cannot Be Overturned," Fox News, October 13, 2020, https://www.foxnews.com/politics/barrett-roe-v-wade-not-super-precedent-that-cannot-be-overturned.

27. 443 U.S. 622.

parents may be permissible with respect to other choices facing a minor, the unique nature and consequences of the abortion decision make it inappropriate "to give a third party an absolute, and possibly arbitrary, veto over the decision of the physician and his patient to terminate the patient's pregnancy, regardless of the reason for withholding the consent." We therefore conclude that if the State decides to require a pregnant minor to obtain one or both parents' consent to an abortion, it also must provide an alternative procedure whereby authorization for the abortion can be obtained.[28]

In *H.L. v. Matheson* (1981),[29] the Supreme Court ruled 6 to 3 regarding a Utah law requiring that prior to undertaking an abortion on an unemancipated minor, a medical person must notify a parent "whenever possible." The law did not give a formal "veto" or require parents to give informed consent, in contrast to the statute challenged in *Bellotti*, and the court determined that mere notification was at least reasonable, if not desirable. "We have recognized that *parents* have an important 'guiding role' to play in the upbringing of their children … which presumptively includes counseling them on important decisions."[30]

In *Hodgson v. Minnesota* (1990)[31] the court ruled that a forty-eight-hour waiting period with a two-parent notification requirement was unconstitutional because it did not "further any legitimate state interest."[32] But the court reaffirmed a long-standing view that children are subject to the care, custody, and control of their parents for good reason:

The State has a strong and legitimate interest in the welfare of its young citizens, whose immaturity, inexperience, and lack of judgment may sometimes impair their ability to exercise their rights wisely … That interest, which justifies … state-imposed requirements that a minor obtain his or her parent's consent before undergoing an operation, marrying, or entering military service … extends also to the minor's decision to terminate her pregnancy.[33]

28. Id., at 634.
29. 450 U.S. 398.
30. Id., at 411 (emphasis added).
31. 497 U.S. 417.
32. Id., at 451.
33. Id., at 445–446.

The issue of parental involvement in abortions was again litigated in *Ayotte v. Planned Parenthood* (2006).[34] In *Ayotte*, a New Hampshire law called the Parental Notification Prior to Abortion Act prohibited a physician from performing an abortion on a pregnant minor (or a woman for whom a guardian or conservator has been appointed) until forty-eight hours after written notice of the pending abortion was delivered to a parent or guardian. The court found that the act was not unconstitutional and provided for sufficient exceptions to address certain rare potentially problematic situations when a parent or guardian could not be located or an abortion was considered an "emergency."

The issue of parental consent is not limited to abortion, however. Since the court decided *Jacobson v. Massachusetts* (1905),[35] it has been established that state governments may require that individuals be vaccinated or be subject to sanctions. This has come to include a nearly universal standard that children who attend public schools be vaccinated in accordance with some state schedule of certain immunizations.

States have also nearly universally provided for parents to exempt their children from immunizations for medical, religious, philosophical, conscientious, or other reasons. Until 2019, only West Virginia and Mississippi prohibited nonmedical exemptions for attendance at public school. Since 2019, four additional states have passed laws removing religious or conscientious exemptions from immunization as a requirement for attending public schools, including California (2015), Maine (2019), New York (2019), and Connecticut (2021).[36]

It is one thing to remove the availability of an exemption for religious reasons. It is quite another thing to affirmatively deceive parents, hiding from them the truth that their children have been immunized without their knowledge or consent and prohibiting notification even when parents have obtained a lawful exemption. This is what is accomplished by the District of Columbia Minor Consent for Vaccinations

34. 540 U.S. 320.
35. 197 U.S. 11.
36. National Conference of State Legislatures, "States with Religious and Philosophical Exemptions from School Immunization Requirements," NCLS website, April 30, 2021, https://www.ncsl.org/research/health/ school-immunization-exemption-state-laws.aspx.

Amendment Act of 2020. The act allows a minor who is 11 years of age or older to consent to receive a vaccine if the minor can meet the informed consent standard; proscribes medical providers from informing parents about the vaccination; denies access to medical records containing the child's vaccination information if the child receives a vaccination without the informed consent of the parent; and even applies when a parent has lawfully exempted a child from vaccination.

Parentalrights.org and Children's Health Defense have filed a lawsuit asserting that the act both violates federal law and deprives parents of their fundamental right to direct the upbringing of their children in violation of the US Constitution. With respect to federal law, the complaint asserts that the National Childhood Vaccine Injury Compensation Act of 1986 is preemptive and supreme, and it requires that health care providers provide parents or legal representatives of any child the vaccine information sheets. The complaint asserts that the affirmative exclusion of parents from notification as well as giving informed consent violates the constitution's substantive due process protections as described above.

Parham v. J. R. (1979)[37] reviewed procedures of Georgia hospitals that cared for minors who were voluntarily committed by their parents for mental health care. The court denied a class action lawsuit demanding an adversarial procedure to approve and maintain a commitment in the face of Georgia law that required review by a professional for the same purpose. The court did rule that a deprivation of liberty of this nature requires third-party review but affirmed the existing procedures were sufficient because "the parent or guardian is presumed to be acting in that person's [the child's] best interests."[38] The court said:

The law's concept of the family rests on a presumption that parents possess what a child lacks in maturity, experience, and capacity for judgment required for making life's difficult decisions. More important, historically it has recognized that natural bonds of affection lead parents to act in the best interests of their children.[39]

37. 442 U.S. 584.
38. Id., at 623.
39. Id., at 602.

Custody/Control/Management

Despite the Supreme Court's long-standing recognition that parents are important in the education and health of their children, other areas of parental decision-making that the court has adjudicated indicate some concern that the court's willingness to protect the family from state intervention is wavering. Most recently, *Troxel v. Granville* (2000) was a plurality decision that held only that "special weight" must be given to parental decision-making in the context of third-party visitation. In this section, we explore issues where there is no dispute between parents but rather between the undisputed parent(s) and third parties or the state itself. (In cases where parents are unable to agree, it is necessary that some decision be made as to what is in the best interests of the child. These cases are beyond the scope of this chapter.)

Although the Supreme Court continues to affirm the fundamental value of parental rights, the court has been willing to uphold state action restricting parental decision-making. In *Prince v. Massachusetts* (1943),[40] a mother was convicted of violating child labor laws for allowing her child to accompany her while she was street preaching and distributing Jehovah's Witness religious materials. Despite acknowledging parental rights, the court cited the state's *parens patriae* role, which can curtail parental authority in certain situations:

The family itself is not beyond regulation in the public interest, as against a claim of religious liberty. And neither rights of religion nor rights of parenthood are beyond limitation. Acting to guard the general interest in youth's well being, the state as *parens patriae* may restrict the parent's control by requiring school attendance, regulating or prohibiting the child's labor and in many other ways. Its authority is not nullified merely because the parent grounds his claim to control the child's course of conduct on religion or conscience.[41]

One of the most significant areas of intrusion in the family is when the state intervenes pursuant to a report of abuse or neglect. Although few dispute a legitimate state role to intervene to protect children from

40. 321 U.S. 804.
41. *Prince*, id. at 166–167.

harm, state-level changes in child abuse and neglect programs resulting from CAPTA have steadily increased cases and conflict between parents and child protective agencies.[42]

In Fiscal Year 2019, 7.9 million children were the subject of allegations of abuse or neglect. Of these, 3.5 million were the subject of state-level investigations. Out of these children, 251,000 (more than 7 percent) were removed at least temporarily from their homes. Nearly 500,000 children at any given time are in state custody. Of the more than 200,000 children who "received foster care services," a third were classified as "non-victims."[43] Abuse is not the major contributor to the state removing children to foster care. Rather, allegations of neglect or parental drug use are the basis for most reported child foster care entry.[44] This is problematic, as definitions of neglect can often be vague and subjective.

The trauma to children and families for unnecessary removal is significant, but unfortunately it has not been a major focus of child welfare policy discussion or practical experience. According to federal statistics, at least two-thirds of reports are unfounded or did not provide evidence of state abuse or neglect.[45] Such a significant number of "false positives" suggest significant overreporting and overinvestigating.

In Fiscal Year 2021, $536 million—about 44 percent of all child welfare spending (not all from CAPTA grants)—came from the federal government. CAPTA funds are to be used for the processing and investigation of reports of child abuse or neglect; legal action; case management; risk assessment materials; technology; training, recruitment, and retention of caseworkers; community-based programs; and

42. Martin Guggenheim, *What's Wrong with Children's Rights?* (Cambridge, MA: Harvard University Press, 2003), 246.

43. US Department of Health and Human Services, Administration for Children and Families, Administration on Children, Youth and Families, Children's Bureau, *Child Maltreatment 2019* (Washington, DC: US Department of Health and Human Services, 2021), xiv, https://www.acf.hhs.gov/cb/research-data-technology/ statistics-research/child-maltreatment.

44. Emilie Stoltzfu, "Child Welfare: Purposes, Federal Programs, and Funding," Congressional Research Service, April 16, 2021, https://crsreports.congress.gov/product/pdf/IF/IF10590.

45. US Department of Health and Human Services et al., *Child Maltreatment 2019*, 18.

interagency collaboration. To qualify for these federal funds, states must show they meet federal requirements. These include statewide laws about processing reports of child abuse and neglect; mandatory reporting by certain persons; protecting infants with prenatal drug/ alcohol exposure; screening, assessment, and investigation of abuse or neglect allegations; state immunity for persons who in good faith report suspected abuse or neglect; confidentiality of reports; agreeing to share information with certain agencies; appointments of guardians *ad litem* to represent children in judicial proceedings; expedited termination of parental rights in certain circumstances; and citizen review panels.[46]

It isn't hard to understand why compliance with these grant qualification requirements would increase conflicts between the state and parents in the context of abuse and neglect proceedings.[47] Anonymous reporting alone is a questionable practice that is easily abused and largely contributes to the increased number. In my fifteen years of practice in this area, I have witnessed numerous cases where anonymous reporting has been used to harass and injure a person. In divorce cases, one party can use CPS as a weapon to affect custody proceedings and to gain custody even when there is a court order to the contrary. According to federal statistics, 0.0 percent of reports are "intentionally false," a stat that seems unlikely. From my professional experience, I am aware of numerous false reports, some of which were malicious. Although it is often a crime to make a false report, law enforcement almost never investigates, let alone prosecutes, such crimes; social services agencies simply ignore and do not report the possibility of false reports. Because these false reports are not investigated and classified, they are not reported—which explains why the federal statistics indicate 0.0 percent.[48]

CAPTA provisions have also increased the length of child abuse proceedings and the power of state agents to remove children from

46. Luis Acosta, "Child Protection Law and Policy: Comparative Summary," Library of Congress website, May 2019, https://www.loc.gov/law/help/child-protection-law/compsum.php#_ftnref5.

47. Krason, id.

48. Id.

their homes, even with scanty or no evidence of abuse or neglect. Additionally, the appointment of guardians *ad litem* to represent either the child or his best interests prior to any determination of parental unfitness seems to run counter to the Supreme Court's jurisprudence that fit parents are deemed to act in their children's best interests.

An early example of how agencies abuse their power is demonstrated in *Duchesne v. Sugarman* (1977).[49] The case began when Pauline Perez was unexpectedly admitted to a hospital for mental health care, and her neighbor was unable to keep the children for more than a day or two. CPS agents placed the children in a hospital and then in a foster home without ever obtaining the mother's consent or a court order. Twenty-seven months passed before a habeas corpus action was initiated, and then the City of New York filed a petition for the custody of the children. Years later, an appeals court reversed the family court's *post hoc* ratification of the removal based on mother's neglect. Despite reversing the finding, the appellate court did not return the children. The administratrix of Perez's estate continued the lawsuit on behalf of the children. The issue in the case was whether a civil rights action was available. The US Supreme Court noted:

Here we are concerned with the most essential and basic aspect of familial privacy—the right of the family to remain together without the coercive interference of the awesome power of the state. This right to the preservation of family integrity encompasses the reciprocal rights of both parent and children. It is the interest of the parent in the "companionship, care, custody and management of his or her children," and of the children in not being dislocated from the "emotional attachments that derive from the intimacy of daily association," with the parent ... [concluding that] the family has been described quite properly as "perhaps the most fundamental social institution of our society." Ms. Perez and her two children were deprived of their right to live together as a family without due process of law. The Civil Rights Act, 42 U.S.C. § 1983, establishes a cause of action against any person who, acting under color of state law, causes an individual to suffer from a constitutional deprivation. We remand for a new trial in which the jury must determine which, if any, of the appellees are liable under § 1983 for the constitutional

49. *Duchesne v. Sugarman*, 566 F.2d 817.

deprivations suffered by the appellants. If liability is established, the extent of damages must also be fixed by the jury.[50]

In *Santoskey v. Kramer* (1982)[51] the court held that substantive due process protecting parental rights required a high standard of proof. It ruled that a New York law requiring only a preponderance of evidence to terminate parental rights was constitutionally deficient and instead established that an evidentiary standard of "clear and convincing" was necessary. The court analogized termination of parental rights to the equivalent of a death penalty in family law, thus demanding a higher standard of proof:

The fundamental liberty interest of natural parents in the care, custody, and management of their child does not evaporate simply because they have not been model parents or have lost temporary custody of their child to the State. Even when blood relationships are strained, parents retain a vital interest in preventing the irretrievable destruction of their family life. If anything, persons faced with forced dissolution of their parental rights have a more critical need for procedural protections than do those resisting state intervention into ongoing family affairs. When the State moves to destroy weakened familial bonds, it must provide the parents with fundamentally fair procedures.[52]

Concerned about the complexity of family law and the risk of drawing federal courts into overseeing more areas of law historically reserved to the states, the dissent instead insisted that the preponderance of the evidence standard did not violate the Fourteenth Amendment's Due Process Clause.[53]

Federal courts continue to be involved in cases relating to state agents' intrusions into families pursuant to abuse and neglect laws. Because many families lack means to obtain lawyers to seek justice for perceived civil rights violations, only a small number of likely meritorious cases are filed. In 1981, in *Lassiter v. Department of Social Services*,[54] the court declined to require the appointment of counsel for indigent parents facing termination of their parental rights, let alone

50. Id., at 825, 833.
51. 455 U.S. 745.
52. Id., at 753.
53. See id., 770–791.
54. 453 U.S. 927.

for the "mere removal" of their children from the home. Even though most removals are protected by due process procedures, in many cases, such procedures are ignored or ineffective.

Juvenile court judges are quick to accept the assertions of investigating social workers or prosecutors and issue verbal or written *ex parte* orders of cooperation or removal. Seeking redress or reversal of such situations is challenging because parents, who are often unfamiliar with the process, are desperate to have their children returned and are willing to do virtually anything to appease the state agents or judges. While undoubtedly there are many situations where removal is appropriate and necessary for the safety of the subject children, the statistics above indicate that many children are removed who should never have been.

Parents are woefully uninformed and uneducated about their constitutional rights when it comes to CPS investigations. CAPTA does contain provisions that require states to take steps to train social workers to inform parents about their rights (such as informing them about the allegations against them) as well as to protect them.[55] Unfortunately, this rarely happens, although in some states, CPS investigators and peace officers take this aspect of their job seriously. Many, however, choose not to believe or are told that the rights of the child come before the rights of parents or that the Fourth Amendment does not apply to social workers in child protection matters. Despite significant litigation in the federal circuit courts setting forth that the Fourth Amendment does indeed apply to social workers,[56] the Supreme Court has never addressed this issue directly.

Even with circuit court precedent, CPS investigators and police officers often do not understand or refuse to abide by these constitutional requirements. The few attorneys who practice in this area (the work is not financially lucrative) are familiar that this is a frequent occurrence. I have been on telephone conferences advising members of the Home School Legal Defense Association (HSLDA) in numer-

---

55. 42 USC 5106a (b) (2) (A) (xviii).
56. See *Andrews v. Hickman County* (4th Cir.), *Calabretta v. Floyd* (9th Cir.), *Gates v. Texas* (5th Cir.), *Roska v. Peterson* (10th Cir.), *Good v. Dauphin County* (3rd Cir.), *Doe v. Heck* (7th Cir.), and *Shulkers v. Kammer* (6th Cir.).

ous situations where I have heard social workers and police officers say things like "the Fourth Amendment doesn't apply to me," or "the Fourth Amendment doesn't apply to child protection," or "I don't give a damn about the Fourth Amendment; I'm coming in to make sure this social worker is able to do her job!" HSLDA has filed several lawsuits in such situations as evidence that these kinds of situations do occur.[57]

Another reason that attorneys for would-be civil rights plaintiffs in these cases have been unable to advance these rights is the doctrine of qualified immunity. A brief discussion of this doctrine is essential to understanding the dearth of federal court cases that reach the Supreme Court. The Institute for Justice explains the concern about this doctrine:

> A web of legal doctrines effectively places government workers above the law by making it nearly impossible for individuals to hold them accountable for violations of constitutional rights. Outside of narrow exceptions, these doctrines give all those employed by the government—police, mayors, school officials, IRS agents, you name it—immunity from lawsuits, even if they act in bad faith.[58]

The latest Supreme Court case involving social worker violations of the Fourth Amendment rights of parents, families, and children was *Camreta v. Green* (2011).[59] The case illustrates the difficulty of the doctrine of qualified immunity, which requires that specific factual situations be clearly established as constitutional rights violations. In *Camreta* the Ninth Circuit held that a social worker's warrantless interview of a minor school child without parental consent violated the child's and parents' constitutional right, but because the law was not "clearly established," the official was entitled to qualified immunity. On appeal the Supreme Court vacated the determination of the violation

57. "When a Knock at the Door Becomes a Nightmare," HSLDA, September 17, 2019, https://hslda.org/post/when-a-knock-at-the-door-becomes-a-nightmare-holly-currys-story.

58. Institute for Justice, Project on Immunity and Accountability website, accessed June 24, 2021, https://ij.org/issues/project-on-immunity-and-accountaility/?gclid=CjOKCQjw2tCG BhCLARIsAJGmZ6Z-WHir63VSu97sfvPR1WgbTwkclolNyHpVdr1dKHZlyy9l4WHD2YaAg C2EALwwcb.

59. *Camreta v. Greene*, 563 U.S. 692.

of the Fourth Amendment on the basis that the child had grown up and moved and thus the case was moot. This means that the issue of warrantless searches in schools absent parental consent remains a circuit-by-circuit issue and not a nationwide issue with respect to being a "clearly established" protection.

The doctrine of qualified immunity says that government agents who are performing their duties should not be liable for damages for violating a citizen's constitutional right(s) unless that right has been "clearly established." This is an extremely high hurdle to overcome. Since the Supreme Court has not weighed in sufficiently, circuit and district courts must go through years of litigation before certain violations become "clearly established" enough to even survive motions to dismiss or summary judgment so that plaintiffs can get to a trial.

Most state constitutions' bills of rights are more extensive than the US Constitution's. Because most states have adopted similar jurisprudential limitations on lawsuits against government officials, however, citizens are similarly limited in their ability to seek vindication of violations of their state constitutional rights. Organizations such as the American Civil Liberties Union, Alliance Defending Freedom, HSLDA, and the Institute for Justice are advocating for the legislative abrogation of this doctrine at the state level.[60] Such laws would help plaintiffs in many cases, since most of the alleged violations brought to federal court are committed by state-level government agents.

The most recent Supreme Court case involving parents' rights originated in Washington State. In *Troxel v. Granville* (2000),[61] parents challenged a third-party visitation law that gave any person the right to petition a court for visitation with a child for any reason. The court found that the law violated the substantive due process protections afforded parents because the law did not give at least some "special weight" to an otherwise fit parent's determination regarding visiting a child. The ruling was 6 to 3, but some commentators—like Michael P. Farris, a founder of both HSLDA and Parentalrights.org—have ob-

60. Colorado General Assembly, Testimony on HB 1287, House Committee on the Judiciary, Public Testimony on Colorado HB 20-1287, March 5, 2020, https://leg.colorado.gov/content/e3bce64e442127c1872585220073d04a-hearing-summary.
    61. 530 U.S. 57.

served that the failure of a majority to recognize the fundamental nature of parental rights has weakened the doctrine. [62]

Following *Troxel*'s failure to clearly reaffirm the fundamental nature of parental rights and the application of strict scrutiny thereto, federal district courts and courts of appeal have presented a confused picture of parental rights. Although state courts have been more protective of these rights, the Supreme Court's historical grand statements regarding the fundamental nature of parental rights under its substantive due process jurisprudence have not resulted in the consistent application of the proper level of scrutiny. Consequently, state actions that have been tested under the court's *Troxel* opinion have resulted in lesser protections and more deference to state action that interferes with parental rights.[63] This confusion led Farris to assert that "the need for clear constitutional standards for parental rights is evident—particularly in the federal courts."[64]

Conclusion

A regular tempo of state and federal court cases combines with state legislative activity in areas that interact with and potentially interfere with parental decisions. Although the Supreme Court has indicated over the past one hundred years that parental rights are among those rights protected by its Fourteenth Amendment substantive due process jurisprudence, recent rulings such as the plurality in *Troxel* have weakened this presumption. Considering the accelerating rate of new state laws in education, health, and child protection, it appears conflict between the state and families over these issues will likely continue and increase without a clearer ruling from the Supreme Court recognizing the fundamental nature of parental rights.

62. See Michael P. Farris, "The Confused Character of Parental Rights in the Aftermath of *Troxel*," accessed June 25, 2021, https://parentalrights.org/wp-content/uploads/2017/06/Aftermath-of-Troxel.pdf.

63. Farris, "Confused Character," 9.

64. Farris, "Confused Character," 15.

3

The Welfare State, the Family, and Parental Rights

Just as the primary existence of God is the ultimate starting and ending point of all inquiry, scientific or philosophical, so too the primary moment of existence of the human being is the ultimate starting and the "end" point of inquiries into man and society. Though God has no "generator, or prior cause," human beings do: their parents, in cooperation with God, the giver of life. Just as God's existence undergirds all philosophy, parenthood undergirds all social analysis, discussion, and synthesis, including the discussion of rights. But parenthood itself only comes about through the new existence of the child. The child confers parenthood on the man and woman. This is fundamental to the proper order of fundamental human rights.

There are two different types of human rights with vast difference in gravitas. Rights are relationship demands by one on another or others and come in two totally distinct forms: fundamental/inalienable human rights and politically granted rights.

Fundamental Rights Are Universal

They are inherent to man's existence. They are not granted to him by any human being, organization, or power. They inhere in his humanity. Thus all everywhere are required to recognize and honor fundamental human rights of all with whom they come in contact, fleetingly or constantly. Fundamental rights have no geographical or political boundaries. They are universal, and transcending all borders, they engulf all nations and peoples.

Political Rights Are Changeable and Geographically Bounded

Political rights are totally different from fundamental rights. They are gifts from a person's political community (particular nation, welfare state, or substate community), which grants the citizen the permit to draw upon the material or legal largesse of his polis, as these gifts are defined in its laws and regulations. These rights do not inhere in the person; they come from his legal standing in the community. Also, the polis, by new laws enacted, may expand, reduce, or eliminate these rights. Furthermore, the citizen of one community does not have standing to draw upon the political gift/rights of another community, unless specifically granted in law to them. Other political communities have no obligation to honor for their own people the political gifts a different society grants to theirs. Thus social security rights change from one nation to another and in some do not exist at all. In a different way, the largesse of the United States has assigned in law to legal immigrants (before citizenship) a status that gives them access to political rights/gifts of largesse as enumerated for such immigrants. There is much discussion lately about the conferring of legal immigrant rights to illegal immigrants. Many have deliberately confused the boundary, even though boundaries can be expanded or tightened by law. Political order needs clarity. Those who desire disorder love confusion.

In the welfare state, since it grants so many political rights, there is a special need to make and promulgate the vast and grave difference between these two types of rights. These distinctions are always critical in addressing the relationship between any and all states and the rights (fundamental or political) of parents, children, and the family, of citizens, immigrants (legal and illegal), and visitors.

Two Sets of Universal, Inalienable Rights within the Family

Beyond the polis and within the family itself, two sets of fundamental/inalienable/universal rights coexist and are in constant play: the rights of parents regarding the raising of their children within their family and their local community and the rights of the child, to his life and to the lifelong intact marriage of his parents, without which he will not become the fully capable and conjugal adult he is meant to become. These fundamental rights of the child are almost universally ignored and are not articulated in the foundational treaties of the United Nations,[1] but because they exist, codified or not, they are foundational to man and central to the argument in this chapter.[2]

There is an existential ranking inherent in the inalienable rights of the family. The rights (and obligations) of parents come into existence only when the existence of their child begins. It is not the conjugal act that confers the right but the fruit of that act—another being—that causes and confers the fundamental human rights of parenthood upon parents. Without a child's existence, they have no parental rights. With his conception, they do. But the child simultaneously has complementary fundamental rights to life *and to their marriage.* In all cases the first can always be honored; not so the second. It is with the total abandonment of the existence of this right that the modern confusion has grown in society and even in practice among many members of

---

1. There was much discussion of this right, but it failed to become part of the treaty. Eleanor Roosevelt was a major obstacle.

2. It is complicated to investigate the rights of parents in a body politic that disregards the rights of the child and in which many parents violate the rights of their own children. They peak with forked tongue: "I demand my standing as parent be honored despite my denying similar honor on my children the ones who confer the status of parent on me (my child)."

the Catholic Church. On these fundamental rights we have less unity than on the totally secondary, limited, changeable, political rights/gifts granted by the state.

As all married parents have found out that, unless they are united on certain issues, their children will drive "a coach and four" through the split. Similarly, the enemies of freedom (the right to do good) are driving a coach and four through the standing of the child, the parent, the marriage, and the family in society.

Though many defend the child's right to life (and they are gradually winning many legal contests), few defend his right to the marriage of its parents. Therein lies the core rights weakness, all-corrupting impact on the last few emerging generations. It is the hidden, undiagnosed, unrecognized cancer eating away at the body politic—at all body politics across the globe. Too many parents abuse the children's *two* fundamental rights. The relational foundations are crumbling.

Consider two sets of facts. In 2021, about 20 percent of Americans in their forties were parents who had aborted at least one of their children,[3] violating the fundamental right to life of their own child, making clear they did not want the onus or rights of being a parent. The modern welfare state facilitates, even protects, these violations. In 2015, by the time the average child reaches age 17, 53 percent of American parents have violated this right. Only 47 percent of American 17-year-olds live in an intact family with both of their biological parents.[4]

Some children, especially those who live in inner city poverty, are the fourth or fifth generation of fatherless families. Today, young unwed parents are totally ignorant of these fundamental human rights, most through no fault of their own, because in many poor communities, there are no married couples. Marriage belongs in other cultures, not theirs. Even Christian clergy in the inner cities have stopped

---

3. The data are more accurate (though limited) for women. The assumption is that a similar percentage of men are fathers of these children. For family and abortion data, see Patrick F. Fagan and Scott Talkington, *The Demographics of Women Who Report Having an Abortion* (Washington, DC: Marriage and Religion Research Institute, 2014), http://marri.us/wp-content/uploads/Demographics-of-Women-Who-Report-Having-an-Abortion.pdf.

4. For five annual reports, based on Census data and starting a decade ago, see "Annual Index of Belonging and Rejection," Marriage and Religion Research Institute, accessed April 23, 2022, http://marri.us/research/annual-index-of-belonging-and-rejection/.

teaching their flocks about the foundational importance of marriage or their child's right to this, even though it is a right that can immediately be grasped once explained and explored.

While Christ never used rights language, he did teach clearly on purity of heart, monogamous marriage, divorce, and celibacy. Furthermore, the early Christians renounced and avoided contraception (widely practiced in depopulating Roman times). These doctrines, insights, and moral imperatives are absent from many Christian communities today.

The Welfare State

Welfare State: An A-Relational Bureaucracy

The fundamental philosophical fact that undergirds social science is that man is a relational being. Conversely, the welfare state is not a relational creature; it is a bureaucratic administrator of regulations that disburse the largesse of the state to those granted the political rights to draw upon them. In many ways it is a-relational. It does not change its behavior as its clients' relationships are changed by its regulated largesse. It is an a-relational organization, animated by abstract laws turned into bureaucratic regulations.

Regarding the development of the welfare state, the words of the Dutch welfare state policy analyst and historian Abram de Swann are worth paraphrasing: "big issues, big needs, big men and women, against a backdrop of big transformations in society" (paraphrased because he did not include the notion of "big mistakes, and big misunderstandings"). This big bureaucratic conglomerate has grown massively without a central strategic principle. By now, it has something for almost everyone. It takes care of the basic needs of the poorest of our poor, of many needs of our poor, of some needs of children, of the credit needs of multinational corporations, and of banks "too big to fail." Yet it has no economic theory underlying the receipt and disbursement of its political rights largesse.

Though the welfare state has grown in different ways in different nations, its motivation is always to care for particular groups in dire need when neither they, the marketplace, their families, their local communities, nor even their own regional governments could. Bureaucracies frequently harness other institutions in the distribution of this largesse: churches, schools, hospital personnel, banks, and law enforcement.

Whatever the short-term results, the long term is always debilitating because the continued largesse engenders dependence and undermines the capacity to produce that makes for capable citizens. These systems of largesse, helpful at the time of crisis, have rarely resulted in capacity development, and when they have (e.g., Wisconsin welfare reform under Governor Tommy Thompson, or smaller but significant welfare reforms in New York City under Mayor Rudy Giuliani), they are overturned by the time the next dependence-inducing regime takes power.

The Population Depletion Effect of the Welfare State

One chart from John Mueller's *Redeeming Economics*[5] points to the welfare state's debilitating dilemma: The higher a nation's social program spending, the lower its fertility rate. This has led to a deep and so far irreversible looming population crisis for all Western democratic welfare states.[6]

The Largesse of the US Welfare State

Materially, our poor are rich by historical standards. According to the government's own data, the average American family or single person identified as poor by the Census Bureau lives in an air-conditioned, centrally heated house or apartment that is in good repair and not overcrowded. They have a car or truck. (Indeed, 43 percent of poor families own two or more vehicles.) The home has at least one widescreen television connected to cable, satellite, or a streaming ser-

5. John Mueller, *Redeeming Economics* (Wilmington, DE ISI Press, 2014), chap. 13.
6. See "Fertility Rate, Total (Births per Woman)—World," The Word Bank, accessed April 23, 2022, https://data.worldbank.org/indicator/SP.DYN.TFRT.IN?locations=1W.

vice; a computer or tablet with Internet connection; and a smartphone (some 82 percent of poor families have one or more smartphones). By their own reporting, the average poor family had enough food to eat throughout the prior year. No family member went hungry for even a single day due to a lack of money for food. They have health insurance (either public or private) and are able to get all "necessary medical care and prescription medication" when needed.

Despite these facts, the United States has a widespread reputation for stinginess toward its poor (even though the poor of the world endanger themselves to get here). Philip Alston, a law professor at New York University and the United Nations' special rapporteur ("assessment expert" on extreme poverty and human rights), recently reported that in the United States, "about 40 million live in poverty, 18.5 million in extreme poverty, and 5.3 million live in third-world conditions of absolute poverty."[7] He further argued before the UN Human Rights Commission that "one of the world's wealthiest countries does very little about the fact that 40 million of its citizens live in poverty."[8] He is wrong on all counts and either uninformed or deliberately misleading. Given his bio,[9] it would be hard for him to be uninformed.[10]

The Welfare State's Faulty Economic Theory

John Mueller fingers the fundamental modern economic problem, which we see writ large in the modern welfare system. According to Mueller, economists have three major "equations" for production,

7. United Nations General Assembly, *Report of the Special Rapporteur on Extreme Poverty and Human Rights on His Mission to the United States of America* (New York: United Nations, 2018), https://undocs.org/A/HRC/38/33/ADD.1.

8. Jamie Bryan Hall, "Don't Believe the UN's Propaganda about 'Extreme Poverty' in the US," Heritage Foundation, July 17, 2018, https://www.heritage.org/poverty-and-inequality/commentary/dont-believe-the-uns-propaganda-about-extreme-poverty-the-us. See also Jamie Hall and Robert Rector, "Examining Extreme and Deep Poverty in the United States," Heritage Foundation, February 20, 2018, https://www.heritage.org/poverty-and-inequality/report/examining-extreme-and-deep-poverty-the-united-states.

9. Wikipedia, s.v. "Philip Alston," last edited February 7, 2022, https://en.wikipedia.org/wiki/Philip_Alston.

10. His UN special rapporteur work was not paid for by the UN. His support comes from elsewhere. It would be interesting to stage a debate between him and Robert Rector, author of *The Paradox of Poverty: We Spent $3.5 Trillion without Changing the Poverty Rate* (Washington, DC: Heritage Foundation, 1992), http://thf_media.s3.amazonaws.com/1992/pdf/hl410.pdf.

consumption, and exchange but not for the *distribution* of income, property, and gifts—the economic choices involved in distributing one's goods between others (e.g., spouse, children, church, charities, and others). Modern economics has no theory of such distribution and takes no notice of gifts to persons—children, individuals in need, churches, schools, charities, nonprofits—up to a third of the economy! In other words, mainstream economics is missing the economic manifestation of relationships, of man's relational nature. No wonder welfare economics is so wrong and commits a form of economic suicide on the poor.

Strategic Mistake on the "Infant Industry"

If the foundation of a home is collapsing, it makes no sense to buy new carpeting for the living room. The foundations of all Western democratic welfare states are crumbling—in their populations—as the World Bank's fertility data make plain.[11]

Many countries are gradually disappearing, taking about three generations to do so but with no escape exit in sight. Among the most hopeless cases is South Korea, with a fertility rate of 0.9.[12] In three generations, its emerging cohort will be one-tenth of today's cohort. Its infant industry is bankrupt.

The international geographic landscape is full of similar illustrations: Ireland, which in the past fifty years has moved from world-high rates of fertility, intact marriage, and weekly worship to typical European soft paganism. During the next thirty years, it will have to import half its needed population (had it not aborted the children it did, it probably would not need to do so[13]). The "Celtic Tiger," now counted as one of the top economies in the world,[14] has forsaken its

---

11. "Fertility Rate, Total (Births per Woman)—World."

12. "Fertility Rate, Total (Births per Woman)—Korea, Rep.," The World Bank, accessed April 23, 2022, https://data.worldbank.org/indicator/SP.DYN.TFRT.IN?locations=KR.

13. For some time, Ireland's abortion rate (abortions were mostly procured overseas) was about 13 percent of all pregnancies.

14. Naomi O'Leary, "Ireland Ranked Second in the World for Quality of Life, Beating Sweden, Germany and UK," *Irish Times*, December 17, 2020, https://www.irishtimes.com/news/ireland/irish-news/ireland-ranked-second-in-the-world-for-quality-of-life-beating -sweden -germany-and-uk-1.4440009.

sine qua non industry, "babies of the future"[15] in which it was a world leader but is now a begging nation. How strange the metrics of modern economics?

The Welfare State Rejects Its Foundation, the Family

The normal developmental goal of the functional family is the future marriage of their child to a virginally chaste,[16] competent, kind, hardworking spouse who has a network of loyal friends who will be present to witness their marriage vows. Though poor families have reached this goal for their children since the beginning of time, even consideration of achieving this goal is totally absent in the planning, execution, and assessment of the modern welfare state's "largesse."

Strategic Rejection of the Father Role

The welfare state especially abuses the father's relationships with his children and their mother, resulting in long-term "sexual suicide" and economic crippling of families.[17] Should the income of the absent father and welfare state largesse to the welfare family be combined, 70 percent of families would move above the poverty line.[18] Still more would leave because a "marriage premium" of 27 percent increase in income happens when a man marries and has children.[19] Given the growth of Western economies since the late 1940s, the United States and others would have long ago left behind material poverty,[20] should marriage have remained a constant of life.

Instead, the poor, young, unmarried father from the inner city is

15. "Fertility Rate, Total (Births per Woman)—Ireland," The World Bank, accessed April 23, 2022, https://data.worldbank.org/indicator/SP.DYN.TFRT.IN?locations=IE.

16. See Chart 7 in Chastity and Monogamy: Correlates and Impacts, at http://marri.us/speeches_powerpoints/.

17. See George F. Gilder, Sexual Suicide (N.Y.: Bantam Books, 1973), later republished (with some modifications) as Men and Marriage (N.Y.: Pelican, 1983). It was prescient. >

18. Patrick Fagan, Kirk Johnson, Lauren Noyes, and Robert Rector, "Increasing Marriage Would Dramatically Reduce Child Poverty," Heritage Foundation, May 20, 2003, https://www.heritage.org/marriage-and-family/report/increasing-marriage-would-dramatically-reduce-child-poverty.

19. K. Antovics and R. Town, "Are All the Good Men Married? Uncovering the Sources of the Marital Wage Premium," American Economic Review 94 (2004): 317–21.

20. One never gets rid of "relative poverty," which is a statistical creation.

inducted and enculturated into a welfare state, a child support enforcement system by which he forfeits much of his paycheck to support his children and their mother(s). This rather than being a hardworking provider for his wife and children. It is one thing to enforce child support on a middle-class man who leaves his family. It is a horse of a different color when it is an integral part of the state-constructed life cycle of the poor male—a nasty rite of passage for most poor fathers.

The Sexual Malformation of Children

The sexual formation of children has massive impact on the whether the families they will later form as adults are of intact marriage based on chaste loyalty or are instead an out-of-wedlock single parent, cohabitating (serial) couple, single aborting parent, or divorced. The modern US welfare state is inimical to intact marriage, which follows on chaste courtship (the universal, transcultural ideal for a healthy marriage). Such is extremely rare among the poor and nowhere held up as the goal for anyone who desires sexual intercourse. Instead, the welfare state—aided and abetted by the US Supreme Court's *Eisenstadt v. Baird* decision—in its treatment of the poor has virtually eliminated intact lifelong marriage. In the poorest part of Washington, DC, within hailing distance of the buildings of the US Congress, only 9 percent of 17-year-olds live in an intact family with their biological parents. The other 93 percent suffers the debilitating experience of their biological parents having rejected each other.[21]

The sexual culture of the welfare state for the poor of America is anti-patriarch (for feminists, the patriarch is the married father). Thus it is also anti-child and anti-mother and has resulted in a continuous depletion of family and social capacity in inner poverty tracks. The Marxist-feminist founders of the National Organization of Women (NOW), who had a great influence on the new welfare policies of the Kennedy, Johnson, Nixon, Ford, and Carter eras, explicitly embraced this family-wrecking strategy, the nation at large being totally unaware

21. Henry Potrykus and Patrick Fagan, *Social Policy Outcomes Mapped across the District of Columbia* (Washington, DC: Marriage and Religion Research Institute, 2013), http://marri.us /wp-content/uploads/Social-Policy-Outcomes-District-of-Columbia.pdf.

of what was being put in place at the deep relational levels. It was much later (2014) before the bald truth of the neo-Marxist takedown of the American family became apparent.[22] By the same sexual revolution, they gradually depleted a large section of the Catholic Church's membership.

The effects of out-of-wedlock births have been well known for some time. In 2001, testifying before the House Ways and Means Committee, I stated, "The impact on the child is significant and can be permanent.... [many are] more likely to suffer from: poorer health as a newborn, and if the mother is young, from an increased chance of dying; retarded cognitive (especially verbal) development; lower educational achievement; lower job attainment; increased behavioral and emotional problems; lower impulse control; retarded social development; increased crime in their community if there is a high level of out of wedlock births. The root cause lies not in poverty but in the lack of married parents."[23]

Twenty years later (2021) the US Census Bureau refers to these effects in the opening paragraphs of a recent report on single parenthood.[24] Ironically, the report's cover portrait depicts a happy situation.

Sexual and Physical Abuse and Neglect

The absence of the father results in massive increases in physical and sexual abuse and in neglect,[25] leaving many boys and girls sexually dysfunctional (incapable of conjugal marriage) for life, often having to bear deep feelings of anger and inclinations toward violence. The 2002–8 television crime series *The Wire* portrayed this sort of family life for inner-city Baltimore. The riots in Ferguson, Missouri (2014),

22. Mallory Millett, "Marxist Feminism's Ruined Lives," *Frontpage Mag*, September 1, 2014, https://archives.frontpagemag.com/fpm/marxist-feminisms-ruined-lives-mallory-millett/.

23. Patrick F. Fagan, "The Federal and State Governments, Welfare and Marriage Issues: Congressional Testimony before the House Ways and Means Committee," May 22, 2001, https://downloads.frc.org/EF/EF08H41.pdf.

24. Paul Hemez and Chanell Washington, "Percentage and Number of Children Living with Two Parents Has Dropped since 1968," US Census Bureau, April 12, 2021, https://www.census.gov/library/stories/2021/04/number-of-children-living-only-with-their-mothers-has-doubled-in-past-50-years.html.

25. See Charts 22 and 23 at Catholic Charities Arlington, Nov. 2013 presentation at http://marri.us/speeches_powerpoints/.

and in Baltimore (2015) were the natural consequence of widespread alienation stemming from sexual and family chaos at the community level.[26]

The young adult son of a friend of mine came within seconds of bleeding to death in 2020 after being chosen as a target for a gang initiation, rite-of-passage murder. His recovery is still ongoing. Though the perpetrators were never caught, any educated adult can write their family biographies.[27]

The Mission of the Social Sciences: To Thrive or to Wither

Since the mission of the social sciences is to discover and illustrate the way man thrives (or withers), there is a moral imperative silently hidden in their robust findings, the unspoken moral norm: "If we want to thrive, we act in these ways; to avoid withering we avoid these ways."

The social sciences clarify insights about mankind that many moderns are uncomfortable agreeing with: that man thrives when he takes self-sacrificing care of his two fundamental relationships, with his God and with his closest neighbors (spouse and children), traditionally summed up as the Two Great Commandments, or the Two Great Loves.

The data, of which the United States has by far the best in the world, are astounding: On virtually every outcome measured in national surveys, adults and children who live in an always-intact-married family have the highest average scores, as do those who worship weekly. When combined into the always-intact-married family that worships weekly, these Americans outrank every other combination on more than 130 different measures of well-being.[28]

The thriving (more worship, marriage, and children) and wilting (less worship, marriage, and children) models are in fundamental

26. See Pat Fagan, "Violence in Baltimore—Social Science Resources for Journalists and Public Officials," Family Research Council, accessed April 23, 2022, https://www.frc.org/marri researchsynthesis/violence-in-baltimore.

27. See also the Heritage Foundation's *The Real Root Causes of Violent Crime: The Breakdown of Marriage, Family, and Community* (Washington, DC: Heritage Foundation, 1995), http://thf_media.s3.amazonaws.com/1995/pdf/bg1026.pdf.

28. For all 130 outcomes, see "Mapping America," Marriage and Religion Research Institute, accessed April 23, 2022, http://marri.us/research/mapping-america/.

competition with each other and have been throughout history, especially since Christianity spread and built an increasingly thriving culture. But the cost of thriving is self-sacrificing love.

The universal natural project for men and women that demands self-sacrifice is raising children within. Such self-sacrifice is most likely when religious beliefs are harnessed, when prayer and worship are pursued freely. Women who worship weekly have the highest fertility rates across the globe, within and among all its religions, peoples, and cultures.[29]

The academy is—by and large—deaf to and even hostile to this data. Hostility to any good data is a cause for alarm in any science. Hostility to data on thriving is a deep, suicidal crisis. Continuous thriving, however, yielding surplus wealth, increases the temptation to indulge desires that wither. As one headmaster put it, "The rich commit the sins the poor can only dream of."[30] Church history is littered with the rise and fall (and rise again) of monasteries that thrived, indulged, and reformed again, sometimes repeating the cycle many times over. Saints initiated these reforms, but the modern welfare state, dismissive and even hostile to religious practice, is rather unlikely to produce such reform. What is more likely to bring reform is privation when largesse is no longer possible.

The elites of the welfare state in academia, legislative bodies, and the marketplace are all afraid of the thriving model, even though avoiding the elixir of sacrificial love is national suicide. Only those who love the truth and selflessly love persons in their families are capable of seeing and telling others what the data say. Most social scientists cannot! In the academy, religiously devout social scientists are those most likely to see and to have the courage to point out what the data say. With their philosophical undergirding in natural law (Aristotle, Augustine, Aquinas, and their descendants), Catholic social scientists are natural leaders, accompanied and sometimes led by others, especially their Evangelical, Orthodox Jewish, and Mormon colleagues.

---

29. Mueller, *Redeeming Economics*, chap. 13.
30. Bob Jackson, one of the early founders of the Heights School in Potomac, Maryland.

Divorce Data and Worse

It is not only among the poor that all is not well. Conjugally, middle-class America is in trouble, too. Cohabitation is the norm before marriage even among Christians,[31] even though this is disastrous for later marriage. Within five years of marriage, the national divorce average for women with two sexual partners prior to their husband is about 50 percent. For men, the rates are different.[32] These data are the most powerful witness in all the social sciences of the need for celibacy until marriage. It protects both spouses but especially the children. Purity of heart and body are foundational to marriage and thus to a well-functioning society (and church congregation).

Divorce, though dropping in rates for child-raising parents, is growing among older baby boomers.[33] For all, divorce's effects are debilitating.[34] Divorce also has results people never see in the research. For instance, a decade ago, in conversation with a director of Catholic Charities from the Denver region, I learned that teenage girls of recently divorced parents in well-to-do Denver neighborhoods were prime targets for entrapment by sex traffickers. I had known of this fate for teenage girls who ran away from home to the big cities, but not for middle-class girls in their own neighborhoods. Hungry for love of a man, they are easily exploited; some, it seems, disappear forever.

The Influential Modeling of the Prior Generation

Adding still further to the confusion of young adults of all income levels is the fact that for the past fifty years the generation ahead of them

---

31. Christian Smith, in one of his three-volume longitudinal reports, finds that the average single Christian (Catholic or Evangelical) in their late twenties who worships weekly has already had sexual intercourse with two different people on average.

32. See Chart 7 in *Chastity and Monogamy: Correlates and Impacts* at http://marri.us/speeches_powerpoints/.

33. Renee Stepler, "Led by Baby Boomers, Divorce Rates Climb for America's 50+ Population," Pew Research, March 9, 2017, https://www.pewresearch.org/fact-tank/2017/03/09/led-by-baby-boomers-divorce-rates-climb-for-americas-50-population/.

34. See Patrick F. Fagan and Aaron Churchill, *The Effects of Divorce on Children* (Washington, DC: Marriage and Religion Research Institute, 2012), http://marri.us/wp-content/uploads/The-Effects-of-Divorce-on-Children.pdf.

has been increasingly avoiding marriage.[35] More and more children are born without the honoring of their second fundamental human right: the marriage of their parents. By 1991 the "great crossover" happened: the age of first birth for women was younger than the age for marriage, and the disparity has continued to widen since then.[36]

Academics' (and Others') Fallen Human Nature Rebellion against "Thou Ought"

Even the best data have serious limitations in persuading those who do not like its implications—those very people most in need of enlightenment. A story will help: One of my closest friends has a gifted son who has been kind to me any time I have been a guest at their home. He is handsome, charming, hardworking, loyal, and successful in his work, which brings him into contact with a large amount of people. He is not promiscuous though has been sexually active for many years—"serial monogamy" with different girlfriends. Once, out of interest in my work, he accompanied me to a presentation of the data on the effects of marriage and religious practice.[37] On the drive back to his home, he made it clear he did not want to discuss the data at all. My interpretation: The moral implications were too powerful if the data were acknowledged. Sadly, he has many identical clones in academia, legislatures, media, high schools, even clergy. Underneath strong data lies a moral imperative, "Do this good, avoid this evil." Fallen human nature, however, resists imperatives that go against indulged desires. Though sexually active with women in their highest fertile years, neither he nor they have any children—all made possible through contraception.

Modernity's Poison Pill

More than any other issue—more even than abortion—contraception is the great "de-sacralizer," the great paganizer, of everything to do with

35. See MARRI demographics, http://marri.us/decomp-family.

36. Jared Bernstein et al., "Knot Yet: The Future of Marriage in the U.S.," Brookings Institute, March 20, 2013, https://www.brookings.edu/events/knot-yet-the-future-of-marriage-in-the-u-s/.

37. "Mapping America."

matters sexual: romance, marriage, vows, babies, divorce, cohabitation, and abortion. The time line of the unfolding US Supreme Court sexual revolution decisions shows that contraception led the way and laid the foundation for everything else that followed,[38] leading to a speedy de-sacralization of sexual intimacy, of family life, and of community life. The worship of God was increasingly pushed to the sidelines, as recent Pew Research Center data on worship and affiliation illustrate yet again.[39] The Pill not only facilitates; it also drives the collapse of marriage and the intact family, replacing it with the plethora of family structures of today. It is the main tool of the paganizing welfare state, never clearer than in the Obama administration's unyielding attempt to force the consciences of the Little Sisters of the Poor.

Contraception caused the sexual revolution, and with it all the changes in culture as each pillar crumbled bit by bit. There is a logic to the effects. Remove the child from the conjugal act, and there are no limits on what this new sexuality means or is intended for. The welfare state—the great initiator, popularizer, funder, defender of all things contraceptive—has undermined and displaced marriage. In doing so, it has become the enemy of the natural family—of marriage, the child, the father, and by default the natural mother.

Simultaneous Withering within the Membership of the Catholic Church

What does contraception do that has effects on the life of the poor? It makes marriage moot as the entrance to finding a spouse and to the enjoyment of sexual intercourse. It leads to unwanted pregnancies and to the frequent desire to abort the child. It leaves children without fathers. It leads mothers into poverty for long periods, and it sidelines their educational progress. It pushes the commandments of God to the side and over time pushes the worship of God aside. It invites

38. *Griswold v. Connecticut* (1965) and *Eisenstadt v. Baird* (1972) preceded *Roe v. Wade* (1973).

39. See "Catholic Attendance," Pew Research, February 25, 2013, https://www.pew research.org/catholic-attendance/; "In U.S., Decline of Christianity Continues at Rapid Pace," Pew Research, October 17, 2019, and https://www.pewforum.org/2019/10/17/in-u-s-decline-of -christianity-continues-at-rapid-pace/.

tubal ligation and vasectomy as permanent rejection of life-giving in partnership with God, severing man from the Source of Life. It undermines the confession of sins and for Christians has introduced a new heresy: "the private interpretation of natural moral law," by which man is morally unanchored from reality and from the foundation of all moral action, the universal "Do good and avoid evil." Its religious implications are deeper and wider than "the private interpretation of the Bible." As Old Testament histories make clear, and the past sixty years illustrates again, the sexual set free from the bonds of marriage is man's royal road to paganism. Modern sexual practices are identical to those of pagan Rome, to which early Christian behavior stood in clear contrast and gradually led to a thriving Europe, founded on sexuality channeled to its two ends: the prime, children, and the secondary, the good of the spouses.[40] The culture of celibacy until marriage that was necessary for that human triumph is no longer widespread even among Catholics and has become relatively rare. Church membership is not yet in a fit state to take on the culture of the paganized welfare state. That was diagnosed more than sixty years ago by someone now very famous, Pope Emeritus Benedict XVI.

In 1958, around the time of the expansion of the welfare state in Western democracies, Joseph Ratzinger wrote a paper titled "The New Pagans and the Church."[41] It was startling for its time and spoke about the secularization (he called it paganization) within the Catholic Church.[42] In other words, Ratzinger was calling pagan what social scientists call secularization. Then, in 1968, Pope Paul VI issued *Humanae Vitae*, which reaffirmed perennial Christian teaching on con-

---

40. Vatican II's documents on the ends of marriage footnotes back to Trent's definitions of prime and secondary, even as it uses pastoral language that blurs the difference. It seems that it is time to focus on the footnote.

41. Joseph Ratzinger, "The New Pagans and the Church," *Homiletic and Pastoral Review*, January 30, 2017, https://www.hprweb.com/2017/01/the-new-pagans-and-the-church/.

42. "The outward shape of the modern Church is determined essentially by the fact that in a totally new way, she has become the Church of pagans, and is constantly becoming even more so. She is no longer, as she once was, a Church composed of pagans who have become Christians but a Church of pagans, who still call themselves Christians, but actually have become pagans ... And there can be no doubt that most of them, from the Christian point of view, should really no longer be called believers, because they follow, more or less, a secular philosophy" (Ratzinger, "New Pagans and the Church").

traception that dated back to Apostolic times. This document brought into the open the secularization-sacralization split in the Church.[43] With its predictive validity, *Humanae Vitae* gives Paul VI Nobel Laureate status in science. It remains an embarrassment to this day, and with the depopulation crisis (only one of the Pill's effects), it is becoming more so with each passing year—within the social sciences; the academy; the business world; the grant-making foundation world; the United Nations; the World Bank; the World Health Organization; UNESCO; and virtually every government in existence.

In 1970 the by then more widely known Professor Ratzinger accurately predicted a much smaller church.[44] In 1972, Pope Paul VI, stricken by the response of Catholic bishops to *Humanae Vitae*, gave his "Smoke of Satan within the Church" homily,[45] his own version of Ratzinger's "pagans in the Church" speech. For both, pagan sexuality is at the core of the secularization of the Church, probably best exemplified in the 2021 document of the majority of the German bishops (unique among nations as welfare state beneficiaries of great largesse), which radically and deliberately departs from Christ's and the Church's moral teaching on conjugal and sexual matters. The paganism within deepens as they (unconsciously) align with their pagan welfare state benefactor.

We Are a Culture of Rejection of Life and Marriage

The United States has the highest percent of children living in single parent homes in the world.[46] Alarmingly, in 2019, about 80 percent of young women 18 to 25 view marriage as an option, not as a goal, and are comfortable with the prospect of raising their children without a

43. Made visible by the many national bishop assemblies, which undermined the reception of the encyclical with their ambivalence while enabling a "private interpretation of natural law"—a veiled form of revolt against the encyclical.

44. Joseph Ratzinger, *Faith and the Future* (New York: Random House, 1970).

45. IX Anniversary of the Coronation of his Holiness Homily of Paul VI, Solemnity of the Holy Apostles Peter and Paul, Thursday, June 29, 1972, https://www.vatican.va/content/paul-vi-it-homilies/1972/documents/hf_p-vi_hom_19720629.html, fifth paragraph from the end.

46. See Stephanie Kramer, "U.S. Has Highest Rate of Children Living in Single-Parent Households," Pew Research, December 12, 2019, https://www.pewresearch.org/fact-tank/2019/12/12/u-s-children-more-likely-than-children-in-other-countries-to-live-with-just-one-parent/.

father. Only 20 percent fully intend to have their children within marriage, and of them many do not necessarily even intend to have any children.[47] These alarming data comport with similar Pew research data.[48]

The capacity for normal courtship leading to marriage is virtually impossible in such communities. The cultivation of chastity and its accompanying byproduct, sexual self-control, are alien ideas and ideals for almost all. These require the presence of fathers in each family and a community culture of chastity.

The demographic crossover from "first child coming before marriage rather than after marriage" occurred in 1991, more than a generation ago.[49] Today, most young people are unwitting violators of the child's fundamental human rights, as they follow in the footsteps of their parents.

Reforms
Restoring a Culture of Chastity for Families of the Church
Restoring a culture and legal system that honors fundamental parental and child rights requires a sexual reformation. All other issues are irrelevant to *solving* the problems of welfare and family rights. The change needed is that of enshrining and expecting young men to be raised as chaste (despite, and because of, the struggle involved) and expecting them to remain celibate until married. Anything less is to concede that reform is impossible and that we condone the killing of children and the denial of their fundamental right to their parents' marriage.

Many will disagree: Marxists, feminists, free-market libertarians,

---

47. Hana Shepherd and Emily A. Marshall, "Childbearing Worldviews and Contraceptive Behavior among Young Women," *Journal of Marriage and Family* 81, no. 5 (2019). This report, from Michigan data, is cause for alarm (and further, deeper study) because Michigan is considered a "median" state by family demographers, so the United States is likely to be close to the same.

48. Deja Thomas, "As Family Structures Change in U.S., a Growing Share of Americans Say It Makes No Difference," Pew Research, April 10, 2020, https://www.pewresearch.org/fact-tank/2020/04/10/as-family-structures-change-in-u-s-a-growing-share-of-americans-say-it-makes-no-difference/.

49. Bernstein et al., "Knot Yet."

and virtually all Democrats and Republicans. Libertarians because they do not want any societal constraints on their sexual desires. Unrestrained sexual expression by the male is a key tool for the patient Marxist-feminist takeover/takedown of society, as was made clear in Mallory Millet's famous exposé on the founders of the National Organization of Women.[50] And so far, no party has claimed championship of celibacy until marriage and monogamy for life. All seem afraid. This is the work of heads of families and the Christian clergy, however. If they form the parade, a political leader will be able to get out front and harness its power.

Catholics, first among all, have got to get contraception right by totally avoiding it and proselytizing for natural conjugality and openness to life.[51] This has always been a mark of being Christian … and still is. Others have inadvertently become pagan. Contraception desacralizes—de-Christianizes—conjugal relations and gradually leads to pagan sex (fornication, abortion, cohabitation, divorce, same-sex coupling, and more). By removing the child as end, contraception unanchors sexual intercourse from nature and renders "perversion" obsolete (once the child is gone) because the purpose becomes pleasure, which is always idiosyncratic.

"Sex gone wild" is man's (male and female) most common way of ceasing to live as a Christian and the most common way of falling back into paganism. It is now made much more tempting than ever in the past with all variants of pornography available free on a mobile phone. If entertained, no male, adolescent, or old man can resist its ever more alluring pull. And as evidenced in Mallory Millet's writing above,[52] the enemies of the family were presciently aware that they could "take down" both family and Church membership simultaneously.

Without a culture of chastity, the most fundamental rights of the child will be violated at massive levels. A chaste culture and its communities of families are superior in every way.[53] Thus it has the moral

50. Millett, "Marxist Feminism's Ruined Lives."

51. A total review of the effects of contraception will be completed this year and published in 2022. Follow this on MARRI.us.

52. Millett, "Marxist Feminism's Ruined Lives."

53. "Mapping America."

standing to claim justice and freedom for this way of life—the freedom to live a superior "baby centered/future centered" lifestyle. The challenge for laity and leaders is how to voice this Christian way attractively, to make Christ (and us) on the Cross attractive through the human happiness he brings with it—man fully alive.

The Fundamental Reform: Forming the Future Husband and Father

The most pressing need is for the Christian patriarch to publicly lead the way, claiming his fundamental human right to his inherent difference on matters sexual by doing the following.

(1) Insist on the removal of sex education from all of their children's classes. They have the superior sexual way, have the right to form their children therein, are the sexual "creators" of each of these children, are members of a community that knows its way sexually, and they produce superior results that all others ought to attempt to emulate. (2) Insist that anything the schools do in this matter is child sexual abuse; therefore fathers become expert at protecting these rights in law. There is Supreme Court precedent for this, when the Amish won for themselves what is now proposed here for all religious families of all faiths.[54] (3) Patriarchs must deliberately form close community identity with similarly minded families of all religions and peoples, who have the goal of virginal marriage for their children, both male and female. (4) Since the raising of children is a community endeavor as well as a family endeavor, the Church's families need to win standing to have their own lifestyle and community. (5) The Christian family's great initiative will be to persuade by their presence and by the happiness of their children and their marriages, inviting all who desire to begin to live the same way, to join them in this most natural way of family and community life. This form of happiness-generating love is available to all (with effort) and is needed by every child on earth. (6) Induct every male and female adolescent into their emerging adult capacity to transmit life by pledging to their future (yet unknown chil-

---

54. *Wisconsin v. Jonas Yoder*, 406 U.S. 205 (1972), https://www.law.cornell.edu/supreme court/text/406/205.

THE WELFARE STATE, THE FAMILY, AND PARENTAL RIGHTS

dren) never to violate their right to life nor their right to the marriage of their parents (whoever that adolescent's future spouse may be). (7) The vocation of the vast majority of Christians is to marriage, life-long marriage, where each spouse is dedicated to the happiness of the other, and both together are dedicated to building strong confident children who in turn are dedicated to putting smiles on each other's faces. (8) In these families the male—the husband and father—must be dedicated to one thing: serving first the happiness of his wife (putting a smile on her face) as the surest way of serving his children. The real patriarch is the exact opposite of the nasty strawman depicted by Marxist feminists (though most of the NOW founding feminists had fathers who fit that nasty description).[55] (9) These husbands and fathers aspire to the title of patriarch—generator, protector, loyal ally, nation-builder, lover of freedom and of love. The enemies of marriage, family, the worship of God, of freedom and liberty were Satanically intelligent in choosing to take down the patriarch. In turn, the rebuilding starts at this targeted core. The central project of each father is to form his boys to be true patriarchs in turn (a true patriarch who is totally dedicated to the happiness of his bride and to the children she wishes to bring into this world with him). He is a man who will have no other woman but her. (10) The Christian family's way of rebuilding society, of re-sacralizing society, is one friendship at a time.[56]

Voucherize Everything

Users have much more competence to tailor the largesse of the state to their unique needs (which doctor, school, hospital, insurance company, or food store to choose for their own maximum benefit, if it is given directly to the intended user in voucher format). Vouchers restore subsidiarity, which is now violated throughout the welfare state. In all comparative studies, vouchers are the way of delivering superior educational outcomes.[57]

55. Aitjpr's personal conclusion from reading their biographies many decades ago.

56. See my "Fantasy Sermon," in *Renewing Catholic Family Life: Experts Explore New Directions in Family Spirituality and Family Ministry* (Huntington, IN: OSV Press, 2020).

57. E.g., Krista Kafer and Kirk Johnson, "What the Harvard/Mathematica Study Says," Heritage Foundation, April 12, 2002, https://www.heritage.org/education/report/what-the-harvard mathematica-study-says.

The "Infant Industry" in Economics

The work of John Mueller is gradually gaining international recognition,[58] as it pinpoints the corrections needed in the practice of economics (properly called the political economy) if the first industry (babies) is to thrive. This is the "industry" from which all others spring.

The spiritual dimension is in play in all relationships throughout life, for relationships are not material phenomena. To benefit optimally, all material goods must be at the service of this relational domain— by rationing in a relational "order of priority," the heart of the needed reform in economics (the good of the household, the good of the polis). John Mueller's child and conjugal-friendly *Redeeming Economics* is the definitive work on this reform. It talks about the "equation for distribution," which covers and then accounts for a large part of every economy. Presently, this is unaccounted for in economics, from the World Bank down to the local community college.

Social Sciences Initiatives

DATA REFORM   The whole US federal data system on welfare-related issues totally misses the centrality of conjugality, and it is incomplete on matters conjugal. It is almost impossible for economists and sociologists to get a good picture of what is happening between males and females and how they become parents and what their family structure pathways are. The Centers for Disease Control and Prevention (CDC) and the National Vital Statistics Reports do not give household data. The Division of Adolescent Health within the CDC ought to be totally restaffed so that the new staff can first gain a clear understanding of these sexual pathways. Based in Atlanta, this division sits in the center of the highest rates of HIV in the country among young adults. If ever there were a case for total reform, that fact alone provides the justification.

Essentially, Congress and the nation are flying blind on welfare. Though we have the greatest data system in the world, we have no data-driven insights on the dynamics of the failure of the welfare state "to win its war on poverty."

58. A Brazilian Portuguese translation is expected in 2022.

SOCIAL SCIENCE SYNTHESIS SOLUTION   What is most needed from social scientists is an academically robust synthesis of all the welfare-relevant topics related to the thriving or wilting of the next generation: the effects of marriage on adults and children (versus the effects of divorce on adults and children), the effects of lifetime monogamy on marriage and the enjoyment of the conjugal relationship; the effects of non-contraceptive sexual relations on the marriage (versus the effects of contraception on male-female relations, marriage, family, neurological substrata, and health); the effects of early infant attachment to both mother and father (versus the effects of non-attachment or weak attachment); the effects of closeness to father on sons and daughters; the effects of closeness to mother on sons and daughters; the effects of religious practice on every one of these outcomes (but also on income, savings, health, happiness, conjugal enjoyment, friendships and happiness). The list could go on.

Social scientists operating from the foundation of natural law need to present this synthesis to the world and keep them updated so that they can be accessed by all politicians, parents, pastors, teachers, doctors, students, policy makers, politicians, journalists, talk show hosts, and directors of companies. It is the vocation of a social scientist to show how man thrives and wilts.

INDEX OF BELONGING AND REJECTION   The index of belonging and rejection is a simple yet powerful indicator of the state of the relational capacity of the nation's youngest adults.[59] It illustrates the proportion of our older teenagers (age 17) who have grown up in the embrace of their biological parents' always-intact marriage. The remainder is the proportion who have experienced (and now suffer from) the rejection of each other by their biological parents, resulting in total abandonment, single parenthood, split cohabitations, or divorce.

The index is the most parsimonious yet powerful[60] measure of the societal health of America. It can be broken down by income, ethnicity, urban/rural, and many other variables.

59. "Annual Index of Belonging and Rejection."
60. See the derivative studies attached to each annual index.

CONGRESS NEEDS TO REFORM THE OFFICE OF THE CENSUS   A corruption of the data by the staff of the Office of the Census is publicly under way and will increase the incapacity of the nation to understand what is happening to families, particularly families of the poor. The packaging of the data (by algorithms) will deprive scholars access the raw familial-conjugality data available annually in the American Community Survey.[61] It will render them more blind.

Summary

Man in his essence is a relational being. To separate the body from the spirit, the relational from the material at any level—intellectually, individually, conjugally, familial or community—is to immediately make a strategic mistake that compounds across all human endeavors. The practical proxies for living at the dually fused levels are marriage and worship properly (honestly) pursued.

Culture of Chastity

Without a culture of chastity, the most fundamental rights of the child are violated. With a culture of chastity, the community of such parents stands out as superior in every way.[62]

The Relational Incapacity of the Welfare State

The collection of taxes and the redistribution of goods is easy for government. Distribution of what is most needed—intimate marital and family relations—is an impossible task for government.

Modern (Welfare State) Economics Mistakes the Household Economy

Without marriage, the household economy does not exist in full, and the national economy wilts in comparison to its potential,

---

61. "IFS Calls on U.S. Census Bureau to Retain ACS As Is," Institute for Family Studies, June 4, 2021, https://ifstudies.org/blog/ifs-calls-on-us-census-bureau-to-retain-acs-as-is.
62. "Mapping America."

Welfare Summary Strategic Misconception

Welfare is a "war" misconceived in its fundamentals, without a strategy (the big moral good to be attained).[63] With incompetent "armies, tactics and maneuvers" (bureaucracies and regulations), it delivers repeated failure to win the "war" declared by President Lyndon Johnson.

Conclusion

We live in a period of transition: a rapid movement of many toward a secularized/paganized view of life, toward a society that is less and less relationally competent. Contraception combined with the decisions of the US Supreme Court have been the two biggest tools in dismantling the "soft" Christian order of the 1940s to build instead a rudderless, Christian-hostile, pagan society.

It remains to be seen whether the remnants of the Christian family can lead the nation—families of all faiths—to first claim in justice before the Supreme Court their own "relational territory" and thence bring more and more families into that relational competence which easily yields material sufficiency.

63. John R. Boyd, *A Discourse on Winning and Losing* (Maxwell AFB, AL: Air University Press, 2018), https://www.airuniversity.af.edu/Portals/10/AUPress/Books/B_0151_Boyd_Discourse_Winning_Losing.pdf.

4

Parental Rights and Decisions about Minor Children's Health Care

MARY RICE HASSON

For most parents, the greatest threat to their parental rights, in the medical context, is likely to come from well-meaning people they already trust.

The tragic case of Charlie Gard is every parent's worst nightmare.[1] Born with a rare genetic disease, Charlie suffered multiple seizures that, according to UK medical experts, left him with a poor quality of life and rendered further medical treatments futile. The hospital refused to release Charlie to his parents' care to pursue alternative treatments elsewhere, insisting that it was in Charlie's best interests to die. Even personal appeals from Pope Francis, offering care for Charlie at a Vatican-connected hospital in Rome, fell on deaf ears. Charlie's parents appealed their case all the way to the European Court of Human

---

1. Debra Goldschmidt and Hilary Clarke, "Baby Charlie Gard Dies after Life Support Withdrawn," CNN, July 29, 2017, https://www.cnn.com/2017/07/28/health/charlie-gard -death/index.html; "Charlie Gard Dies in Hospice, Parents Say, Fox News, September 26, 2017, https://www.foxnews.com/world/charlie-gard-dies-in-hospice-parents-say.

Rights, to no avail. The hospital eventually won judicial approval to end Charlie's life-sustaining treatments.[2] Put differently, "Charlie was essentially kidnapped, so that the authorities would be sure that he died on schedule."[3] Stripped of their right to make critical medical decisions on his behalf, the state permitted Charlie's parents to be at his bedside—as powerless onlookers—for his final hours.

It is tempting to regard the Charlie Gard saga as the horrific by-product of the United Kingdom's nationalized health system, where government bureaucrats wield outsize authority over health care and the law curtails the rights of parents, in certain situations, to make medical decisions for their own children. But the United States has had its share of high-profile cases where hospitals have sought court permission to override parents and end a child's life-sustaining treatment.

Jahi McMath, for example, was a healthy 13-year-old when she entered Children's Hospital in Oakland, California, for routine surgery to remove her tonsils and adenoids. In recovery, Jahi seemed alert—even asking for a popsicle—before suddenly hemorrhaging and going into cardiac arrest.[4] Within days, the hospital declared her "brain dead" and sought to "pull the plug" on Jahi's life support. Citing her religious beliefs, Jahi's mother refused to accept the declaration of "brain

2. The Charlie Gard case was decided under precedent inapplicable to US laws, such as the Convention for the Protection of Human Rights and Fundamental Freedoms, Council of Europe, and UK laws and court rulings. The UK High Court initially heard the case and appointed a guardian to represent his "best interests," presumably in opposition to the parents' decisions. At every level, it was clear that the courts vested the power to determine Charlie's best interests not in Charlie's parents but in others. Charlie's parents argued that the UK courts erred in deciding the case under a "best interests" standard, as opposed to a more limited standard that would override parental rights only if the parents' preferred course of medical treatment was likely to cause the child "significant harm." The European Court of Human Rights acknowledged the parents' "parental responsibility," which gave them "the power to give consent for their child to undergo treatment," but held that, "as a matter of law, overriding control is vested in the court exercising its independent and objective judgement in the child's best interests. In making that decision, the welfare of the child is paramount." See "Charles Gard and Others v. the United Kingdom," Global Health and Human Rights Database, accessed April 24, 2022, https://www.globalhealthrights.org/charles-gard-and-others-v-the-united-kingdom/.

3. Phil Lawler, "The State-Imposed Death of Charlie Gard: Not Just a Tragedy but an Injustice," *Catholic Culture*, June 30, 2017.

4. "Court Blocks Hospital from Disconnecting Jahi McMath from Life Support," CNN, December 30, 2013, https://www.cnn.com/2013/12/30/health/jahi-mcmath-girl-brain-dead/index.html.

death" or to consent to the removal of her daughter's life support. She insisted her daughter showed signs of life. The hospital went to court, seeking permission to disconnect Jahi's ventilator, arguing that any apparent signs of life were merely the result of the mechanical devices still pumping her heart. Jahi's "brain death," the hospital said, was irreversible.

Jahi's family sought to transfer her to another facility out of state, declaring, "we believe that, in this country, a parent has the right to make decisions concerning the existence of their child: not a doctor who looks only at lines on a paper, or reads the cold black and white words on a law that says 'brain dead' and definitely not a doctor who runs the facility that caused the brain death in the first place."[5] In an unusual settlement, the court let the hospital issue a death certificate but ordered Jahi be kept on a ventilator and released to her mother's care.[6] Jahi's family moved her to a New Jersey hospital, where she remained until her death in 2018, five years after being declared "brain dead." Jahi's mother has no regrets about her fight to secure care for her daughter and insists "Jahi wasn't brain dead or any kind of dead … She was a girl with a brain injury and she deserved to be cared for like any other child who had a brain injury."[7]

Like Jahi's family, the mother of Tinslee Lewis, a seriously ill toddler from Fort Worth, Texas, battled the medical establishment for the right to direct her daughter's care. Tinslee suffers from a serious heart defect and requires continuous, sophisticated medical care. The hospital caring for her petitioned the court for an expiration date on Tinslee's care. After spending nearly $24 million in state funds on her treatments, the hospital argued that Tinslee is in pain, recovery is hopeless, and treatment must end. Because the hospital described

5. "Court Blocks Hospital."

6. W. Smith, "There's Something about Jahi," *Human Life Review*, accessed April 24, 2022, https://humanlifereview.com/theres-something-about-jahi/.

7. "Girl Declared Brain-Dead Five Years Ago Dies in New Jersey," NBC News, June 29, 2018, https://www.nbcnews.com/health/health-news/girl-declared-bbrain-dead-5-years-ago-dies-california-n8877716. Despite the characterization of Jahi as a "corpse," she continued to mature and even underwent puberty. Celeste McGovern, "Jahi McMath Dies Four Years after Being Declared Brain-Dead," *National Catholic Register*, July 16, 2018. https://www.ncregister.com/news/jahi-mcmath-dies-four-years-after-being-declared-brain-dead.

Tinslee's treatments as "medically futile," the state fund paying for her care questioned whether "Texas should be spending tax dollars" on keeping Tinslee alive.[8] Tinslee's mother insisted that no matter who is paying the bill, only a parent should decide whether to end a child's life-sustaining care.[9] The court battle ended in April 2022, when the parties agreed Tinslee's mother could take her home. Texas Right to Life, an advocate for Tinslee's continued care, expressed gratitude that the hospital finally "worked with the family to improve Tinslee's health" so the child could be treated at home, where she reportedly is "doing great" and giving her family kisses.[10]

The Stakes

Cases like those of Charlie Gard, Jahi McMath, and Tinslee Lewis make headlines because the stakes are high: life or death. As states, hospitals, and health insurers increasingly foot the bills for expensive medical treatments, some inevitably will balk at parents' requests for life-prolonging treatments for medically fragile children and will seek court mandates to displace parents as medical decision-makers. Parents' rights in these contexts are incredibly important, not because there is a moral obligation to use "extraordinary means" to extend a child's life (there isn't), but because "the decision about whether to pursue extraordinary care should rest with the rightful authority," typically the parents.[11] Fortunately, most parents will never have to make

8. "Hospital Seeks New Trial to Remove Toddler from Life Support," ABC News, May 3, 2021, https://abcnews.go.com/Health/wireStory/hospital-seeks-trial-remove-toddler-life-support-777469184.

9. "Hospital Seeks New Trial."

10. Kaley Johnson, "'Tinslee Is Home': Toddler Discharged from Fort Worth Hospital after Lengthy Court Battle," *Fort Worth Star-Telegram*, April 15, 2022, https://www.star-telegram.com/news/local/fort-worth/article260358560.html.

11. Fr. Shenan Bouquet, "The Case of Charlie Gard," *Human Life International*, July 8, 2017, https://www.hli.org/2017/07/case-charlie-gard/. The Catholic Church teaches that "nutrition and hydration, even if medically assisted, is normally ordinary care ... Ordinary medical care is largely an intervention that is generally accepted as effective and not terribly burdensome or expensive. This varies from place to place and even as a result of scientific breakthroughs ... Extraordinary means would involve severe burdens, physical or psychological or financial. Extraordinary means such as experimental treatments would not have a very high chance of effectively helping the patient." John Haas and Joseph Meaney, "Discerning Ordinary vs.

life-or-death medical decisions for a child, and even fewer will face the prospect that a physician, hospital, or the state will try to strip away their decision-making power at critical junctures.[12]

Even so, these dramatic cases underscore the critical importance of protecting parents' rights. Writing about the Charlie Gard case, Fr. Shenan J. Bouquet, the president of Human Life International, identified the "fundamental issue" at stake: "A struggle for power. That is: The hospital, and the UK government, believe that the state, and not Charlie's parents, should have the power to decide what is best for Charlie (and, presumably, others like him)."[13]

The "power struggle" is not confined to critical care. For most parents, the greatest threat to their parental rights, in the medical context, is likely to come from well-meaning people they already trust: a child's pediatrician, a school-based health provider, or a counselor. Unlike the intensity of end-of-life decision-making, the sustained threat to parents' rights plays out over years, like a silent stalker following a child through adolescence. Before exploring the rocky adolescent terrain, however, a quick overview of the nature of parental rights is in order.

Parental Rights and Responsibilities, in Brief

Most parents are likely familiar with the general rule regarding their children's medical care: Parents have the right to make medical decisions for children who are under the age of legal majority, typically 18. "Obtaining informed permission from parents or legal guardians be-

Extraordinary Means in Catholic Bioethics: President Messages," National Catholic Bioethics Center, October 30, 2020.

12. A consistent fact pattern in which medical authorities, backed by the power of the state, will override the wishes of parents involves a life-or-death situation where the parents are Jehovah's Witnesses and refuse consent for a lifesaving blood transfusion for a child. In these cases, courts typically override the parents' wishes and permit the hospital to transfuse the child, although in at least one case where an older teen shared his parents' religious beliefs against accepting a transfusion, the courts declined to intervene. For a brief treatment of the issue, see D. Winiarski et al., "Risks and Legal Issues in Caring for Minor Jehovah's Witness Patients," American Society for Health Care Risk Management, March 29, 2018, https://forum.ashrm.org/2018/03/29/risks-and-legal-issues-in-caring-for-minor-jehovahs-witness-patients/.

13. Fr. Shenan Bouquet, "The Case of Charlie Gard," *Human Life International*, July 8, 2017, https://www.hli.org/2017/07/case-charlie-gard/.

fore medical interventions on pediatric patients is now standard with-in our medical and legal culture."[14] The law affords parents significant latitude in decision-making under a general rationale, consistent with natural law, that parents have a *right* to make medical decisions be-cause they have a *responsibility* to care for their children.[15]

In light of the bond between parent and child, parents presumably know the child's needs best, have the strongest motivation to act in a child's best interests, and are well positioned to follow through with the requisite care. Philosopher Melissa Moschella explains that "paren-tal rights are really about parents' authority to make decisions about what is in the best interests of their children. Because children are not mature enough to make important decisions for themselves, someone needs to have the authority to make decisions on their behalf. Defend-ers of parental rights believe that childrearing authority belongs pri-marily to parents and that the state should not interfere with parents' decision-making except when parents have clearly shown themselves to be unfit."[16]

Put differently, parental authority is God given and inherent in the parent-child relationship. Parental authority precedes the state; that is, the state neither grants nor delegates authority to parents over their children. Parents possess this authority simply by virtue of be-ing parents. The right is not absolute, and conflicts arise, for example, when parents reject recommended medical advice and refuse care for a child, for religious reasons or otherwise. Even then, physicians (and courts) are reluctant to override a parent's decision unless the child's life is at stake or the parent's decision threatens serious harm to the child's present or long-term health. The state's role is to respect parents as the primary authorities in their children's lives and support them in raising their children. Only when parents fail in their duty, by either

14. Aviva L. Katz et al., "Informed Consent in Decision-Making in Pediatric Practice," *Pediatrics* 138, no. 2 (2016): e20161485, doi:10.1542/peds.2016-1485.

15. Melissa Moschella, "Parental Rights, Gender Ideology, and the Equality Act," Heritage Foundation, March 16, 2021, https://www.heritage.org/gender/report/parental-rights-gender-ideology-and-the-equality-act. See also M. Moschella, *To Whom Do Children Belong? Parental Rights, Civic Education, and Children's Autonomy* (Cambridge: Cambridge University Press; repr. ed., 2017).

16. Moschella, "Parental Rights."

neglect or harmful actions, should the state step into the parental role (*parens patriae*) to protect and care for children.[17]

In a line of cases stretching over a hundred years, the US Supreme Court recognized the "fundamental right" of parents to raise, care for, and educate their children.[18] The court has acknowledged that parental rights precede the authority of the state ("the custody, care and nurture of the child reside first in the parents"[19]) and are grounded in the Western cultural and legal tradition ("our jurisprudence historically has reflected Western civilization concepts of the family as a unit with broad parental authority over minor children").[20] The court makes the commonsense point that parents possess maturity and judgment, while minors do not ("presumption that parents possess what a child lacks in maturity, experience, and capacity for judgment required for making life's difficult decisions"[21]). Twenty years ago, the Supreme Court recounted its extensive history supporting parental rights and capped it off by declaring, "In light of this extensive precedent, it cannot now be doubted that the Due Process Clause of the Fourteenth Amendment protects the fundamental right of parents to make decisions concerning the care, custody, and control of their children."[22]

Parents' enjoyment of these fundamental rights gives rise to certain presumptions under the law: parents are *presumed* to be fit parents unless proven otherwise, and they are *presumed* to be acting in the best interests of their child (the court "historically ... has recognized that natural bonds of affection lead parents to act in the best interests of their children"[23]). The state bears the burden of proving otherwise. Further, these presumptions do not "evaporate" or become "subordinated" to the state simply because a child's individual liberty interests

17. *Parens patriae* is a term that describes the "power of the state to act as guardian for those who are unable to care for themselves, such as children or disabled individuals." "Parens Patriae," Legal Information Institute, accessed April 24, 2022, https://www.law.cornell.edu/wex/parens_patriae.

18. *Troxel v. Granville*, 530 U.S. 57, 65–66 (2000).

19. *Prince v. Massachusetts*, 321 U.S. 158, 166 (1944).

20. *Parham v. J. R.*, 442 U.S. 584, 602 (1979). See also *Wisconsin v. Yoder*, 406 U.S. 205, 232 (1972).

21. *Parham*, at 602.

22. *Troxel*, at 66.

23. *Parham*, at 602.

also are involved, or because the state has a generalized concern about abusive parents, or because the parents have not always been "model parents."[24] Nor can the state impose a "decisional framework" that "directly contravene[s] the traditional presumption that a fit parent will act in the best interest of his or her child."[25] Finally, the state cannot "discard wholesale" the presumption that parents are acting in the child's best interests.[26] Evidence, typically showing actual or imminent risk of abuse or serious harm, is required to rebut that presumption.

In sum, parents have a natural right to make decisions regarding the upbringing and care of their children, including their medical care. The law recognizes parental authority and presumes parents will make decisions with child's "best interests" in mind (or at least avoiding significant harm), and courts defer to parental judgment about what is "best," regardless of whether the child agrees.[27] In light of parents' fundamental rights, the Constitution limits the power of state to "inject itself into the private realm of the family," absent evidence that the parents have failed to "adequately" care for their child.[28] The court emphatically rejects as "repugnant to American tradition" the "statist

24. "The law's concept of the family rests on a presumption that parents possess what a child lacks in maturity, experience, and capacity for judgment required for making life's difficult decisions. More important, historically it has recognized that natural bonds of affection lead parents to act in the best interests of their children. 1 W. Blackstone, Commentaries 447; 2 J. Kent, *Commentaries on American Law* 190." *Parham*, at 602. Regarding the possibility of abuse, the *Parham* court observed that parental rights give rise to a "'high duty' to recognize symptoms of illness and to seek and follow medical advice," citing *Pierce v. Society of Sisters*, 268 U.S. 510, 535 (1925). "As with so many other legal presumptions, experience and reality may rebut what the law accepts as a starting point; the incidence of child neglect and abuse cases attests to this. That some parents 'may at times be acting against the interests of their children,' as was stated in *Bartley v. Kremens*, 402 F. Supp. 1039, 1047–1048 (ED Pa.1975), *vacated and remanded,* 431 U.S. 119 (1977), creates a basis for caution, but is hardly a reason to discard wholesale those pages of human experience that teach that parents generally do act in the child's best interests." *Parham*, at 602, 603. In *Santosky v. Kramer* the court noted that the "fundamental liberty interest of natural parents in the care, custody, and management of their child does not evaporate simply because they have not been model parents or have lost temporary custody of their child to the State. Even when blood relationships are strained, parents retain a vital interest in preventing the irretrievable destruction of their family life." *Santosky v. Kramer*, 455 U.S. 745, 753 (1982).

25. *Troxel*, at 69, citing *Parham*, at 602. In other words, the state cannot attempt to accomplish procedurally what it is not permitted to do substantively.

26. *Parham*, at 603.

27. *Parham*, at 603.

28. *Troxel*, at 68.

notion that governmental power should supersede parental authority in *all* cases because *some* parents abuse and neglect children."[29] The fundamental rights of specific parents cannot be burdened or overridden because of a theoretical risk that *some parents, somewhere* might abuse their children in similar factual situations.

In the medical realm, paternalistic practices of old have fallen by the wayside, in recognition of patient autonomy and rights in tort law to prevent undesired contact or bodily harm. As a result, the modern practice of medicine imposes legal and ethical duties on providers to disclose critical information to patients and obtain the patient's informed consent before undertaking medical treatments.[30] When the patient lacks actual or legal capacity to give consent, then "parents or other surrogates provide 'informed permission' for diagnosis and treatment," explains the American Academy of Pediatrics (AAP), "with the assent of the child as developmentally appropriate."[31] Thus parental decision-making on a child's behalf includes the power to *give* or *refuse* permission for a child to receive a particular medical intervention. In practice, parental authority over a minor child's health care, and the right of a minor to give consent on his or her own behalf, is governed by state laws (which vary significantly) and some federal requirements (e.g., Title X).[32]

29. *Parham*, at 603 (emphasis added). Most recently, the Supreme Court gave a nod to parental rights in an education-related case, where the school imposed punishment on a cheerleader's vulgar comments, which were made on social media, outside of school. *Mahanoy Area School District v. B.L.*, 594 U.S. (2021). In this case the Supreme Court held that although schools possess some authority to impose limits on on-campus speech, they cannot punish a student for posting vulgar messages on social media. The court distinguished between the "zone of parental ... responsibility" and the "zone of ... school-related ... responsibility" (slip op., at 7) and noted that schools possess limited delegated authority (*in loco parentis*) from parents, describing the "doctrine of *in loco parentis*" as "treat[ing] school administrators as standing in the place of students' parents under circumstances where the children's actual parents cannot protect, guide, and discipline them" (slip op., at 7).

30. According to the AAP technical report *Informed Consent in Decision-Making in Pediatric Practice*, "the required elements of disclosure during the consent process [include]... mandating disclosure of risks, the nature of the medical condition, details of the proposed treatment, the probability of success, and possible alternative treatments. The standard of what information must be included in discussions leading to informed consent or informed refusal of treatment has evolved over time and varies somewhat from state to state" (Katz et al., "Informed Consent").

31. Katz et al., "Informed Consent."

32. When the federal government offers certain medical services, for example, the pro-

Parents' ordinary experiences with pediatricians, specialists, and hospitals during a child's first ten years of life give them confidence that "doctors advise but parents decide."[33] The familiar administrative routines common to most health care settings communicate a reassuring message that, absent an emergency, providers will not treat a child without first obtaining the parent's permission. Before a child can receive the typical vaccines required for school enrollment, for example, the child's physician must explain the vaccine's purpose, side effects, and benefits to parents. Only after parents sign forms documenting their understanding and giving the physician permission to vaccinate their child will the physician proceed. Parents of school-aged children know that the school nurse will not give their children Tylenol for a headache without first calling to ask permission. And when a young child needs surgery or complicated medical treatments, parents typically expect multiple conversations with the child's physician, reviewing risks, benefits, and alternatives before giving written approval for their child's planned procedure.

It is natural for parents to look to their child's physicians for guidance and expertise and expect their parental decisions to be respected. (The AAP, however, describes physicians and parents as "co-fiduciaries" of the child's "health matters," implying an equality at least in terms of ethical obligations.)[34] Clinicians who treat prepubescent children of-

---

vision of contraception at federally funded Title X clinics, federal regulations on access, and confidentiality come into play. Several helpful charts that analyze state laws regarding minor's rights to consent to medical care and governing disclosure of protected health information are available as follows. The Guttmacher Institute gives a state-by-state analysis of the kinds of reproductive-related medical care that minors (under 18) can consent to on their own (i.e., no parental consent). "An Overview to Consent to Reproductive Health Services by Young People," Guttmacher Institute, updated July 1, 2021, https://www.guttmacher.org/state-policy/explore/overview-minors-consent-law. The CDC provides information about minor consent to services for STIs and HIV: "State Laws That Enable a Minor to Provide Informed Consent to Receive HIV and STD Services," HIV Legal Landscape, Centers for Disease Control and Prevention, January 8, 2021, https://www.cdc.gov/hiv/policies/law/states/minors.html. The Department of Health and Human Services provides fact sheets, frequently asked questions, and other guidelines on HIPAA Privacy Rules; see "Summary of the HIPAA Privacy Rule," US Department of Health and Human Services, last reviewed July 26, 2013, https://www.hhs.gov/hipaa/for-professionals/privacy/laws-regulations/index.html.

33. Elizabeth S. Scott and Clare Huntington, "Children's Health in a Legal Framework," *Future of Children* 25, no. 1 (spring 2015).

34. Katz et al., "Informed Consent."

ten encourage a "shared decision-making" approach between parents and physicians. In this model the physician informs and guides but typically "defers the decision to caregiver views of what is 'best' provided they are reasonable and do not lead to harm for the child."[35]

The Perils of Adolescence

As parents round the corner on a child's first decade of life, they may feel confident that, barring a crisis, their right to make medical decisions for their minor children (under 18) is secure.[36] It's the calm before the storm. Once the child moves into adolescence (typically defined as 12–18 years old), the paradigm shifts, and parental control over a child's medical care becomes increasingly tenuous, at least in "sensitive" areas of an adolescent's life. There, the general rule respecting parents' rights collapses under the weight of exceptions.

While the sexual revolution was encouraging young people to experiment ("if it feels good, do it"), the Supreme Court and many states were restricting the rights of parents to be involved in a minor child's decisions about contraception and abortion and, by implication, sexu-

35. The shared decision-making approach presumes that the decision tree offers "multiple ethically reasonable approaches." It rests on a shared commitment to patient autonomy (or parental authority exercised on behalf of the child) and "the child's best interests (beneficence)," where "both parties bring knowledge, values, and preferences to the discussion and work collaboratively … facilitating information exchange to decide what is best for the child, within the context of family goals." A. Patel, D. M. Feltman, and E. T. Paquette, "Integrating Public Health Ethics into Shared Decision Making for Children during the Novel Coronavirus Disease-19 Pandemic," *Journal of Pediatrics* 231 (2021): 259–64, https://doi.org/10.1016/j.jpeds.2020.11.061, https://www.ncbi.nlm.nih.gov/pmc/articles/PMC7706416/.

36. The rights of parents over their minor's care, of course, have never been regarded as absolute. In addition to the state's *parens patriae* power (state intervention to protect minor children whose parents failed to fulfill their obligations), states recognize some minors as legally "emancipated" and thus capable of making their own decisions, and typically permit physicians to render emergency care for minors to preserve life or prevent serious injury, even in the absence of parental consent. These exceptions to parental rights are not controversial and will not be addressed further in this chapter, except to note that state law defines and governs the status of "emancipated" minors, who typically are treated as legal adults for all purposes and thus not subject to parental authority. Generally, a minor can be accorded emancipated status by court order, military service, marriage, or parenthood. Emergency care requirements are addressed both by state and federal laws; see "Emergency Medical Treatment and Labor Act (EMTLA)," Centers for Medicare and Medicaid Services, last modified December 1, 2021, https://www.cms.gov/Regulations-and-Guidance/Legislation/EMTALA.

al activity.[37] It is beyond the scope of this chapter to detail the history and evolution of the court's troubling jurisprudence on abortion and contraception, except to say that court decisions striking down state age barriers and invalidating "blanket" parental consent requirements as unconstitutional gave rise to the "mature minor" concept and set the stage for today's expansive exceptions to parental authority over children's medical care.[38]

Since the 1970s, policy makers, legislatures, and health care professionals have collaborated to shut parents out of adolescent decision-making. They carved out entire swaths of teenage life, labeled it "sensitive," and rendered it "out of bounds" for parental advice, limits, or support, absent a teen's willingness to involve the parents. It is not a coincidence that "adolescent medicine" emerged as a discrete medical specialty during the 1970s, in the wake of the sexual revolution

37. The International Planned Parenthood Federation sums up the progressive approach toward youth sexuality and parental rights: "Sexuality and sexual pleasure are important parts of being human for everyone—no matter what age, no matter if you're married or not and no matter if you want to have children or not ... Young people's capacities to make decisions for themselves evolve over time and must be recognized, especially when it comes to sexuality. Governments and leaders have a duty to respect, protect and fulfil all sexual rights for everyone ... [Young people are entitled to] autonomy to make decisions about one's sexuality in line with the evolving capacity of young people and without forceful interference from parents, guardians or other adult figures ... [Young people are entitled to] privacy and confidentiality at sexual and reproductive health services ... Privacy and confidentiality of information about young people's sexual behaviour, sexual orientation, HIV status, contraceptive use, history of sexually transmitted infections, pregnancy or abortion ... [and to] give their consent before any personal sexual health information is disclosed to parents, families, spouses, partners or communities." "Exclaim: Young People's Guide to 'Sexual Rights: An IPPF Declaration,'" International Planned Parenthood Federation, accessed May 31, 2022, https://www.ippf.org/resource/exclaim-young-peoples-guide-sexual-rights-ippf-declaration, p. 20 and Annex 2.

38. Supreme Court jurisprudence on abortion and contraception has resulted in a tangled set of constitutional criteria that courts apply to evaluate state laws that attempt to regulate the provision of abortion and contraception, including to minors. *See Carey v. Population Services International*, 431 U.S. 678 (1977), which *inter alia* invalidated minimum age restrictions on contraception. "An Overview to Consent to Reproductive Health Services by Young People," Guttmacher Institute, updated July 1, 2021, https://www.guttmacher.org/state-policy/explore/overview-minors-consent-law. Legal precedents governing abortion and contraception have been well analyzed elsewhere and are beyond the scope of this chapter. The courts have upheld various state "informed consent" laws that require physicians to provide women with information about the abortion procedure, attendant risks and outcomes, and fetal development. *Planned Parenthood of Southeastern Pennsylvania v. Casey*, 505 U.S. 833 (1992). See also "Minnesota Governor Vetoes Informed Consent Bill," Charlotte Lozier Institute, June 13, 2018, https://lozierinstitute.org/minnesota-governor-vetoes-informed-consent-bill/#_ftn23.

and dramatic cultural and legal changes.[39] By 2004 the Society for Adolescent Medicine boasted of its success in "making confidential care available to adolescents, particularly for sensitive concerns such as sexuality [and reproduction], sexually transmitted infections (STIs), substance abuse, and mental health."[40] From the perspective of the experts, fencing parents out of adolescent medical care in favor of adolescent "autonomy" was now "a well-established tradition ... in the United States."[41]

Apart from minor's access to abortion and contraception (under sweeping constitutional protections for the choice whether to "bear or beget" a child), legal carve-outs to parental permission requirements for minors' "sensitive" health matters are typically justified in one of two ways: as "public health" necessities (an aspect of the state's police power) or under the "mature minor" rationale.[42] The end result is the

39. "Behavioral trends were also associated with rising rates of sexually transmitted infections (STIs), teenage pregnancy, substance abuse, accidents, and violence. The field thus had to develop special interdisciplinary skills to address the unique intertwining of complex medical, developmental, and psychosocial issues characteristic of the adolescent patient." Jessica Rieder, MD, et al., "Adolescent Medicine: Emergence of a New Specialty," *Virtual Mentor* 7, no. 3 (2005): 249–52, doi:10.1001/virtualmentor.2005.7.3.msoc1-0503, https://journalofethics.ama-assn.org/article/adoles cent-medicine-emergence-new-specialty/2005-03.

40. In its position paper the Society for Adolescent Medicine said, "A well-established tradition has developed in the United States of making confidential care available to adolescents, particularly for sensitive concerns such as sexuality, sexually transmitted infections (STIs), substance abuse, and mental health. This tradition has been carried on by a wide variety of health care professionals in diverse settings. It is well grounded in ethics, clinical practice, and research. In addition, legal protections for confidential care have been embodied in federal and state laws" (citations omitted). "Confidential Health Care for Adolescents: Position Paper of the Society for Adolescent Medicine," *Journal of Adolescent Health* 35, no. 1 (2004): doi:10.1016/j.jadohealth.2004.03.00.2.

41. Society for Adolescent Medicine, "Confidential Health Care for Adolescents."

42. The state's police power has long been recognized to permit the state to impose mandatory vaccination rules or other measures necessary to preserve public health. *Jacobson v. Massachusetts*, 197 U.S. 11 (1905). It has been invoked to justify minors' testing and treatment for STIs, in light of the expressed reluctance of some minors to seek appropriate medical care if their parents will be informed or required to provide consent. The "mature minor" doctrine permits a minor to consent to specific medical procedures or testing, even though the minor lacks capacity to give legal consent more generally. When the mature minor rule is invoked, the minor is presumed or adjudged to have the requisite maturity and capacity for decision-making regarding the specific issue at hand. Numerous Supreme Court decisions involving state laws requiring parental notice or consent included discussion of "mature minor" concepts and mechanisms (such as the judicial bypass) to determine a minor's capacity to give informed consent. See, e.g., *Bellotti v. Baird*, 443 U.S. 622 (1979) and *Planned Parenthood Assn. v. Ashcroft*, 462 U.S. 476 (1983).

same: to permit minors to give legal consent, on their own, to certain types of controversial medical care. From a parental perspective, the end result is to deprive parents of the opportunity to guide, correct, or support their children in making significant life decisions or in bearing the consequences of earlier decisions.

Shocking Expansion of Laws Permitting Minor Consent

Laws in all fifty states permit minors—in most cases, as young as 12 years of age—to consent to and access testing and treatment for sexually transmitted infections (STIs), without parental involvement.[43] Many of these statutes are decades old, from a time when child abuse and sexual assault were underrecognized and underreported, and some states permitted minors as young as 14 to marry. The public health rationale for permitting STI testing or treatment without requiring parental consent or notice is premised on the belief that easy testing and treatment reduces the spread of STIs and their associated costs to society, and that adolescents are less likely to receive testing and treatment if their parents would be involved.

But there is no evidence that keeping parents in the dark regarding adolescent STI testing or treatment has played any role in decreasing adolescent STIs. For starters, STI rates have not decreased: they are at an all-time high, with adolescents and young adults accounting for nearly half of new cases.[44] No reported studies appear to have assessed whether parental intervention might result in lower overall STI rates, whether by deterring youth sexual activity over time, increased parental monitoring of risky behaviors, or parental oversight to ensure that the minor complies with treatment and risk reduction efforts. Research justifications for permitting minors to receive STI testing and treatment without parental involvement seem to rest mostly on adolescent speculation. Although a recent study, for example, reported

43. "State Laws That Enable."

44. Centers for Disease Control and Prevention, "New CDC Report: STDs Continue to Rise in the U.S.," press release, October 8, 2019, https://www.cdc.gov/nchhstp/newsroom /2019/2018-STD-surveillance-report-press-release.html.

that 22 percent of sexually experienced 15- to 17-year-olds said they "would not seek sexual or reproductive health care because their parents might find out," the authors cautioned that "a causal relationship between confidentiality concerns and receipt of STD services cannot be inferred."[45] Given that the direct lifetime medical costs of new STIs total $16 billion (not counting other related social costs), and society's greater awareness that sex involving minors may involve exploitation, abuse, or even sex trafficking, it is past time for a new approach: restore parental involvement in STI testing and treatment for minors and assess the impact on STI incidence and outcomes.

There is an additional reason to be concerned over the STI exception to parental consent requirements: In a growing number of states, the STI exception specifically extends to testing, treatment, and preventive services for HIV.[46] When state law is silent—not specifically permitting minors to receive HIV testing and treatment without parental consent—medical providers become de facto gatekeepers, exercising their own judgment about whether to provide the minor with HIV testing or treatment and whether to inform parents. According to the latest tallies from the Centers for Disease Control and Prevention (CDC), no jurisdictions specifically prohibit minor consent to HIV testing, treatment, or prevention, which leaves the door wide open for medical providers to promote the use of HIV-prevention (PreP) medications or HIV treatment drug regimens to adolescents, without parental knowledge. This is an extraordinary stretching of the STI exception. The health ramifications for a minor who undergoes testing and treatment for common STIs are vastly different from the serious, lifelong consequences of HIV-related prevention and treatment.

Consider the sexually active minor, a male who has sex with other

45. J. S. Leichliter, C. Copen, and P. J. Dittus, "Confidentiality Issues and Use of Sexually Transmitted Disease Services among Sexually Experienced Persons Aged 15–25 Years—United States, 2013–2015," *Morbidity and Mortality Weekly Report* 66 (2017): 237–41, doi:http://dx.doi.org/10.15585/mmwr.mm6609a1, https://www.cdc.gov/mmwr/volumes/66/wr/mm6609a1.htm. See also D. M. Reddy, R. Fleming, and C. Swain, "Effect of Mandatory Parental Notification on Adolescent Girls' Use of Sexual Health Care Services," *JAMA* 288, no. 6 (2002): 710–14, doi:10.1001/jama.288.6.710, PMID 12169074.

46. "An Overview of Consent to Reproductive Health Services by Young People," Guttmacher Institute, July 1, 2021, https://www.guttmacher.org/state-policy/explore/overview-minors-consent-law.

males and engages in receptive anal intercourse with no condom. His behavior puts him at high risk for becoming infected with HIV. (In 2018, 69 percent of people diagnosed with HIV in the United States were "gay, bisexual and other men who have sex with men (MSM)," with young people ages 12–24 accounting for 20 percent of US HIV diagnoses.)[47] Additionally, "HIV diagnoses among adolescents and young adults in the US increased by six percent" from 2012 to 2016, even though HIV diagnoses held steady among older adults.[48]

Public health experts are panicking but are loath to tell young people not to have sex or not to have risky sex. Instead, one of the new strategies "to reduce the alarming rates of new adolescent HIV infections in the U.S. and to improve the health of adolescents who are at increased risk for contracting HIV" is to expand existing minor consent laws to permit adolescents to consent to HIV prevention (meaning PreP) and treatment (anti-retroviral medications, including "PEP, an after-the-exposure preventive dosing").[49]

But the PreP protocol carries significant risks. Significant increases in STI rates are associated with taking PreP, along with serious side effects.[50] The PreP medication Descovy, for example, has side effects that include worsening of hepatitis B infection, kidney problems/ failure, severe liver problems, too much lactic acid, nausea, diarrhea, headache, and more.[51] Truvada, another common PreP medication, lists the same serious side effects as Descovy, with the addition of bone thinning and risk of fractures—a particular concern for adolescents, who are generally still growing.[52] Moreover, there are no long-term studies documenting the outcomes of PreP use in adolescents.

47. O. Olateju, D. Dunn, P. McLaine, and S. Barrett, "Revision of Maryland Minor Consent Law on Human Immunodeficiency Virus Infection Prevention: An Outcome of Advocacy," *HIV/AIDS Research and Treatment Open Journal* 7, no. 1 (2020): 10–17, doi:10.17140/ HARTOJ-7-134.

48. Olateju et al., "Revision of Maryland Minor Consent Law."

49. Olateju et al., "Revision of Maryland Minor Consent Law."

50. M. W. Traeger et al., "Association of HIV Preexposure Prophylaxis with Incidence of Sexually Transmitted Infections among Individuals at High Risk of HIV Infection," *JAMA* 321, no. 14 (2019): 1380–90, doi:10.1001/jama.2019.2947.

51. "Important Safety Information about Descovy for PreP," Descovy, accessed April 24, 2022, https://www.descovy.com/treatment.

52. "What Are Possible Side Effects of Truvada?," Truvada, accessed April 24, 2022, https:// www.truvada.com/what-is-truvada/side-effects.

A minor who tests positive for HIV is in a precarious position, which becomes even more precarious when he must face an HIV diagnosis alone, without parental support, guidance, or intervention. Although medical advances have reduced the lethality of an HIV diagnosis, HIV remains a serious, incurable disease, with long-term effects on many bodily systems. It requires *lifelong* medication to reduce transmissibility of the virus and to maintain overall health. Medication is costly, and treatment regimens require commitment and maturity; even among adults, continuing adherence to medication and treatment protocols is inconsistent, and rates of compliance tend to decrease over time. Young people infected with HIV have "the lowest rates of antiretroviral (ARV) therapy uptake and adherence, and the lowest level of awareness of their HIV status."[53] Adolescents with HIV also "may be at increased risk for poor medication adherence, for difficulty achieving viral suppression, for viral rebound, and for loss to follow-up ... Adolescents may bear other risks such as transmitting the virus to others, developing antiretroviral resistance, and having a compromised immune system."[54]

In contrast, most (non-HIV) STI infections are curable. Even serious infections like syphilis often require only a short course of inexpensive antibiotics. Aside from HIV, the few incurable STIs (e.g., herpes) are not deadly and do not typically require lifelong medication for the person to remain functionally healthy. It is unconscionable to keep parents in the dark when their adolescent (of any age) is engaging in behavior that puts him at high risk of acquiring HIV; it is equally unconscionable to treat the at-risk adolescent with HIV-prevention (PreP) or treatment drugs, all of which have serious side effects and potentially lifelong consequence, without involving the adolescent's parents.

Inevitably, activists working to undermine parental rights raise the specter of abusive parents, parents who will harm or reject a vulnera-

---

53. Olateju et al., "Revision of Maryland Minor Consent Law."

54. Olateju et al., "Revision of Maryland Minor Consent Law," citing M. R. Tanner et al., "Preexposure Prophylaxis for Prevention of HIV Acquisition among Adolescents: Clinical Considerations," *MMWR Recommendations and Reports* 69, no. 3 (2020): 1–12, doi:10.15585/mmwr.rr6903a1.

ble child because of conflicts over a child's sexual behavior or identity. This argument is a red herring. Society already has mechanisms in place to report suspected child abuse and to protect vulnerable children in imminent danger of harm. And the Supreme Court has rejected the notion that generalized concerns can be leveraged to deprive parents of their fundamental rights.[55] Policy makers and parents should reject those arguments as well.

In addition to their efforts to expand minor self-consent laws to cover HIV prevention and treatment protocols, activists are zeroing in on vaccine laws. Even before the COVID-19 pandemic, public pressure to permit minors to consent to vaccines was on the rise, influenced by public health experts pushing increased vaccination rates among adolescents for the human papillomavirus (HPV) and in response to the growing ranks of "antivaxxers."[56] As COVID-19 vaccines became available, the pressure on states increased. A CNN review in May 2021 found that "Five states—Alabama, Iowa, North Carolina, Oregon and Tennessee—either allow some ages in that group to consent for themselves or leave requirements up to individual vaccine providers."[57]

The District of Columbia passed a regulation in 2020 that permitted minors, from age 11 onward, to consent to receive vaccines so long as the minor is capable of giving informed consent, defined as understanding the purpose of the vaccine and its risks and benefits.[58] The truly insidious aspect of the DC law, however, is its demonstrated intent to disregard and override decisions that the parent *already* has made about the child's vaccines. The regulation states that when "a minor student is utilizing a religious exemption for vaccinations or is opting out of receiving the Human Papillomavirus vaccine," but then receives a vaccine under the new law, the health care provider must

55. *Parham*, at 602.

56. Michael Ollove, "Teens of 'Anti-Vaxxers' Can Get Their Own Vaccines, Some States Say," *Stateline*, June 24, 2019, https://www.pewtrusts.org/en/research-and-analysis/blogs/state line/2019/06/24/teens-of-anti-vaxxers-can-get-their-own-vaccines-some-states-say.

57. "COVID: States That Do Not Require Parental Consent for Vaccine for Ages 12 to 15," CNN, May 14, 2021, https://www.mercurynews.com/2021/05/14/covid-states-that-do-not-require -parental-consent-for-vaccine-for-ages-12-to-15/.

58. "B23-0171—Minor Consent for Vaccinations Amendment Act of 2020," Council of the District of Columbia, accessed May 30, 2022, https://code.dccouncil.us/us/dc/council/laws/ 23-193.

submit the vaccine record directly to the child's school, not the parent. The school, in turn, must keep the child's vaccine status "confidential." In other words, despite a parent's specific objection to a particular vaccine, the state "empowers" an 11-year-old child to decide otherwise and presumes the child is capable of giving valid informed consent to receive the vaccine. Under the guise of facilitating the child's "autonomy," the state deliberately overrides the parent's known decision about what's best for the child by elevating the child to the position of "decision maker." But no child makes a decision about taking a vaccine without seeking adult guidance, especially a child of 11 years. The DC law blocks parental influence while elevating the influence of unknown others (under the pretense that the child is capable of giving informed consent) and requiring health care providers to collude with the child's school, and implicitly the Department of Health, to hide the child's vaccine status from the parents. Two lawsuits were soon filed on behalf of parents alleging that the law violated their parental rights and religious freedom. In March 2022, a federal judge enjoined the law, prohibiting the government from permitting minors to receive vaccines without parental consent while the cases play out in court.[59]

There's more. The pressure is on to create further "minor consent" exceptions, now focused on "gender transitions." Advocates of "transgender medicine" seek to prioritize the "developing autonomy" of a transgender-identifying child when parents object to "gender-affirming care."[60] (Adolescents who identify as transgender or nonbinary often seek so-called gender-affirming care, which involves medical and surgical interventions that alter the body's appearance and destroy its functions in order to reinforce the adolescent's distorted identity perceptions.) A recent article in the *Journal of Medical Ethics*, for exam-

59. Cami Mondeaux, "Judge Blocks DC from Allowing Children to Get Vaccinated without Parental Consent," *Washington Examiner*, March 21, 2011, https://www.washington examiner.com/restoring-america/fairness-justice/judge-blocks-dc-from-allowing-children-to -get-vaccinated-without-parental-consent.

60. S. Dubin et al., "Medically Assisted Gender Affirmation: When Children and Parents Disagree," *Journal of Medical Ethics* 46 (2020): 295–99, https://jme.bmj.com/content/46/5/295; M. Priest, "Transgender Children and the Right to Transition: Medical Ethics When Parents Mean Well but Cause Harm," *American Journal of Bioethics* 19, no. 2 (2019): 45–59, doi:10.1080 /15265161.2018.1557276, PMID 30784385.

ple, claimed that when parents and children disagree over whether a transgender-identifying child should begin "gender-affirming care," one of three legal mechanisms should be used to override parental decision-making authority—"legal carve-outs to parental consent, the mature minor doctrine and state intervention for neglect."[61]

These exceptions—public health or mature minor rationales—did not come about because parents lobbied for them or because of new scientific discoveries about adolescent development and maturity.[62] As every parent knows, an adolescent's "sensitive concerns" are the precise areas that beg for parental intervention, especially in light of adolescent tendencies toward experimentation, impulsive decision-making (especially when emotions run high), emotional extremes, short-term thinking, peer-driven behaviors, and insecurity. The truth is that "these minor consent laws reflect policy judgments" that align with the agendas of the powerful sexual and reproductive rights industry (and, more lately, lesbian, gay, bisexual, transgender, or queer [LGBTQ] groups) while perpetuating useful fictions. In other words, "certain minors have attained a level of maturity or autonomy ... to make their own medical decisions," and public health requires minor self-consent because "adolescents generally are unlikely to seek certain 'sensitive' but essential services unless they ... do so independently of their parents."[63] Parents have been displaced as the primary medical

61. Dubin et al., "Medically Assisted Gender Affirmation." In at least one case, parents have lost their parental rights because of claims that their refusal to support a gender transition amounted to abusive behavior. Ryan T. Anderson, "Parents Just Lost Custody of Teenage Daughter Who Wants to 'Transition' to a Boy: What You Need to Know," Heritage Foundation, February 20, 2018, https://www.heritage.org/gender/commentary/parents-just-lost-custody -teenage-daughter-who-wants-transition-boy-what-you-need.

62. Scientific evidence undercuts the fiction that minors have the capacity to give informed consent as if they were adults. Research on the adolescent brain shows that so long as adolescents are on an even keel emotionally, they can comprehend information and make rational decisions from about age 14 on. But the parts of the brain that respond to emotional stimuli, control impulsiveness, and similar functions do not fully mature until the twenties, and the typical strong emotional responses experienced in adolescence surely affect the teen's decision-making. Joel E. Frader, MD, MA, FAAP, and Erin Flanagan, MD, FAAP, "American Academy of Pediatrics Bioethics Resident Curriculum: Case-Based Teaching Guides, Session 4. Minors as Decision-Makers," American Academy of Pediatrics, last updated August 24, 2021, https://www.aap.org/en/learning/bioethics-case-based-teaching-guides-for-resident-training/.

63. "Confidential Health Care for Adolescents: Position Paper of the Society for Adolescent Medicine," Journal of Adolescent Health 35, nos. 1, 5 (2004): doi:10.1016/j.jadohealth.2004.03.002.

decision makers for adolescents in these areas, their authority supplanted by the child's supposed (and sudden) "autonomy." Why? Because policy makers, legislators, and self-appointed activist-experts in the medical field believe it to be in adolescents' "best interests."

Where is all this headed? What are the emerging threats to parental rights in the medical arena? The next (and final) section briefly highlights two serious but "under-the-radar" challenges to the rights of parents to make medical decisions for their children: adolescent office care and minors' health records.

Adolescent Office Care

An adolescent's routine office visit to a medical provider or clinic certainly sounds innocuous. Today's medical clinics and offices, however, aim to be "youth-friendly" and "LGBTQ-friendly," descriptions that have little to do with the cheerfulness of office staff and everything to do with confidentiality (keeping information from parents) and normalizing a range of sexual behaviors and "gender diversity." According to the American Academy of Pediatrics (AAP), "quality health care" for adolescents is "inextricably intertwined" with "confidentiality and privacy."[64] In fact, the AAP recommends that private insurers and government payers "reward" providers who deliver "desired measurable outcomes" for "adolescent access to care" (read: contraception) and "confidentiality."[65]

One troubling feature of adolescent health care is the now-standard practice of health care providers to request "time alone" with an adolescent. According to the AAP Committee on Adolescence, "beginning with the 11- to 14-year-old patient visits, the pediatrician should explain the office confidentiality policy to the adolescent and parent at the onset of the visit, which includes providing the adolescent time alone with the pediatrician ... This provides opportunity for confidential sexual

64. "Achieving Quality Health Services for Adolescents, Committee on Adolescence," *Pediatrics* 138, no. 2 (2016): e20161347; doi:10.1542/peds.2016-1347, https://pediatrics.aappublications.org/content/138/2/e20161347.
65. "Achieving Quality Health Services."

and behavioral health risk history and counseling."[66] "Time alone" is a scripted intrusion into parental space, justified by claims that adolescents will not be forthcoming about risky behaviors or health care needs if parents are present or likely to find out what was said. This justification might ring true for a particular adolescent at a particular time, but it is surely not true for every child all the time.

Moreover, some studies show that adolescent girls, in particular, "expressed feelings of fear and awkwardness about how their providers presented the concept of time alone, such that, they were reluctant to agree to it, felt uncomfortable disclosing information, and were concerned about prying questions from parents afterward."[67] In addition, studies of parent attitudes have found that parents often misunderstand the confidentiality constraints. Some parents erroneously assume that providers will "disclose any information they think the parent might want to know, even if the adolescent prefers the parent not be told," especially information about STI testing and treatment.[68] Other parents mistakenly "believed confidentiality meant information was kept private between adolescent, provider, *and* parent."[69] A recent European study, where similar confidentiality practices are taking hold, found that "parental attitudes towards health-care related confidentiality and consent for adolescents are mixed. Although parents recognize the benefits associated with confidentiality for their children, they also view such health-care related information as a parental right and are uncomfortable not knowing what is discussed in these confidential consultations."[70]

Regrettably, the powerful medical associations influencing ado-

66. Arik V. Marcell and Gale R. Burstein, "Sexual and Reproductive Health Care Services in the Pediatric Setting," *Pediatrics* 140, no. 5 (2017): e20172858, doi:10.1542/peds.2017-2858.

67. S. Pampati, N. Liddon, P. J. Dittus, S. H. Adkins, and R. J. Steiner, "Confidentiality Matters but How Do We Improve Implementation in Adolescent Sexual and Reproductive Health Care?," *Journal of Adolescent Health* 65, no. 3 (2019): 315–22, https://doi.org/10.1016/j.jadohealth.2019.03.021.

68. Pampati et al., "Confidentiality Matters."

69. Pampati et al., "Confidentiality Matters."

70. D. De Coninck, K. Matthijs, P. de Winter, and J. Toelen, "Late Adolescents' Own and Assumed Parental Preferences towards Health-Care Related Confidentiality and Consent in Belgium," *PloS ONE* 16, no. 6 (2021): e0252618, https://doi.org/10.1371/journal.pone.0252618, https://www.ncbi.nlm.nih.gov/pmc/articles/PMC8171959/.

lescent care—the American Academy of Pediatrics and the Society for Adolescent Medicine, among others—are not listening to parents. Adolescent specialists and pediatricians aim to engage in these intrusive conversations with *every* adolescent—assuming the parent complies with the request to leave the exam room. What happens in these conversations? It varies, according to whether the provider is activist minded or respects the parental role (and beliefs) and how closely the provider follows the professional script. The AAP encourages pediatricians to see their role as "helping teenagers sort through their feelings and behaviors. Young people need information about healthy, positive expressions of sexuality, and pediatricians should assist adolescents as they develop their identities and to avoid the consequences of unwanted pregnancy and sexually transmitted infections (STIs), regardless of sexual orientation."[71] It is unclear how many parents are at peace with being displaced in that role by their child's physician, instead of the physician undertaking a supportive role toward the parents and family as a whole.

The AAP guidance on "Office-Based Care for LGBTQ Youth" (2013) instructs providers *not* to inform parents of an adolescent's LGBTQ identity or behaviors, lest exposure put the child at risk.[72] "Pediatricians should ... provide the context that being LGBTQ is normal, just different ... Pediatricians and their office staff should encourage teenagers to feel comfortable talking with them about their emerging sexual identities and concerns about their sexual activities. Care should be confidential, and it is not the role of the pediatrician to inform parents/guardians about the teenager's sexual identity or behavior; doing so could expose the youth to harm."[73]

Dr. Johanna Olson-Kennedy, a leading "gender specialist" at Los Angeles Children's Hospital, recently spoke to a national audience of pediatricians, sharing her recommendations for office conversations with youth who identify as LGBTQ. She noted that any visit—a physical, a strep throat swab, or a trip to the emergency room—provides

71. David A. Levine, "Office-Based Care for Lesbian, Gay, Bisexual, Transgender, and Questioning Youth," *Pediatrics* 132, no. 1 (2013): e297–e313; doi:10.1542/peds.2013-1283.

72. Levine, "Office-Based Care."

73. Levine, "Office-Based Care."

the chance to ask adolescents about their sexuality and "gender." (She also said there is no consensus on the appropriate age to begin such conversations.) Olson-Kennedy suggests that physicians ask the child questions like the following: "Do you like boys, or girls, both, or maybe you're not sure yet?" "It's important for you to know that you can have a crush on whoever you want to." "I see that your chart has you listed as a girl [or boy]. How do you feel about that?" "Are you comfortable talking with me about your gender?"[74] Of course, Olson-Kennedy shoos the parents from the room before opening these conversations.

Kaiser-Permanente recently took intrusive "confidential" questions, and disregard for parents' rights, to a new level. Kaiser piloted a "systematic gender identity screening during adolescent well checks" at several clinics in California. During check-in, adolescents filled out a confidential form with three questions about "gender identity," including whether parents were aware of the adolescent's identity. The adolescent's "responses to the gender identity screen were then discussed in detail" with the physician "during the confidential portion of the visit *before* the parents entered the examination room."[75] Adolescents who underwent "gender identity screenings" were almost *seven times* more likely to report a transgender identity than adolescents in clinics that did not do gender screenings.[76] The study concluded that confidentiality (without parents being present) is a "critical factor" for gender identity screenings, presumably because parents might not be "accepting of the adolescent's gender identity."[77] The recommendation? Pediatric practices should "implement systematic gender identity screening" during "adolescent well checks," in order to "facilitate the delivery of gender-affirming care for adolescents and families in need."[78] The disparity between the number of children identifying

74. Johanna Olson-Kennedy, MD, "Conversations with LGBTQ Youth: The Role of the Pediatrician," virtual presentation, American Academy of Pediatrics National Conference and Exhibition, 2020.

75. Josephine S. Lau, MD, et al., "Screening for Gender Identity in Adolescent Well Visits: Is It Feasible and Acceptable?" *Journal of Adolescent Health* 68, no. 6 (2021): 1089–95, https://www.sciencedirect.com/science/article/pii/S1054139X20304377; emphasis added.

76. Lau et al., "Screening for Gender Identity."

77. Lau et al., "Screening for Gender Identity."

78. Lau et al., "Screening for Gender Identity."

as "transgender" in response to the medical provider's prompt compared to the number identifying as transgender without a prompt raises troubling questions. It is normal for children in early adolescence to experience confusing feelings, doubts, and questions about "who they are." Kaiser's interest in implementing gender screenings during ordinary well visits suggests they have chosen an ideological approach to identity concerns; they seem all too eager to move vulnerable adolescents into the transgender pipeline, with scant concern for the consequences.

The "confidential" adolescent office visit, of course, opens the door for the minor to receive a range of medical procedures (vaccinations, contraceptive implants), prescriptions (birth control, STI antibiotics), referrals (abortion, "gender-affirming" counselors), and counseling (drug use, mental health concerns), all unbeknownst to parents. "Parental rights" are reduced to rights that exist on paper, not in practice, when it comes to adolescents and "sensitive concerns."

Confidentiality, HIPAA, and Electronic Medical Records

Parents who think that the law protects their right to access their minor child's complete health records are in for a rude surprise. Usually around a child's 12th birthday, parents find themselves walled off from important health-related information about their children. They may discover they are barred from retrieving a child's medical records or diagnostic tests without the child's consent or that the online information available to them is minimal. Parents may not even know that they've been locked out of critical information about their child's health.

Parental rights to access a minor's medical records are closely tied to laws (predominately state laws) regarding medical consent and confidentiality. The general rule is that the person with the power to consent to medical services is the person with the power to control access to protected health information and medical records. For example, because minors generally have the right to access contraceptives, and to consent on their own to their use, information and medical records about minors' contraceptive use are typically treated as confidential—meaning parents usually have no legal right to that information.[79] Similar legal constraints exist regarding information about testing and treatment for sexually transmitted infections, abortion, substance use treatment and counseling, and mental health counseling.

Parents of older teens are likely familiar with the frustrations of navigating federal rules around "protected health information" under the Health Insurance Portability and Accountability Act of 1996 (HIPAA). As soon as a child turns 18, parents lose all power to access their son or daughter's medical records or even to discuss their care with a physician, absent the child's specific consent. HIPAA does provide important safeguards that ensure an individual's right to access their own health records and require the provider to keep the patient's protected health information secure and confidential.[80] Even when a child is still a minor, however, parental rights to access the child's medical records may be limited. For example, parents who agree to a child's receipt of confidential services or confidential conversations with a provider may forfeit their rights as the child's "personal representative" under medical privacy laws and lose access to the relevant medical records pertaining to those confidential services or conversations.

According to the US Health and Human Services Office for Civil Rights, a parent might be "prevented" from being their child's "personal representative under HIPAA or prevented from accessing their medical records" in several situations: (1) if the child "independently consented to a health care service, no other consent is required by law," and the child "has not requested" that the parent "be treated as the

---

79. It is important to check specific state laws governing minor capacity to consent, as rights may vary with age or according to specific kinds of medical care. In addition, laws governing federal Title X family planning clinics, which provide contraception to minors without parental consent, also require confidentiality regarding Title X services for minors. The Supreme Court struck down a minimum age requirement to access contraceptives in *Carey v. Population Services International*, 431 U.S. 678 (1977). For a general overview of state laws regarding minor's ability to consent to various services, see "An Overview of Consent to Reproductive Health Services by Young People," Guttmacher Institute, July 1, 2021, https://www.guttmacher.org/state-policy/explore/overview-minors-consent-law.

80. Health Insurance Portability and Accountability Act of 1996, Public Law 104–191, https://aspe.hhs.gov/report/health-insurance-portability-and-accountability-act-1996.

personal representative"; (2) state law "allows minors to obtain a health care service without the consent of a parent, guardian, or other person acting *in loco parentis*, and [the] child, a court, or another authorized person has consented to that treatment; or (3) [the parent] voluntarily agreed that [the] child's information would be kept confidential from [the parent]."[81]

Parents are blocked from information about their child's health at both ends of the system—input and output. For example, "youth-friendly" medical offices often use iPads or other electronic devices that permit adolescents to check in without a parent seeing the information ("input") they enter. Check-ins may include questions about the child's "gender identity," sexual orientation, and preferred pronouns. (The American Academy of Pediatrics makes a point of telling health care providers that "intake forms and questionnaires should not assume heterosexuality."[82])

In terms of "output," accessing what is already in the records, parents encounter built-in barriers in electronic health records (EHR) systems. Nearly all medical practices now rely on EHR systems, in part because of federal requirements and incentives from the Centers for Medicare and Medicaid Services (CMS).[83] EHR systems can improve patient care, but they present problems too, notably for minors' medical care. Since state laws permit minors to consent to receive certain kinds of treatment without parental knowledge or approval, EHR systems are designed with functionality that blocks parental access to particular kinds of information. The EHR systems used by individual medical practices and health care systems vary, but their features typically permit private messaging between physician and patient (e.g., direct messaging between the minor and physician), segment confidential information (including lab results, treatment notes, etc.), filter information provided through online portals, restrict access by user

81. "Am I My Child's Personal Representative under HIPAA?" Office for Civil Rights, Department of Health and Human Services.

82. Levine, "Office-Based Care."

83. Department of Health and Human Services, *Electronics Health Records Systems 2020*, Report 202002131000 (Washington, DC: Health and Human Services Cybersecurity Program, Office of Information Security, 2020).

(separate log-ins for adolescents and their parents), and coordinate with billing software to exclude confidential information from insurance "Explanation of Benefits" documents. The net result is a complicated process that often interferes with parents' abilities to coordinate care for a minor child.[84] Parents might not even know that a portion of the child's medical record is invisible to them.

Final Thoughts

Nearly ten years ago, TV personality Melissa Harris-Perry provoked outrage when she "exhorted Americans to put aside the 'private notion of children,' where 'your kid is yours' and 'kids belong to their parents or kids belong to their families.' Instead, Harris-Perry insisted, 'Kids belong to whole communities.'"[85] Back then, I warned parents and conservatives not to misread Harris-Perry's remarks as a grand plan to put children under state control. The Left has a simpler, much more effective plan to mold innocent children in the progressive image: "putting children in supposed control over their own lives."[86]

Adolescent medicine may be a valuable medical specialty, but it has spawned activist "professional" groups, like the Society for Adolescent Health and Medicine, that advance a radical "sex and gender rights" agenda under the guise of the "emerging autonomy" and "evolving" decision-making capacities of children—and marginalize parents in the process.[87] School-based health centers, teen telehealth options,

84. Jennifer L. Carlson, Rachel Goldstein, Tyler Buhr, and Nancy Buhr, "Teenager, Parent, and Clinician Perspectives on the Electronic Health Record," *Pediatrics* 145, no. 3 (2020): e20190193, doi:10.1542/peds.2019-0193, https://pediatrics.aappublications.org/content/145/3/e20190193.

85. Mary Rice Hasson, "Youth Rights and the Shrinking Power of Parents," Ethics and Public Policy Center, Fall 2013, https://eppc.org/publication/youth-rights-and-the-shrinking-power-of-parents/.

86. Hasson, "Youth Rights."

87. The American Academy of Pediatrics references the "emerging autonomy" of the adolescent. See Katz et al., "Informed Consent." Article 5 of the UN Convention on the Rights of the Child recognizes child "rights" alongside parental rights, which must be exercised "consistent" with the child's autonomy and "evolving capacity" to exercise his or her own rights. Article 5 reads, "Parties shall respect the responsibilities, rights and duties of parents or, where applicable, the members of the extended family or community as provided for by local custom, legal guardians or other persons legally responsible for the child, to provide, in a manner

and app-based medical portals enable medical providers to communicate directly and confidentially with adolescents, bypassing mom and dad completely.

Adolescents do not magically become mature, rational decision makers by virtue of excluding parents from their conversations. The truth is that adolescent decisions are always mediated by adults. The only question is which adults will guide their decisions—their parents, or unrelated adults with an agenda?

As Fr. Bouquet writes, "The Catholic Church has always defended the primary rights of parents over the welfare and education of their children. Wherever those rights have been eroded, totalitarianism has not been far behind."[88] Parental rights over medical decision-making for their children have indeed been eroded—significantly. It is troubling to imagine what comes next.

---

consistent with the evolving capacities of the child, appropriate direction and guidance in the exercise by the child of the rights recognized in the present Convention." According to a UNICEF report on *The Evolving Capacities of the Child*, the "evolving capacity" language "challenges any presumption of ownership of the child by parents, and introduces a role for the State in helping achieve appropriate protection of children within their families and to encourage children's participation in decision-making." Gerison Lansdown, *The Evolving Capacities of the Child* (Paris: UNICEF Innocenti Research Centre, 2005), vii, https://www.unicef-irc.org/publications/384-the-evolving-capacities-of-the-child.html. Although the United States is not a signatory to the UN Convention on the Rights of the Child, the medical community in the United States takes a mirror approach to that of the convention, subordinating or limiting parental rights, and elevating "children's rights," according to the "evolving capacities" of the child.

88. Fr. Shenan Bouquet, "The Case of Charlie Gard," Human Life International, July 8, 2017, https://www.hli.org/2017/07/case-charlie-gard/.

5

Parental Rights and Abortion

ANNE HENDERSHOTT

If every law tells a story about a society, then studying our laws should tell the story of who we are and what we believe. In the best of worlds, our laws would contain a moral story that proclaims the ideals and principles of the people who live by these laws. Our laws would convey our understanding of the common good and represent our willingness to work toward the good life for everyone. In the real world, however, we must acknowledge that many of our most important laws—especially those surrounding parental rights and the life issues—do not necessarily reflect the values and beliefs of a majority of the people and instead reveal the will of those with the power to shape the laws that we all are forced to follow.

Among the most contentious of these laws are the laws surrounding the rights of adolescents to what the abortion advocates call "confidential health care" when considering abortion. And although most states have laws that ostensibly protect parental involvement in the abortion decisions by their minor children, the reality is that parents have no rights at all to have input into these life-or-death decisions.

According to the Guttmacher Institute, thirty-eight states currently require parental involvement in a minor's decision to have an abortion. Twenty-one states require only parental consent; three of these require both parents' consent. Eleven states require only parental notification; one of these requires that both parents be notified. Seven states permit a minor to obtain an abortion if a grandparent or other adult relative is involved in the decision. Eleven states require identification for parental consent; four states require proof of parenthood; two states require a minor's identification to have an abortion. Thirty-seven states that require parental involvement have an alternative process for minors seeking an abortion through a judicial bypass procedure that allows a minor to obtain approval from a court. Most states that require parental involvement make exceptions under certain circumstances, including a medical emergency or in cases of abuse, assault, incest or neglect. [1]

Although the majority of states require some kind of parental involvement in a minor's decision to have an abortion, most require the consent or notification of only one parent, usually twenty-four or forty-eight hours before the procedures. In a handful of states, both parents must give permission, but most states do not require it. In some states, a grandparent or other close relative like an aunt or uncle can give permission. Some states require the minor and a parent to provide government-issued identification to the abortion provider and/or as part of notarizing the parental consent form. In other states, there are no parental notification requirements at all for the child who wants an abortion without letting her parents know. [2]

Indeed, for nearly fifty years—since *Roe v. Wade*—it has been legal for a minor child—even those children living in states with strict parental notification requirements—to get an abortion without her parents' knowledge. As far back as 1976, in *Planned Parenthood of Central Missouri v. Danforth*, the US Supreme Court ruled that states may not give parents an absolute veto over their child's decision to have an

---

1. "Parental Involvement in Minors' Abortions," Guttmacher Institute, September 1, 2021, https://www.guttmacher.org/state-policy/explore/parental-involvement-minors-abortions.
2. "Parental Involvement in Minors' Abortions."

abortion. In several rulings the Supreme Court has allowed minors to receive court approval—what is known as "judicial bypass"—for abortion procedures without their parents' knowledge or consent. Judicial bypass requires judges to use specific criteria when determining whether to grant a waiver of parental involvement. Although the waiver is almost always granted to the minor child, these criteria can include the young person's intelligence, emotional stability, and understanding of the possible consequences of obtaining an abortion. Many states require a judge to use the unusually strict legal standard of "clear and convincing evidence" to determine whether a minor is sufficiently mature and the abortion is in her best interest prior to waiving the parental involvement requirement. The result of the judicial bypass is that a child—even one as young as 13 years old—has what amounts to an unfettered access to abortion in every state in the nation. And even though specific states may require the permission of a parent, federal laws surrounding abortion mandate that in order to be constitutional, any state law mandating parental involvement must allow teens to go to court to request a waiver of that requirement. And in nearly all cases, the courts are ready, willing, and able to provide that waiver.

This is the legacy of *Roe v. Wade*. Today, nearly fifty years after the 1973 US Supreme Court decision, there are no laws that tell a more compelling or more contradictory story. For the pro-choice side, abortion laws express fundamental beliefs about life and liberty for women and young girls. For the pro-life side, these same laws tell a tragic story of the failure of our democratic institutions to protect the life of the unborn child—and the life of an overwhelmed pregnant minor. For the critics of the court, the ruling in *Roe v. Wade* reflects the politics and personal views of the justices—justices who were shaped by an increasingly progressive culture—rather than a careful reading of the Constitution. In fact, the late constitutional law expert Bernard Siegan believed that rather than engaging in a careful reading of the Constitution to guide them, some of the justices made a political decision based up on their own personal beliefs, as influenced by significant others. In his book *The Supreme Court's Constitution*, Siegan suggested that in the case of *Roe v. Wade*, a "major problem confronted by the majority Justices was how best to rationalize constitutionally this enormously important decision, destined to strike down, in whole or in part the statues of every state in the Union."[3] Siegan concluded that instead of interpreting a particular provision of he Constitution as requiring invalidating a statute, the justices sought to find a constitutional basis for a decision they had already determined in advance. In his dissent, in fact, Justice Byron White criticized the decision as "an exercise in raw judicial power."[4] We are experiencing that same raw judicial power today in terms of the role that the courts have assumed in usurping parental rights when it comes to the influence of parents on the abortion decisions of their own minor children.

Regardless of the motivations of the justices, *Roe v. Wade* has had tremendous repercussions for parental rights. From the earliest days of *Roe*, minors have had the right to obtain an abortion without parental consent unless otherwise specified by state law. State legislation that mandates parental involvement (parental consent or notification) as a condition of service when a minor seeks an abortion has generated some controversy. But US Supreme Court rulings have upheld the claimed constitutional right of minors to choose abortion. Although the court has also held that it is not unconstitutional for states to impose requirements for parental involvement, it has also mandated that "adequate provision for judicial bypass" must be available for minors who believe that parental involvement would not be in their best interest. Even though there has been renewed activity within some states like Florida to include mandatory parental consent or notification requirements in state and federal abortion-related legislation, these attempts are unlikely to succeed so long as *Roe v. Wade* stands.[5] Subsequent Supreme Court decisions affirmed a state's right to pass laws that require parental involvement in a minor's decision to have an abortion, but only if they were accompanied by judicial bypass proce-

3. Bernard Siegan, *The Supreme Court's Constitution: An Inquiry into Judicial Review and Its Impact on Society* (New Brunswick, NJ: Transaction, 1993), 149.

4. Siegan, *Supreme Court's Constitution*, 150.

5. Committee on Adolescence, "The Adolescent's Right to Confidential Care When Considering Abortion," *Pediatrics* 139, no. 2 (2017): http://pediatrics.aappublications.org/content/139/2/e20163861.

dures that also allow a minor to receive court approval for an abortion without her parents' knowledge or consent.[6]

Judicial Bypass Is a "Rubber Stamp" Giving Minors Access to Abortion

While *Roe v. Wade* provided the guidelines for the constitutional protection of a woman's right to choose an abortion, in the earliest days following *Roe*, the Supreme Court had still not settled on whether these same rights applied to a minor child seeking an abortion. In the 1976 case of *Planned Parenthood v. Danforth* the Supreme Court rejected a Missouri statute that required an unmarried minor to obtain the consent of a parent before having an abortion. Yet the decision was only 5 to 4, and even the majority hinted that a less restrictive statute might be acceptable.[7] The specific provisions of the Missouri statute that had been attacked were (1) a provision defining viability for purposes that any abortion not necessary to preserve the life or health of the mother should not be performed unless the attending physician would certify with reasonable medical certainty that the fetus is not viable; (2) a provision requiring that a woman, prior to submitting to an abortion during the first twelve weeks of pregnancy, must certify in writing her consent to the procedure and that her consent was informed, freely given and not the result of coercion; (3) a provision requiring the prior written consent of the spouse of a woman seeking an abortion during the first twelve weeks of pregnancy unless the abortion were certified by a physician to be necessary for preservation of the mother's life; and (4) a provision with respect to the first twelve weeks of pregnancy when the pregnant woman is unmarried and under 18 years of age, for the written consent of a parent or legal guardian unless the abortion were certified by a physician as necessary for the preservation of the mother's life; and (5) a provision prohibiting the saline amniocentesis technique of abortion, in which amniotic fluid is

6. *Hodgson v. Minnesota*, 497 U.S. 417 (1990).
7. Satsie Veith, "The Judicial Bypass Procedure and Adolescents' Abortion Rights: The Fallacy of the Maturity Standard," *Hofstra Law Review* 23, no. 2 (1994): 4.

inserted into the amniotic sac after the first twelve weeks of pregnancy.

The complaint charged that the provisions of the bill were invalid because "they deprived the plaintiffs and their patients their constitutional rights—including the privacy of the doctor-patient relationship, the physician's right to the free exercise of medical practice and the right of a woman to determine whether to bear children, the right to life of their patients, and the right to receive adequate medical treatment all in violation of the First Fourth, Fifth, Eighth, Ninth, and Fourteenth Amendments to the U. S. Constitution."[8] The US Supreme Court ruled that the viability definition provision was a matter for the judgment of the responsible attending physician and was not unconstitutional because it did not circumvent the permissible limitations on state regulation of abortions. It also ruled that the pregnant woman's consent provision was not unconstitutional since the state could validly require a pregnant woman's prior written consent for an abortion to ensure awareness of the abortion decision and its significance. Still, the court ruled that husbands have no rights over the decision of the woman to abort her unborn child. Writing that the spousal consent provision was unconstitutional because the state was unable to regulate or proscribe abortions during the first stage of pregnancy, when a physician and patient make such a decision, the court ruled that the state could not delegate authority to any particular person, even a pregnant woman's spouse, to prevent abortion during the first stage of pregnancy. The prohibition on saline amniocentesis was ruled as unconstitutional because it failed as a reasonable regulation for the protection of maternal health, being viewed instead an unreasonable or arbitrary regulation. And most importantly, with regard to our parental rights concerns, the court ruled that the parental consent provision was unconstitutional because the state did not have the constitutional authority to give a third party an absolute and possibly arbitrary veto over the decision of a physician and his patient to terminate the patient's pregnancy, regardless of the reason for withholding the consent.[9]

8. Gary Hartman, Roy Mersky, and Cindy L. Tate, *Landmark Supreme Court Cases* (New York: Facts on File, 2004), 6–7.

9. Hartman et al., *Landmark Supreme Court Cases*, 7.

This right for a minor to access abortion without her parents' knowledge or permission was solidified in 1979 when the US Supreme Court in *Belotti v. Baird* invalidated a Massachusetts parental consent statute even though the statute provided that a teenager who could not obtain the consent of her parents could attempt to obtain a court order authorizing the abortion "for good cause shown." The majority of the justices on the Supreme Court throughout the 1980s believed that the right of privacy only protected a woman's ability to choose to have an abortion without certain types of government interference. This continued throughout the 1990s—and if anything, the right of minors to access abortion without parental permission was simply taken for granted. In fact, there began to be renewed calls for the judicial bypass to be eliminated in favor of just allowing the child to access abortion without her parent's or the court's permission. An article published in 1994 in the *Hofstra Law Review* maintained that although the court upheld the right of a teen to obtain an abortion without parental permission, "the most significant aspect of *Bellotti* lay in dicta in the plurality opinion written by Justice Lewis Powell." The 1994 *Hofstra Law Review* article suggested that "while finding the statute of mandating parental consent unacceptable, Powell assisted future legislatures desiring to require parental involvement in the abortion decisions of teenagers by describing the kind of alternative route to authorization, or 'bypass option' that would make such a statue constitutional."[10] The *Bellotti* bypass procedure became the basis for current constitutional law on abortion rights of minors. The court has since upheld several parental consent and notification statues that include some version of the *Bellotti* bypass procedure.

The *Bellotti* bypass is actually a compromise between the traditional legal deference to parental authority over important decisions of minors and the view that the right to choose abortion should accompany the condition of pregnancy, regardless of the age of the pregnant woman. The procedure centers on the concept of "maturity"—the state may not mandate parental or judicial approval of the abortion decisions of all pregnant teenagers because the "unique nature" of the abortion

---

10. Veith, "Judicial Bypass Procedure."

decision requires that mature teenagers be allowed to make that choice themselves. In other words, in the case of abortion, the presumption that all teenagers are unable to make important decisions for themselves must be replaced by a case-by-case determination of maturity. Satsie Veith, the author of the *Hofstra Law Review* article, suggests that the "maturity standard" used in judicial bypass is "problematic." She calls it a "senseless burden" that unfairly targets vulnerable teenagers:

Pregnant adults need not demonstrate their "maturity" before obtaining an abortion ... Studies of adolescent and adult decision-making indicate that teenagers are as competent as adults in making decisions about medical treatment in general and abortion in particular. Differences in the way adolescents make decisions seem to derive not from lack of ability but from their social role as dependents, a role which only reinforced by mandated interference of adults in their abortion decisions. Evidence also indicates that though teenagers are somewhat more likely than adults to suffer negative reactions following abortions, these reactions are generally mild.[11]

Clearly, the court is reluctant to infringe on the constitutional right to an abortion—even if the child is 13 years old. Judicial bypass provides the "look" of parental rights and oversight, but the reality is that parents of daughters intent on obtaining an abortion really have no input at all into the decision their daughters may make to terminate a pregnancy. As Justice Thurgood Marshall commented, "It is difficult to conceive of any reason, aside from a judge's personal opposition to abortion, that would justify a finding that an immature woman's best interests would be served by forcing her to endure pregnancy and childbirth against her will." In fact, surveys indicate that judges almost never deny permission for an abortion to a minor judged to be "immature." Veith concludes that "If the goal of the bypass procedures is to prevent immature teenagers from having an abortion when it is not in their best interests, it would seem that the procedure is a pointless rubber stamp ... However, the procedure is worse than pointless, it is an added difficulty in the lives of pregnant teenagers. It sometimes presents very real problems of access ... The procedure is bound to add to delay in obtaining the abortion, even if the teenager has access

11. Veith, "Judicial Bypass Procedure."

to the court and does not procrastinate out of anxiety, and delay adds to the medical and psychological risks of the abortion ... the discomfort of the court appearance itself should not be forgotten. A pregnant teenage girl can be terrified of an appearance before a judge who has the power to deny her the right to an abortion. No matter how gentle and understanding the judge may be, the message of the entire experience must be that the teenager is at least suspected of doing something wrong, or of being a bad, untrustworthy person."[12] From Veith's perspective and the perspective of most abortion advocates, judicial bypass procedures actually endanger pregnant teenager girls in the name of protecting them: "It has failed in its stated objectives to liberate mature and protect immature pregnant teenagers. The irony is that children are vulnerable and in need of protection, quite often because of adults. The judicial bypass procedures not only fail to give them protection, it is itself an example of the victimization of children."[13]

Likewise, *Pediatrics*, the official journal of the American Academy of Pediatrics, has long lobbied against any parental notification requirements for minors seeking abortion. In fact, in an article promoting the adolescent's right to confidential access to abortion, the Committee on Adolescents suggested:

There is no evidence that mandatory parental involvement results in the benefits to the family intended by the legislation. No studies show that forced disclosure results in improved parent-child relationships, improved communication, or improved satisfaction with the decision about the pregnancy outcome.[14]

In states with parental notification laws, adolescents who are unwilling to inform their parents or use judicial bypass mechanisms often go out of state to obtain abortion services. The authors of the *Pediatrics* article decry this practice, contending the onerous burden of judicial bypass has "adverse psychological and social impact" on adolescents. Claiming that "there is increasing evidence of the negative effects of delayed abortion on both the emotional health of mothers and the

12. Veith, "Judicial Bypass Procedure."
13. Veith, "Judicial Bypass Procedure."
14. Committee on Adolescence, "Adolescent's Right."

developmental status of unwanted children," the *Pediatrics* adolescent committee wrote in their *Pediatrics* article that the delay that judicial bypass requires results in later-stage abortions, which are themselves associated with a greater risk of psychological outcomes than first-trimester abortions:

American studies have recently corroborated European research that shows that women who are denied abortions only rarely place their unwanted infants up for adoption and may harbor resentment and anger toward their children for years. Despite strong social pressure not to acknowledge that a child is unwanted, more than one-third of the women confessed to having strong negative feelings toward their children. Compared with the offspring of willing parents, the children of those who did not obtain requested abortions were much more likely to be troubled and depressed, to drop out of school, to commit crimes, and to have serious illnesses. Compared to their peers who were allowed to terminate their pregnancies, adolescents who bear children are at significantly higher risk of educational deficits and economic disadvantage.[15]

Impact of Laws Requiring Parental Involvement for Abortion

Since the earliest days following *Planned Parenthood v. Danforth*, the greatest concern from the pro-choice side has always been whether the parental involvement laws would actually harm minors. Pro-choice feminists have argued that parental notification would diminish the reproductive autonomy of minor women. Suggesting that parental notification would jeopardize a minor's ability to "have control over her own body," pro-choice advocates have long decried such laws and have criticized the uncomfortable position judicial bypass requirements have placed minors in. In an attempt to document these harms, the Guttmacher Institute, with funding from the Educational Foundation of America and the Robert Sterling Clark Foundation, commissioned a major research study designed to determine whether minor children seeking abortion are indeed harmed by mandatory parental involve-

15. Committee on Adolescence, "Adolescent's Right."

ment and judicial bypass.[16] Not surprisingly, the Guttmacher Institute—the research arm of Planned Parenthood—suggested that the
judicial bypass is problematic because they believed it would cause a
delay in the ability of the pregnant teen to terminate her pregnancy. Yet
in their review of the literature on the impact of laws requiring parental involvement for abortion, Guttmacher concluded that "the clearest
documented impact of parental involvement laws is an increase in the
number of minors traveling outside their home states to obtain abortion services in states that do not mandate parental involvement or
that have less restrictive laws."[17] Guttmacher documented such travel
in Massachusetts, Mississippi, and Missouri. For example, in Massachusetts—prior to liberalizing their parental notification requirement—29 percent of minors who had abortions did so in neighboring
states, most in response to parental consent requirements. In South
Carolina, where the law applied only to minors younger than age 17,
and a grandparent could satisfy the consent requirement, no out-of-
state travel was detected. Yet in Texas, with a strong parental rights
involvement surrounding abortion, relatively few minors traveled out
of state.[18] Perhaps that may have been because of the great distance of
parts of Texas from other states.

Still, even Guttmacher had to admit that several studies of parental involvement laws have shown that they "reduce abortion rates by
causing minors either to continue unwanted pregnancies or to take
steps to avoid pregnancies ... The clearest result is from Texas where
the abortion rate decreased and the birthrate increased among women
slightly younger than age eighteen in comparison with women slightly
older than this age." The Texas study illustrates that in some cases the
laws may encourage some minors to continue unwanted pregnancies.
In Texas, there are resources to help pregnant teens desiring to end
their pregnancies, including Jane's Due Process, a 501(c)(3) organization dedicated to providing teens with information regarding confi-

16. Amanda Dennis, Stanley K. Henshaw, Theodore J. Joyce, Lawrence B. Finer, and Kelly
Blanchard, *The Impact of Laws Requiring Parental Involvement for Abortion: A Literature Review* (New York: Guttmacher Institute, March 2009).

17. Dennis et al., *Impact of Laws*.

18. Dennis et al., *Impact of Laws*, 27.

dential pregnancy termination services, ensuring legal representation for pregnant minors in Texas. According to the website, "Janes Due Process strives to guarantee that every pregnant minor knows that she has the right to seek legal help and to be treated with respect and sensitivity by those who work in the legal system."[19] In an op-ed posted on their website, Tina Hester, then chief executive officer of Jane's Due Process, decried parental involvement laws in Texas and elsewhere, claiming that many of the young girls she counsels and shepherds through the judicial bypass system could be "murdered" by their parents if they were to find out about their pregnancies: "One Muslim teen told me her father, if he knew, would perform an honor killing."[20]

Health Outcomes of Children Born to Teens Affected by Parental Involvement Laws

While Guttmacher Institute research initially suggested that parental involvement laws were associated with an increase in child abuse and maltreatment by mothers who gave birth to "unwanted" children because of the parental involvement laws, this correlation was not replicated in other studies: "There was no clear correlation between these laws and child abuse or maltreatment. In fact, in a similar study two years later, the authors found that such parental involvement laws actually led to a decrease in child abuse and maltreatment. They attributed this to fewer teenagers having children, inferring that the presence of these laws in a state leads to a change in the sexual or contraceptive behavior of these youth." To their credit, Guttmacher concluded that the literature review revealed "no studies that evaluated increased costs in obtaining abortion due to delays, travel or bypass proceedings, the impact on minors of being forced to consult their parents or minors' opinions about the parental involvement laws."[21]

It is possible—even likely—that over time, minors adjust to pa-

19. Jane's Due Process website, accessed April 25, 2022, janesdueprocess.org.
20. Tina Hester, "Op Ed from Our Executive Director," *Jane's Due Process*, June 10, 2015, https://janesdueprocess.org/blog/op-ed-executive-director-tina-hester/.
21. "Parental Involvement in Minors' Abortions."

rental involvement laws and may even become more conservative in their sexual behavior by avoiding early sexual intercourse or using contraception. Parental rights opponents have claimed that parental involvement in their children's abortion decision removes their child's autonomy and threatens their well-being. Some—including the Committee on Adolescents in the American Academy of Pediatrics—have argued that parental involvement in abortion decisions leads to unwanted children who are at risk of being abused and neglected. The Committee on Adolescents have also suggested that judicial bypass is detrimental to the emotional well-being of the pregnant teen because the court proceedings are "burdensome, humiliating and stressful and create an undue burden for adolescents seeking abortion." None of the research supports such beliefs. In fact, even the Guttmacher Institute has suggested that minors may indeed benefit from parental involvement in their children's abortion decisions. This is something that parental rights advocates have always known.

It is difficult to predict the future of whether parents will ever have a voice in the abortion decisions made by their own pregnant daughters. But as we have seen in the 2021 Supreme Court case of *Dobbs v. Mississippi*, and the controversial new law passed in Texas that ostensibly prohibits abortion after a fetal heartbeat is detected, there is great optimism from the pro-life community—and the parental rights community—that parental rights will begin again to take precedence in the abortion decisions of their children. Conversely, some developments make the future of parental rights and the abortion decisions of minor children look bleak. California's Governor Gavin Newsom, having survived a recall attempt, was emboldened by abortion rights supporters to sign two bills on September 22, 2021, that are major gift to the abortion industry. The first one, AB 1356, makes it illegal to film or photograph patients or employees within 100 feet of an abortion clinic. The second one relates directly to parental rights because AB 1184 allows insured individuals, including minors, to keep "sensitive services" confidential from the insurance policyholder, generally the parents of the minor undergoing the abortion. The new statutory provision requires insurance companies to accommodate a request for confidential communication of medical information, regardless of whether "disclosure would endanger the individual."[22] It specifically mentions "sexual and reproductive health" and "gender-affirming care" as potentially sensitive services. Newsom concluded his announcement by lauding the state of California as a "national leader on reproductive and sexual health protections and rights." Promising to make his state a haven for both in- and out-of-state women seeing abortion, Newsom's actions will have far-ranging consequences for the future of parental rights on the abortion decisions of their own daughters, as well as parental notification and permission on the gender transition treatment and surgical procedures provided secretly to their children.

22. "Newsom Vows to Make California a 'Reproductive Freedom State,'" *The Guardian*, September 23, 2021, https://www.theguardian.com/us-news/2021/sep/23/gavin-newsom-california -reproductive-freedom-abortion-law.

6

Transgenderism's Assault on Parental Rights

MICHELLE CRETELLA

Transgenderism is a modern-day Pied Piper, assaulting parental rights and stealing children away, not under cover of night but in broad daylight. The wholesale indoctrination of our children by transgender activists is carried out 24/7 thanks to social and mainstream media, as well as schools, public libraries, and woke corporations. Our children are growing up immersed in a society-wide cult of gender ideology. In this chapter, I address four questions. What defines this cult? How did it pervade society? Are there any signs of hope? And what can parents do?

Transgenderism refers to the cult of gender ideology that has been enforced around the world by sexual revolutionaries in positions of power. Gender ideology is that aspect of the sexual revolution most at war with reality and its Creator. According to gender ideology, human beings are not a unity of body and soul, but rather a duality of independent spiritual and physical entities, of which the spiritual takes precedence. Accordingly, the high priests and priestesses—donning therapists' credentials or white coats, stethoscopes, syringes, and scalpels—preach with the utmost seriousness that "some girls have penises, and some boys have vaginas." Because, these anointed experts infallibly declare, all people are conceived with an innate sexed identity—a masculine or feminine essence—that may differ from their physical, biological sex. And this disconnect causes their brains to be on a different page from their bodies. (Apparently, the human brain is not a physical part of the human body despite all of its nucleated cells having the same sex chromosomes and hormonal milieu as the cells of every other bodily organ.) Consequently, this alleged spiritual essence not only trumps physical reality itself, but also overrides every other human person's accurate perception of physical reality. As utterly incredible as this may seem, realize that gender ideology is not entirely new. Rather, it is a re-presentation of the ancient pagan heresy of Gnosticism. The Reverend N.T. Wright summarized our situation well in a 2017 letter to the editor of the *London Times*:

The confusion about gender identity is a modern, and now internet-fueled, form of the ancient philosophy of Gnosticism. The Gnostic, one who "knows," has discovered the secret of "who I really am," behind the deceptive outward appearance ... This involves denying the goodness, or even the ultimate reality, of the natural world. Nature, however, tends to strike back, with the likely victims in this case being vulnerable and impressionable youngsters who, as confused adults, will pay the price for their elders' fashionable fantasies.[1]

Although the movement to normalize adult transsexuality goes back decades, 2013 is the year that the American Psychiatric Association (APA) officially replaced the diagnosis of gender identity disorder (GID)for children, adolescents, and adults with the diagnosis of gender dysphoria (GD). That year marked the APA's publication of the fifth edition of the *Diagnostic and Statistical Manual of Mental Disorders* (*DSM-5*). The *DSM* has been long regarded as the world's "Bible of mental illness." Along with the name change in 2013, the fifth edition made it clear that it was no longer a mental illness to believe a person is something other than one's biological sex. Rather, one is

---

1. As cited by A. Van Mol, "Transgenderism: A State-Sponsored Religion?," Public Discourse, January 24, 2018, https://www.thepublicdiscourse.com/2018/01/20547/.

only considered to have "gender dysphoria" if he or she is emotionally disturbed or socially dysfunctional as a result of this belief. In other words, if people believe they are something other than their actual sex but are able to happily live out their lives in that mentally confused state, they do not have a mental disorder, according to the *DSM-5*. The proponents of the new diagnosis of gender dysphoria made clear that many of them did not wish to include even that term but were forced to do so, since a diagnosis code is required for health insurance companies to pay for the expensive puberty blockers, cross-sex hormones, and surgical interventions many of these traumatized patients desire. Once *DSM-5* normalized gender identity disorder, sexual revolutionaries were free to enforce gender ideology across public institutions under the banner of tolerance.

Since 2013, the fields of medicine, psychology, and education as well as corporate America, Silicon Valley, and the mainstream media have embraced transgenderism with an unparalleled religious zeal. Together they have propagandized much of society into believing that gender ideology constitutes evidence-based medicine. Accordingly, professionals, laypersons, parents, and children alike are taught that when children of any age—even as young as 18 months—consistently and persistently insist that they are not their biological sex, everyone, as a matter of scientific fact and human kindness, must affirm that claim or else be guilty of a degree of bigotry that will drive these children to suicide. According to the transgender cult, children are to be socially affirmed in opposition to physical reality based on their word alone; they are to be given new names, pronouns, clothing, and hairstyles in accordance with sex stereotypes to affirm their mistaken belief. As they reach the earliest stages of puberty (between the ages of 8 and 12 years), they should be allowed to "consent" to toxic puberty blockers that impair brain development and are also sterilizing when given in conjunction with or followed by cross-sex hormones. Between 12 and 17 years of age, youth should be allowed to "consent" to cross-sex hormones as well as mutilating and/or sterilizing surgeries. These surgeries include but are not limited to mastectomies, hysterectomies, and castration, even against parents' wishes.

This is possible because of the mature minor doctrine and legal carve-outs to parental consent in state law, as well as gender experts' penchant for overlooking minors' mental illness and spinning their gender dysphoria into a tale of parental neglect.[2] In common law, a mature minor is "a teenager who demonstrates adequate maturity [and therefore] may choose or reject some forms of care, including contraceptive and pregnancy care, mental health and chemical dependency consultations, and treatments for sexually transmitted diseases. In these instances the consent of the parent or guardian is not necessarily needed."[3] Many states have legal carve-outs rooted in this concept—laws that allow minors of a certain age to consent to certain medical interventions without parental consent. The magic age for legal carve-outs in many states is 16 years, but it is younger in some. In fact, since January 2015, the state of Oregon has paid for transition interventions for residents 15 years of age or older who are insured by state Medicaid.[4] Gender experts may also seek to involve child protective services against transgender-hesitant parents based on the lie that children will commit suicide without trans-affirmative counseling and transgender drugs. I would not have believed this possible were it not for the numerous calls from parents received by the American College of Pediatricians over the last several years. I will share some of those stories now.

One call came in the summer of 2016. Mrs. M's voice was heavy with tragic emotion. "Please, Dr. Cretella, you have to help me save my little girl from being sterilized and cutting off her breasts. I already told her I love her more than life itself. I just don't want her to do something so drastic at 15 … stuff that she can never undo." Then she broke down sobbing. Mrs. M was going through a bitter divorce after eighteen years of a difficult marriage. Although her daughter had a history of intermittent depression and anxiety since middle school,

2. S. Dubin, et al., "Medically Assisted Gender Affirmation: When Children and Parents Disagree," *Journal of Medical Ethics* 46 (2020): 295–99.

3. Medical Dictionary, s.v. "Mature Minor," retrieved June 23, 2021, https://medical-dictionary.thefreedictionary.com/mature+minor.

4. Dan Springer, "Oregon Allowing 15-Year-Olds to Get State-Subsidized Sex-Change Operations," Fox News, May 2, 2016, https://www.foxnews.com/politics/oregon-allowing-15-year-olds-to-get-state-subsidized-sex-change-operations.

she never had any signs of gender confusion. It was only in the midst of the bitter divorce, after increased withdrawal and Internet binging, that "Ann" decided she was "really a boy" and always had been. Her pediatrician referred her to the closest gender clinic for evaluation.

At the first appointment, in front of her parents and gender clinic staff, Mrs. M explained, "Ann rewrote her childhood. She claimed to have struggled with thoughts of being trapped in the wrong body and acting like a boy since she was 5. Nothing could be further from the truth. She was always a 'girly girl' but that day she attributed all of her depression and anxiety to 'internalized transphobia' that would be cured by 'transition.' And if she didn't get put on meds and cleared for a mastectomy, she would kill herself. Her dad and I were in shock."

Rather than engaging in a thorough medical and psychological evaluation, however, the gender doctor instead recommended that Ann begin puberty blockers and cross-sex hormones that day. Ann's father was willing to follow this "expert's advice," while the mother wanted to do as much as possible to avoid such drastic interventions. The mother refused to consent and wanted to pursue psychotherapy around the divorce, which seemed to be the actual trigger. But the judge adjudicating the couple's divorce was prepared to side with the gender experts who recommended awarding sole custody and medical decision making to Mr. M. In recent years, there have been and continue to be hundreds of cases like this in divorce courts across America. And, sadly, most judges award custody to the parent who acquiesces to the transgender ideologues in white coats. It is not only parents suffering through divorce who are losing their rights to transgenderism, however; intact families, too, are affected.

In the spring of 2017, Mr. and Mrs. S. reached out to the American College of Pediatricians (ACPeds) seeking expert witnesses to help them retain custody of their daughter. Cincinnati Children's Hospital Medical Center sought to terminate their parental rights due to the parents' refusal to allow their 17-year-old daughter to begin testosterone injections or call the child by her chosen male name.

The case began when the parents took their daughter, who had lived as a gender-conforming female until 2016, to Cincinnati Children's Hospital Medical Center for treatment of the teen's depression and anxiety, where they were "surprised and confused" by the diagnosis of gender dysphoria. The legal dispute began in February 2017, when family services alleged parental neglect and abuse and sought temporary custody of the child. The allegations of neglect and abuse stemmed from the parents' refusal to allow their daughter to receive testosterone injections or call their daughter by her chosen male name. Those allegations were eventually dropped, but the child was nonetheless placed in the temporary custody of family services and ordered to remain in residence with her transgender-affirming grandparents.

Shortly after that, Cincinnati Children's Hospital recommended the 17-year-old begin testosterone injections at the hospital's Transgender Health Clinic. In addition to referencing their Catholic religion, the parents objected by citing their observations of their own child and the results of their own medical research, including letters from physicians testifying that transgender interventions could cause permanent harm to their daughter. Family services then sought to terminate the temporary custody arrangement and grant full legal custody to the grandparents. Both maternal grandparents, who wrongly believed transgender identity is innate and immutable, filed petitions for full legal custody in December 2017.

Sadly, on February 23, 2018, despite the testimony of several physicians, including the ACPeds president, Dr. Quentin Van Meter, Hamilton County, Ohio, judge Sylvia Sieve Hendon awarded custody of the 17-year-old girl to her grandparents. In her decision, Judge Hendon wrote, "It is unfortunate that this case required resolution by the Court as the family would have been best served if this could have been settled within the family after all parties had ample exposure to the reality of the fact that the child truly may be gender-nonconforming and has a legitimate right to pursue life with a different gender identity than the one assigned at birth."

Transgenderism has made shocking inroads in American schools since 2016. That is the year President Obama issued his "Dear Colleague letter" to all superintendents and implied schools risked losing federal funding if they failed to treat gender identity just as they treat matters pertaining to sex under Title IX. Despite the letter having no legal standing, a lawsuit by thirteen states blocking enforcement, and the Trump administration revoking the guidance, virtually all schools "fell in line" in 2016 and continue to tow the line today. Part of this "falling in line" meant forbidding school staff from speaking to parents about a student's gender identity unless the student gave permission for staff to do so. Schools won't dispense Tylenol, ibuprofen, or Benadryl without a parent's written permission. Yet most schools will help students obtain contraception, test for sexually transmitted diseases, obtain abortions, seek mental health interventions, and since the Obama administration's "guidance," also pursue transgender-affirming social interventions, counseling, and referrals without parental knowledge. For example, recently in Massachusetts, a schoolteacher had an 11-year-old student who was struggling with social issues and her gender identity. The teacher sought the advice of her principal and was told that local policy, like that of the Massachusetts Department of Education, forbade her from telling the parents that their daughter claimed she was a boy. Despite this, the teacher knew the parents had a God-given right to know and informed them. The parents were incensed that they would otherwise not have been told of their daughter's struggle and have filed a lawsuit against the school. The teacher, in the meantime, was fired for violating the school's policy.

Events like this are not restricted to liberal states. In Florida, the parents of a 14-year-old girl were seeking a psychological evaluation of their daughter to resolve her rapid-onset gender confusion after three of her friends announced they were transgender. Unbeknownst to the parents, school officials were already affirming their daughter as a boy. School staff had met multiple times with their daughter to discuss how her new gender identity could be affirmed at school. In addition to discussing her "new name" and "new pronouns," school officials explained that she had a "right" to access male-only spaces, including the boys' restrooms, locker rooms, and sports teams. Staff also stated that she had the "right" to room with her 14-year-old male classmates on overnight school trips. School officials did all of this without informing the parents.

Each of these cases represents a brazen attack on the rights of parents who love and want what is best for their children. They are an assault on parents who reject transgenderism's lie that it is good for their children to psychologically divorce themselves from reality, and to chemically and surgically mutilate their bodies.

There Are Signs of Pushback and Reasons for Hope

Many medical organizations around the world, including the Australian College of Physicians,[5] the Royal College of General Practitioners in the United Kingdom,[6] and the Swedish National Council for Medical Ethics[7] have characterized prescribing puberty blockers and cross-sex hormones in youth as experimental and dangerous. World-renowned child psychiatrist Dr. Christopher Gillberg has referred to this as *"possibly one of the greatest scandals in medical history."*[8] His neuropsychiatry research group at Gothenburg University has called for "an immediate moratorium on the use of puberty blocker drugs because of their unknown long-term effects."[9] Partly in response to these warnings, Finland, Sweden, and the United Kingdom have taken steps to limit these interventions in youth, citing risk of harm.[10] In December 2020 the High Court of the United Kingdom

5. "Australia Launches Inquiry into Safety and Ethics of Transgender Medicine," BioEdge.org, August 18, 2019, https://www.bioedge.org/bioethics/australia-launches-inquiry-into-safety-and-ethics-of-transgender-medicine/13182.

6. Royal College of General Practitioners, *RCGP Position Statement: The Role of the GP in Caring for Gender-Questioning and Transgender Patients* (London: Royal College of General Practitioners, June 2019), https://www.rcgp.org.uk/-/media/Files/Policy/A-Z-policy/2019/RCGP-position-statement-providing-care-for-gender-transgender-patients-june-2019.ashx?la=en.

7. Kjell Asplund, Letter to the Department for Social Affairs, April 26, 2019, https://www.transgendertrend.com/wp-content/uploads/2019/04/SMER-National-Council-for-Medical-Ethics-directive-March-2019.pdf.

8. Jonathon Van Maren, "World-Renowned Child Psychiatrist Calls Trans Treatments 'Possibly One of the Greatest Scandals in Medical History,'" September 25, 2019, https://thebridgehead.ca/2019/09/25/world-renowned-child-psychiatrist-calls-trans-treatments-possibly-one-of-the-greatest-scandals-in-medical-history/.

9. Van Maren, "World-Renowned Child Psychiatrist."

10. D. M. Cummings, "Swedish Hospital No Longer Gives Puberty Blockers or Sex Hormones to Children," Lifesite News, May 6, 2021, https://www.lifesitenews.com/news/swedish-hospital-no-longer-gives-puberty-blockers-sex-hormones-to-children.

ruled in the case of Keira Bell, which barred hormonal interventions in youth under the age of 16 and decreed that physicians must seek court approval for hormonal interventions in youth between 16 and 18 years of age.[11] Sweden's Karolinska University Hospital similarly prohibited these interventions in children less than 16 years of age, stating the interventions are "potentially fraught with extensive and irreversible adverse consequences such as cardiovascular disease, osteoporosis, infertility, increased cancer risk, and thrombosis."[12] Finland has issued similar guidelines.[13] In the United States, a diverse group of Americans consisting of radical feminists, transgender-identified adults, de-transitioned young adults, parents of gender-dysphoric children, physicians, therapists, and policymakers have put forth legislation in multiple states to prohibit transgender interventions in minors. Arkansas was the first state to sign such a bill into law. Unsurprisingly, the Biden administration's Department of Justice has sued Arkansas, alleging the law violates the Equal Protection Clause of the Fourteenth Amendment.

Parents Are Not Powerless

Being forewarned allows us to parent proactively. Parents must pray without ceasing, be informed, discipline children in a firm and loving manner, consider homeschooling, and not let the media raise their kids. Withhold screens from your children as long as possible. Eat as a family, and talk with one another. Do not allow television sets, cell phones, or other devices at the kitchen table or in the bedroom. Watch visual media together in a common room as a family. When children need Internet access, be sure to use content filters and parental con-

11. "Summary of Ruling of UK High Court in Keira Bell Case," Judiciary of England and Wales, accessed June 7, 2021, https://www.judiciary.uk/wp-content/uploads/2020/12/Bell-v -Tavistock-Clinic-and-ors-Summary.pdf.

12. "Care of Children and Adolescents with Gender Dysphoria," National Board of Health and Welfare, accessed May 25, 2022, https://www.socialstyrelsen.se/globalassets/share point-dokument/artikelkatalog/kunskapsstod/2022-3-7799.pdf.

13. "Medical Treatment Methods for Dysphoria Associated with Variations in Gender Identity in Minors—Recommendation," Council for Choices in Health Care in Finland, accessed June 7, 2021, https://palveluvalikoima.fi/documents/ 1237350/22895008/Summary_minors_ en.pdf/aaf9a6e7-b970-9de9-165c-abedfae46f2e/Summary_minors_ en.pdf.

trols. For high school-aged children, purchase a monitoring system for their devices.

For parenting resources, visit the ACPeds website, Best4Children. org, and click on the Resources tab. For educational videos and articles pertaining to gender identity, visit the Gender Confusion and Transgender Identity page (it can be reached by typing it into the search bar). If your children attend a public or private school (even if that school is Christian), download the *Back to School for Parents Guide*, by the Family Policy Alliance. This resource is a "busy parent's guide to what's happening in your children's classrooms and practical steps you can take to protect them."[14] Each section covers different topics, such as how to protect your child from inappropriate or biased material in the classroom, what to do when you find offensive or explicit books in your school library, and how to guard your child's safety in school restrooms and locker rooms. The guide explains your rights as parents and your children's rights. It offers guidance on how to talk with your child about difficult subjects and includes suggestions about how to successfully advocate on behalf of your child. The guide also includes links to additional helpful articles and resources.

14. Family Policy Alliance, *Back to School for Parents Guide* (Colorado Springs: Family Policy Alliance, 2021), https://familypolicy alliance.com/press-releases/back-to-school-for-parents -new-guide-offers-parents-help-and-hope-to-face-challenging-school-situations/.

7

Parental Rights in Public Education

CHUCK KOKIKO AND GEORGE ASH

Background

When it comes to educating Ohio's 1.7 million school age children, families have choices. The state recognizes learners have unique needs and encourages families to make informed choices about the best education for their children. In addition to Ohio's public school option, families may consider community (charter) schools; chartered non-public (private) schools; non-chartered, non-tax (parochial/religious) schools; department-sponsored schools; and homeschooling. Each opportunity provides choice for the families to engage their parental rights.

A community or charter school is a publicly funded school free to Ohio residents. Community schools may be in-person, where students attend at a physical location, or operate as an online or electronic e-school. These options do not require the permission of the local school district for student enrollment. A chartered nonpublic or

The authors wish to acknowledge Mark Jackson, Esq., for his contributions, research, consultation, and expertise in writing this paper.

private school must have a valid charter granted by the state Board of Education for operation. Private schools must comply with Ohio's operating standards. Since they do not receive state or local tax dollars, families are required to pay tuition in most cases. In the case of a non-chartered, non-tax (parochial/religious) school, the school is not charted by the state owing to truly held religious beliefs, nor do they receive state or local tax dollars, unless they qualify for state and federal program funding or indirectly receive funding through special scholarships granted to student applicants. Department-sponsored community schools operate in the same manner as a community school; however, the Ohio Department of Education serves as the direct sponsor of the school and provides the necessary oversight. The final form of school choice in Ohio is homeschooling. While US courts have concluded that there is no constitutional right of parents to educate their children at home without reasonable governmental regulation, Ohio adopted standards that allow parents to request approval for home-based instruction.[1] To be approved for the home school option, parents indicate they are interested in educating their children at home. Parents are required to meet legal requirements of homeschooling to ensure their children will meet educational requirements and notify their local school district superintendent of this intent. The superintendent is tasked with evaluating the proposed curriculum to be taught and the qualifications of the person teaching the child. The superintendent must maintain a record evidencing the determination to approve a child for homeschooling. Upon demonstrating that the educational requirements will be satisfied, the school district superintendent releases the child from compulsory education (33 Ohio Rev Code [2019]). A superintendent may revoke or recall an excuse from compulsory education if the superintendent finds substantial evidence that the parent has ceased to provide proper home instruction (33 Ohio Rev Code [2013]).

During the 2018–19 school year, Ohio had 610 public school dis-

1. See Clonlara, Inc. v. Runkel, 722 F.Supp. 1442 (E.D. Mich. 1989); and State v. Schmidt, 29 Ohio St.3d 32 (1987). But see Wisconsin v. Yoder, 406 U.S. 205, 92 S.Ct. 1526 (1972); and State v. Whisner, 47 Ohio St.2d 181 (1976).

tricts with an enrollment of 1,553,963 students. Of these, 102,569 students attended Ohio's community schools. The 176 chartered public schools were attended by 166,608 students, and 32,887 opted to be homeschooled.

Another option families have is to pursue state-issued school vouchers, which are scholarships of various amounts to help offset the cost of private schools (33 Ohio Rev Code [2021]). The vouchers to private schools are available to students attending low-performing public schools as determined by Ohio's School Report Card System. Additional scholarships are available for low-income families who have children with learning or developmental disabilities (33 Ohio Rev Code [2016]). The purpose is to provide an opportunity for parents to choose a school that will meet the student's needs.

The Cleveland Scholarship Program was enacted in 1996 and is specific to children within the Cleveland public school system who wish to attend a private school in Cleveland (33 Ohio Rev Code [2015]). For students in grades K–8, the maximum scholarship is $4,650, and a high school student may receive up to $6,000. Parents are responsible for any tuition cost above this award amount. For families above the 200 percent federal poverty level, parents will need to pay the tuition difference or participate in volunteer service activities in lieu of cash payments.

The Traditional Ed Choice Scholarship Program began in Ohio back in 2005. The current program is limited to 60,000 state-funded scholarships for students who attend Ed Choice-designated public schools as published by the Ohio Department of Education. Similar to the Cleveland Scholarship Program, Ed Choice is set up at $4,650 for students grades K–8, and a high school student may receive up to $6,000 for grades 9–12. Ed Choice scholarships are linked to data provided on Ohio School Report Cards. In 2020–21, eligibility was specifically derived from 2013–14, 2017–18, and 2018–19 school years. One must note that the report card data were influenced by two separate factors in Ohio. First, schools fell under Ohio's safe harbor laws during the years 2014–15, 2015–16, and 2016–17 as the state issued a new methodology in calculating school report cards. Most recently, the COVID-19 pandemic affected schools' administration of state assessments during the 2019–20 school year, so no report card grades were issued for the year. The number of school buildings on the eligible list was set to dramatically increase from 517 school buildings to 1,200, based on new school report card criteria. A coronavirus relief bill passed in March 2020 by the Ohio legislature froze the number at 517 buildings. Proponents of the program favor school choice, especially when students are attending low-performing schools. Those against the program argue that the scholarship amount often exceeds what the district receives in state per pupil funding, thus taking local tax dollars from the district. Furthermore, once a student leaves the district, the scholarship is guaranteed until the student graduates, even if the eligible school building moves off the Ed Choice list. According to the Ohio Department of Education, 22,608 students participated in the Ed Choice Program during the 2018–19 school year, at a cost of $107.65 million.[2]

Ed Choice expansion is an additional option for families who do not qualify for the traditional Ed Choice program. The family must have a gross family income equal to or below 200 percent of the federal poverty guideline and specific grades depending on the year. For example, a family of four making a gross annual income of $52,400 would be considered at the 200 percent of the poverty guideline.[3] This permits parents the opportunity to choose where the child attends school.

The Ohio Autism Scholarship was launched in 2004 as the nation's only private school choice program designed for students with autism.[4] The maximum amount of the voucher is up to $27,000. According to Ed Choice, 1 percent of students are eligible statewide, and 3,789 students participated in the program during the 2018–19 school

2. "Scholarship Historical Information," Ohio Department of Education, last modified March 2, 2022, http://education.ohio.gov/Topics/Other-Resources/Scholarships/Historical-Information.

3. "2022–2023 Income Eligibility Requirements for EdChoice—Expansion," Ohio Department of Education, last revised January 18, 2022, https://education.ohio.gov/getattachment/Topics/Other-Resources/Scholarships/EdChoice-Scholarship-Program/2022-2023-Federal-Poverty-Guidelines-EdCh-Expansion-FY2023.pdf.aspx?lang=en-US.

4. "Ohio Revised Code 3310," Ohio Laws and Administrative Rules, accessed May 31, 2022, http://codes.ohio.gov/orc/3310.

year, attending 1 of 265 participating service providers.[5] The average voucher issued was $22,996 for 2017–18, at a rate of 196 percent of public school funding per student. Current rules indicate there are no income limits, testing mandates, or enrollment caps. Students must be between the ages of 3 and 21, reside in the state, and have been diagnosed with an autism spectrum disorder and on a current individualized education program (IEP) while being enrolled in a public school system.

Opting Out of Testing

Mandated testing is a topic of contention, given that the average student takes 112 tests between kindergarten and the twelfth grade. Some argue the end result becomes schools and teachers focusing on the demands of the test as opposed to the needs of students or providing a comprehensive educational experience. According to the Every Student Succeeds Act (ESSA) 2015, states are required to assess 95 percent of all students, including 95 percent of each subgroup in a school, with federally mandated annual state tests in English and math. If fewer than 95 percent of eligible students take the test, the lowest possible score will be assigned to non-test takers.

When students opt out of state testing, school districts can be subject to funding implications and improvement plans, as well as other actions. The result is to discourage students from opting out of mandated tests. In response to the dilemma, school districts have taken a variety of approaches depending on the state—none of which have been approved by the US Department of Education. In some cases, states create two lists for school reports. The first contains the mandated denominator of 95 percent, while the second contains only those students who actually took the test. The intent is that federal funds aimed at improving schools with low test scores or ratings go to those schools with low scores as opposed to those who have large numbers of students opting out of testing.

5. "Autism Scholarship Program," Ed Choice, accessed May 31, 2022, https://www.ed choice.org/school-choice/programs/ohio-autism-scholarship-program/.

A second approach by schools was to establish plans to increase the number of students taking the tests. Interventions to address low scores are then implemented on the basis of causal factors such as poor performance or a large number of opt-out students. The final approach taken in some states was to penalize schools that did not reach the 95 percent standard. In such cases the school was automatically lowered a grade or rating level in the state's report card system. The end result is that parents are permitted to opt out of state testing, but schools are penalized for the action. Ten states (Alaska, California, Colorado, Idaho, North Dakota, Minnesota, Oregon, Pennsylvania, Utah, and Wisconsin) have laws specifically allowing parents to opt their children out. No states have laws prohibiting a parents' ability to opt out of state tests for their child.

Free and Appropriate Education and Child Find

Section 504 of the Rehabilitation Act of 1973 protects the rights of individuals with disabilities in programs and activities that receive federal financial assistance, including federal funds. Section 504 provides that "No otherwise qualified individual with a disability in the United States ... shall, solely by reason of her or his disability, be excluded from the participation in, be denied the benefits of, or be subjected to discrimination under any program or activity receiving Federal financial assistance."

The US Department of Education enforces Section 504 in programs and activities that it funds. Recipients of these funds include public school districts, institutions of higher education, and other state and local education agencies. The Department of Education has published a regulation implementing Section 504 (34 C.F.R. Part 104) and maintains an Office for Civil Rights (OCR), with twelve enforcement offices and a headquarters office in Washington, DC, to enforce Section 504 and other civil rights laws that pertain to recipients of funds. The Section 504 regulation requires a school district to provide a "free appropriate public education" (FAPE) to each qualified person with a disability who is in the school district's jurisdiction, regardless of the nature or severity of the person's disability. There are several required components as part of FAPE. These include educating the student in the least restricted environment (LRE), developing an IEP, procedural due process, nondiscriminatory assessment, and parental participation in the process. Each school district must periodically review a child's IEP, but not less than annually, to determine whether the annual goals for the child are being achieved and revise the IEP as appropriate (34 Code of Federal Regulations [2017]).

The Individuals with Disabilities Education Act, or IDEA, includes what is known as the Child Find mandate. Schools are required to identify, locate, and evaluate all students from birth to age 21 with disabilities, regardless of the severity. The responsibility lies with the public school district even if the child is not enrolled in the school district or the school district is not providing special education services to the child. Child Find is a continuous process of public awareness activities, screening, and evaluation designed to locate, identify, and evaluate children with disabilities who need Early Childhood Intervention (ECI) Programs (Part C) or Special Education and Related Services (Part B).

Specifically, 34 C.F.R. Section 300.131 addresses Child Find for parentally placed private school children with disabilities. Each local education agency (LEA) must locate, identify, and evaluate all children with disabilities who are enrolled by their parents in private (including religious) schools, elementary schools, and secondary schools located in the district served by the LEA, in accordance with paragraphs (b) through (e) of the section, and 34 C.F.R. §§300.111 and 300.201. The Child Find process must be designed to ensure the following: (1) the equitable participation of parentally placed private school children and (2) an accurate count of those children. In carrying out the requirements of this section, the LEA must undertake activities similar to the activities undertaken for the agency's public school children. The cost of carrying out the Child Find requirements in this section, including individual evaluations, may not be considered in determining whether an LEA has met its obligation under §300.133.

Family Educational Rights and Privacy Act

The Family Educational Rights and Privacy Act (FERPA) (20 U.S.C. § 1232g; 34 CFR Part 99) is a federal law that governs and protects the privacy of student education records. The law applies to all schools that receive federal funds in an applicable program through the US Department of Education (20 US Code [2007]). Each state defines the types of information that public schools must maintain about students and the formats in which that information must be recorded or kept (33 Ohio Rev Code [2007]). Education records, subject to certain exceptions, are directly related to a student and are maintained by an educational agency or institution, or a party acting for the agency or institution (34 Code of Federal Regulations [1988]). FERPA provides parents with specific rights when it comes to their child's education records (20 U.S. Code [2012]). The rights transfer to the student once he or she reaches the age of 18 or attends school beyond high school level (20 U.S. Code [1988]). The eligible party, either the parent or eligible student, has the right to inspect education records of the student (20 U.S. Code [2012]). The school is not required to provide copies of the records. The exception may be if the requesting party cannot physically review or inspect the records for reasons such as travel distance. In this case the school may charge a fee to provide a copy of the records. Student records may be amended should a correction or inaccuracy need addressed, the information in the record is misleading, or the information in the record is a violation of the student's privacy rights (20 U.S. Code [1988]). If the school deems the correction necessary or inappropriate, the parent may request a formal hearing. Should the change be denied, the parent then can place in the file a statement of their view of the contested information. In most cases, release of protected student information requires written permission (20 U.S. Code [2012]). A parental consent to release an education record must be signed, dated, specify the records that may be disclosed, state the purpose of the disclosure, and identify the party or class of parties to whom the disclosure is to be made (34 Code of Federal Regulations [2004]).

FERPA does permit disclosure of records without consent to specific parties under certain conditions. The parties and conditions are as follows (34 Code of Federal Regulations [2011]). (1) Directory information if an annual FERPA notice has been issued to the parents. Directory information is information contained in an education record of a current student that would not generally be considered harmful or an invasion of privacy if disclosed. (2) School officials with legitimate educational interest. (3) Other schools to which a student is transferring. (4) Specified officials for audit or evaluation purposes. (5) Appropriate parties in connection with financial aid to a student. (6) Organizations conducting certain studies for or on behalf of the school. (7) Accrediting organizations. (8) Compliance with a judicial order or lawfully issued subpoena, if a reasonable effort is made to notify the parent of the order or subpoena in advance of compliance. (9) Appropriate officials in cases of health and safety emergencies. (10) State and local authorities, within a juvenile justice system, pursuant to specific state law.

All rights under FERPA are granted to both parents equally, even in situations of divorce where one parent has been designated as the custodial or residential parent (34 Code of Federal Regulations [2011]). An educational institution or school may only limit the FERPA rights of a parent if the institution or school has been provided with evidence that there is a court order, state statute, or legally binding document that specifically revokes the parent's rights (34 Code of Federal Regulations [2011]).

Student Enrollment and Custody

Generally, a student's "school district of residence" is determined by state laws that designate where a student may enroll in school. The IDEA also contains similar default rules for students with disabilities. In Ohio, a child must be admitted in the school district in which the child's parent resides (33 Ohio Rev Code [2017]). There is a "presumption of equality," meaning that both parents hold equal rights and responsibilities for care and custody of their children unless a court order provides otherwise (33 Ohio Rev Code [1991]).

For instances where parents are separated or divorced, or their marriage has been dissolved or annulled, "parent" in those cases means residential parent and legal custodian of the child (33 Ohio Rev Code [2017]). In situations of shared parenting, where both parents share in some or all of the aspects of the physical and legal care of the child in accordance with a court-mandated parenting plan, courts may designate one of the residences to serve as the child's home for enrollment purposes (33 Ohio Rev Code [2017]). Where a shared parenting plan has been established, however, and no parent has been specifically designated as the parent for residential purposes, either parent will be deemed to be the parent eligible for student enrollment (33 Ohio Rev Code [2011]). The applicable law also makes designations if a child is in the legal custody of a governmental agency or grandparent; is homeless; lives in a institution, foster home, group home, or other residential facility; or is living in other situations (33 Ohio Rev Code [2017]).

Some school districts may offer "open enrollment" opportunities for students who do not reside in the district to enroll (33 Ohio Rev Code [2013]). Rules establishing eligibility and open enrollment procedures are determined by the specific school district. Parents have the option to send their child to the school they think is best through the open enrollment option.

Required Vaccinations

Laws requiring vaccinations for children in public and private schools and day care settings, college/university and health care workers, and patients are determined at the state level. There are nine criteria for exemptions from school vaccination requirements: medical or religious exemptions, philosophical exemptions expressed, exempted student exclusion during outbreak, parental acknowledgment of student exclusion during an outbreak, exemptions not recognized during an outbreak, parent notarization or affidavit, enhanced education exemption, medical exemptions expressly temporary, or permanent or annual health care provider recertification for medical exemptions.

Some states permit medical or religious exemptions by law. For example, Delaware's religious exemption process requires applicants to prepare an affidavit of religious belief, which includes a statement that "this belief is not a political, sociological or philosophical view of a merely personal moral code." In Ohio, to enroll in a public school, evidence must be presented that the student has been immunized against mumps, poliomyelitis, diphtheria, pertussis, tetanus, rubeola, and rubella or is in the process of being immunized (33 Ohio Rev Code [2015]). Kindergarten students must present evidence of immunization against hepatitis B and chicken pox (33 Ohio Rev Code [2015]). Furthermore, all students must be immunized, or in the process of being immunized, against meningococcal disease at the age recommended by the state Department of Health (33 Ohio Rev Code [2015]). A student may be exempted from an immunization requirement if the child's physician certifies in writing that such immunization against the applicable disease is "medically contraindicated" (33 Ohio Rev Code [2015]). Further, if a student has previously had mumps, rubella, or chicken pox, the student's parent or physician can present a signed statement to the school district of that fact, and the student will not need to be immunized for the respective illness (33 Ohio Rev Code [2015]).

Ohio law also allows for students to be exempt from the immunization requirements based upon certain objections by a parent or guardian. Specifically, a student whose parent or guardian presents a written statement in which the parent or guardian declines to have the student immunized for religious reasons. Courts found that a student's right to enroll in school without immunization on the basis of a parent's written objection is not absolute. At least one court has upheld a school board's refusal to admit a student whose parents objected to immunization for nonreligious reasons.[6]

6. Hanzel v. Arter, 625 F.Supp. 1259 (S.D.Ohio 1985); State ex. Rel. Mack v. Bd. of Ed. of Covington, 1 Ohio App.2d 143 (2nd Dist. 1963; Baldwin's Ohio School Law, §21.15 (2020–2021 Ed.).

8

The Assault on Parental Rights by Sex Education in the Schools

CATHY RUSE

Did you know that some public schools teach children they could be born in the wrong body?[1] That young teens watch videos with techniques to give pleasure to their sex partners?[2] That students learn how to get secret abortions without telling their parents?[3]

Most of us remember what sex education was like when we were in school. A couple of uncomfortable hours. Line drawings showing

This chapter is adapted from a pamphlet first published by the Family Research Council (www.frc.org).

1. John Domen, "Fairfax Co. School District Passes Proposals to Modify Sex Ed, Dress Codes," WTOP News, June 15, 2018, https://wtop.com/fairfax-county/2018/06/school-district -considers-changes-to-sex-ed-dress-codes/.

2. Clare Chretien, "Parents Furious over Obscene Sex Ed Lesson for 14-Year-Olds: The High School Freshmen Were Taught about Sex Toys, and Oral and Anal Sex," LifeSiteNews, May 1, 2018, https://www.lifesitenews.com/news/parents-furious-after-sex-ed-lesson-for-14 -year-olds-includes-penis-pleasur.

3. Cassy Fiano-Chesser, "Explosive Video: ACLU Coaches Teachers on How to Help Students Get Secret Abortions," Live Action, July 11, 2019, https://www.liveaction.org/news/ video-aclu-coaches-teachers-secret-student-abortions/.

human growth and development. Admonitions to be careful, respect others, and save sex for marriage.

Things are different today. The "facts of life" have not changed, but "inclusivity" and "sex positivity" and other popular buzz-word concepts have changed sex education.

Talking to children about sexuality is a highly sensitive endeavor. It is emotionally charged, even under the best of circumstances. As a nation, we have "outsourced" sex ed. Frankly, most parents really don't want to have these awkward conversations with their children. Parents instinctively don't want to disturb the natural innocence and sexual latency period before puberty. When education "experts" offer to handle the topic, it can be appealing. Especially when they promise us that lessons will be ordered around saving sex for marriage, creating strong families, and protecting children's health and well-being.

It sounds reasonable. But does it really work this way? A major new study reveals failure rates as high as 87 percent for school-based sex ed programs.[4] Even worse, some programs result in increased sexual activity, increased number of sex partners, and increased sexual experimentation by students.[5]

And yet school systems are devoting significant classroom time to them—more than seventy hours per child in one district[6]—even while American public schools are failing to fulfill their core mission. A recent national assessment by the US Department of Education revealed that a shocking two-thirds of American students can't read at grade level, and reading scores were on the decline in thirty-one states.[7] We are experiencing a profound crisis in student achievement.

Well-funded international pressure groups have been extraordinarily successful in pushing what they call "Comprehensive Sexuality Education" (CSE) into American public schools, an agenda-driven

4. Irene H. Ericksen and Stan E. Weed, "Re-Examining the Evidence for School-Based Comprehensive Sex Education: A Global Research Review," *Issues in Law and Medicine* 34, no. 2 (2019): 161–82, https://institute-research.com/published-cse.php.

5. Ericksen and Weed, "Re-Examining the Evidence."

6. ParentAndChild.org, accessed April 13, 2020, https://www.parentandchild.org/.

7. US Department of Education, "Statement from Secretary DeVos on 2019 NAEP Results," press release, October 30, 2019, https://www.ed.gov/news/press-releases/statement-secretary-devos-2019-naep-results.

curriculum that sexualizes children. In CSE, youth sex is normalized, and the concept of "sexual rights" and radical sexual ideology for youth is advanced. The Sexuality Information and Education Council of the United States (SIECUS), the oldest architect of institutional sex ed and a leading proponent of CSE, recently rebranded its messaging to capture this new sex-positive approach: "Sex Ed for Social Change."[8]

Education has given way to indoctrination. Consider the emergence of no-opt-out laws and policies that revoke the right of parents to opt their children out of sexuality-based lessons. California[9] and Illinois[10] have taken this radical step. When Illinois parents started keeping their kids home during a week celebrating LGBTQ (lesbian, gay, bisexual, transgender, queer, or questioning) issues, the school board vice president suggested, publicly, that they might consider not telling parents when it would occur: "Not telling people the time of the curriculum is an option."[11]

Parents have two main concerns about sex ed today: that it sexualizes children and that it is loaded with LGBTQ indoctrination. This chapter reveals troubling examples of each problem, discusses the powerful organizations behind it all, and then offers some action steps for parents to consider in their fight to protect the health and innocence of their children.

8. SIECUS, "SIECUS Announces Major Rebrand, Changing Conversations around Sex Ed after 55 Years," press release, November 12, 2019, https://siecus.org/siecus-rebrand -announcement/.

9. Mary Margaret Olohan, "California Implements Extreme New Sex Ed Curriculum," *Daily Signal*, July 9, 2019, https://www.dailysignal.com/2019/07/09/california-implements -extreme-new-sex-ed-curriculum/.

10. Joy Pullmann, "How Illinois Schools Teach Preschoolers to Celebrate Transgenderism," *The Federalist*, October 9, 2019, https://thefederalist.com/2019/10/09/how-illinois -schools-teach-preschoolers-to-celebrate-transgenderism/.

11. Joy Pullmann, "6 Crazy School District Responses to Parents Mad about LGBT Indoctrination of Preschoolers," *The Federalist*, October 18, 2019, https://thefederalist.com/ 2019/10/18/6-crazy-school-district-responses-to-parents-mad-about-lgbt-indoc tration-of -preschoolers/.

The Sexualization of Children

Year after year, sex ed programs push the limits on what is appropriate, both in terms of the material presented to students and the age at which it is presented. In many school districts today, lessons introduce sexual concepts to very young children and promote risky sexual behavior to vulnerable teens and pre-teens.

What was once simply imparting science-based information and skills to save sex until marriage has now become creating young radical sexual ideologues with the desire to exercise their "sexual rights." Preparing children to have sex with multiple partners over the course of a lifetime seems to be a basic assumption underlying much of sexual education content. This is not in line with Christian and other faith views on sexuality and marriage.

"How-To" Sex Workshops for Kids

Throughout the country, sex education is increasingly introducing elements of sex instruction for students. And many parents are completely in the dark.

The California State Board of Education, for example, recently adopted a Health Education Curriculum Framework that includes recommendations for radical sex and gender education instructional materials; this framework is intended to be guidance for the state's public schools. Lessons offer "tips" like "foreplay can be enjoyable in itself and can lead to orgasm for both partners without having intercourse."[12]

New curriculum in Austin, Texas, encourages even prepubescent children to consider "vaginal intercourse," "oral intercourse," and "anal intercourse."[13] Angry parents have gone to school board meetings demanding to know who gave the school district the right to teach their child how to have anal and oral sex.[14]

12. Olohan, "California Implements."
13. David Walls, "Exposed: Why Austin ISD Must Scrap Radical Sex-Ed Targeted at Young Children," Texas Values, June 27, 2019, https://txvalues.org/2019/06/27/exposed-why-austin-isd-must-scrap-radical-sex-ed-targeted-at-young-children/.
14. Todd Starnes, "Texas School District Implements Pornographic Sex Education Policy,"

Schools in Indiana actually send teens shopping for condoms, with a worksheet to fill out comparing brands, prices, lubrication, and whether or not they are comfortable shopping in the store.[15]

Parents in a rural Virginia high school were outraged when they learned their ninth-grade daughters were shown videos teaching "penis pleasure," how to "stimulate a prostate" inside the anus, and the joys of "sex toys."[16] The video was created by a YouTube star with ties to Planned Parenthood.

Speaking of Planned Parenthood, the nation's largest abortion business is also in the business of pushing its own version of radical sex ed. Planned Parenthood claims to be "the single largest provider of sex education in the United States."[17] It's "Get Real" curriculum includes instructions for seventh graders on how to use grocery store polyethylene cling wrap as a dental dam for oral sex.[18]

Teaching Kids How to Consent to Sex

A troubling trend in sex education is the push to teach "sexual consent," presumably to equip kids to resist committing, or being a victim of, sexual assault. Many parents aren't buying it, however.

Consider this statement from a "Get Real" trainer at Planned Parenthood League of Massachusetts: "Building skills around consent means moving beyond the 'how to say no' model of teaching refusal skills to also *teach young people how to ask for consent*."[19] Massa-

Townhall, October 29, 2019, https://townhall.com/columnists/toddstarnes/2019/10/29/texas-school-district-implements-pornographic-sex-education-policyn2555504.

15. Megan Fox, "Parents Stage Walkout over Planned Parenthood's Graphic, Violent Sex Ed in Public Schools," PJ Media, April 3, 2018, https://pjmedia.com/parenting/parents-stage-walk-planned-parenthoods-graphic-violent-sex-ed-public-schools/.

16. Amanda Prestigiacomo, "Parents Outraged: 9th Graders Shown This 'Sex Ed' Video about Blowjobs, Sex Toys, G-Spot," Daily Wire, April 26, 2018, https://www.dailywire.com/news/parents-outraged-9th-graders-shown-these-sex-ed-amanda-prestigia-como.

17. "How Planned Parenthood Teaches Sex Education," Planned Parenthood, accessed May 11, 2020, https://www.plannedparenthoodaction.org/issues/sex-education/how-planned-parenthood-teaches-sex-education.

18. "Protection Methods Chart," Planned Parenthood League of Massachusetts, updated June 2015, https://www.mafamily.org/wp-content/uploads/2015/06/GetReal_Curriculum_DD.pdf.

19. Teagan Drawbridge-Quealy, "Best Practices of Sex Education in Get Real 2nd Edition,"

chusetts politicians are considering a statewide sex ed curriculum mandate with lessons for students on how to "make healthy decisions about relationships and sexuality, including affirmative and voluntary consent to engage in physical or sexual activity."[20]

In Fairfax County, Virginia, eighth graders are guided in extensive discussions about obtaining mutual consent before engaging in sex— in an *abstinence* lesson![21] The word "consent" appears twenty-five times.

Consenting to a sex act does not make that act healthy, acceptable, or safe—especially when the actors are children. The "consent" movement seems less about avoiding assault and more about promoting sex and sexual rights. Proponents sometimes admit this: "Consent education … respect[s] young people's right to sexual agency and self-determination," according to the Guttmacher Institute, a research group founded by Planned Parenthood.[22] "Teaching about consent is key to pushing back against abstinence-only messages."

A sex ed teacher in Brownsville, Tennessee, told a reporter that consent must be enthusiastic and freely given, but it can also be revoked. "It's OK to say yes, then in the heat of the moment, change your mind."[23] True enough. But do parents agree that it's okay for their children to say yes to sex? And doesn't a focus on consenting to sex assume a paradigm of acceptable sexual activity not bound to marriage and family?

ETR, April 4, 2019, https://www.etr.org/blog/best-practices-of-sex-education-in-get-real-2nd -edition/ (emphasis added).

20. "Bill H.410—An Act Relative to Healthy Youth," 191st General Court of the Commonwealth of Massachusetts, accessed April 27, 2022, https://malegislature.gov/Bills/191/H410.

21. Fairfax County Public Schools, Family Life Education, Grade 8, Human Growth and Development, Lesson 3. Not publicly available online.

22. Sophia Naide, "State Lawmakers Say Yes to Consent Education," Guttmacher Institute, January 15, 2020, https://www.guttmacher.org/article/2020/01/state-lawmakers-say-yes -consent-education.

23. Cydney Adams, "America's Sex Ed Controversy: Can You Teach Consent?" CBS News, April 28, 2019, https://www.cbsnews.com/news/sex-education-consent-abstinence-cbsn -originals/.

Aren't They Supposed to Teach Abstinence?

The expectation of parents is that sex education for their children will focus on abstinence, and teaching sexual abstinence is often required by state law. But that doesn't mean the experts writing or teaching the lessons will honor the purpose of the law or those parent expectations.

For example, parents in Fairfax County, Virginia, naturally assumed their eighth graders' abstinence lesson encouraged kids to remain abstinent until marriage. But curriculum drafters had another kind of abstinence in mind—abstinence until your next steady boyfriend or girlfriend. The lesson plan includes a decision-making exercise that guides them to be "sexually abstinent *until in a faithful, monogamous relationship*" (emphasis added). The stated objective of the lesson—*the information parents are given*—says the lesson will provide "the benefits of abstaining from sexual activity until marriage." The word "marriage," however, doesn't appear anywhere in the lesson.[24] Students never hear that the point of abstinence is to reserve sex for marriage.

Tenth graders in Fairfax County get lessons about fake abstinence, too. One lesson teaches: "The best choice for teenagers . . . is to practice abstinence from sexual activity until they are in a mutually monogamous relationship."[25]

Even when the abstinence-until-marriage message is conveyed, it can be obscured by other messages that undermine it. What is the takeaway for students after being led in discussions on themes like "when two people decide to engage in sexual activity" and "when a couple decides to become sexually active" and "deciding whether or not to be sexually active is a very personal decision"?[26] The message given to students is clear: Saving sex for marriage is not a community expectation or value.

24. "Eighth Grade Family Life Education (FLE)," Fairfax County Public Schools, accessed March 3, 2020, https://www.fcps.edu/year-at-a-glance/eighth-grade-family-life-education-fle.

25. Fairfax County Public Schools, Family Life Education, Grade 10, Human Growth and Development, Lesson 4. Not publicly available online.

26. Quotes taken from Fairfax County Public Schools' Eleventh Grade Family Life Education (Lesson 1) and Second Grade Family Life Education (Lesson 2). Not publicly available online.

Secret Abortions: Your Parents Never Have to Know

Tragically, court decisions have made abortion legal for teens. Schools often include lessons promoting abortion as a legitimate/positive option. Many states even require this by law.

In Fairfax County, Virginia, students hear about their right to abortion in several lessons. One lesson for tenth grade explains how girls can get an abortion without telling their parents if they go before a judge, and that there are helpful organizations that will give them a lawyer to take them to the judge *for free.*[27] Virginia law requires that students be taught about both adoption and abortion, but for more information on making an adoption plan, the lesson script in Fairfax County refers students to Planned Parenthood.[28]

In California, schools have partnered with Planned Parenthood and the American Civil Liberties Union to instruct students on how to get secret abortions without telling their parents, according to a video released by the California organization Our Watch.[29]

Schools in Indiana actually send students to visit clinics with a worksheet to fill out about services provided, including a place to fill out the bus route they took to get there (presumably to avoid parental detection).[30]

Sex Education and LGBTQ Indoctrination

The starkest change to sex education today is that it is now saturated with "LGBTQ sexuality." Marriage, sex/gender, and sexuality are the subject of profound debate in the culture and the courts. Yet many school districts have effectively *chosen sides* on these issues and are us-

27. Fairfax County Public Schools, Family Life Education, Grade 10, Human Growth and Development, Lesson 3. Not publicly available online.

28. Fairfax County Public Schools, Family Life Education, Grade 10, Human Growth and Development, Lesson 3. Not publicly available online.

29. "Sex Ed for Kids Episode 1," OurWatch, accessed February 27, 2020, https://www.ourwatchnow.com/videos.

30. Fox, "Parents Stage Walkout."

ing sex education as the vehicle to enforce conformity with their views.

Remember, SIECUS's new brand is "Sex ed for social change." Lessons can be highly manipulative—carefully designed to get children to approve of the concept of sexual rights and fluid sexual "identities" and to reject their religious beliefs, the authority of their parents, and even physical reality itself. And these lessons are given to young children today.

Homosexuality

The LGBTQ movement demands that homosexual relationships be presented to children as good, healthy, and equal in every way to heterosexuality within man-woman marriage. Many sex ed developers and providers are all too happy to comply.

Parents in Illinois were alarmed when they learned that their preschool children were being instructed, "If you have two mommies, they can be called LESBIANS."[31]

In Austin, Texas, schools introduce sexual orientation and gender identity concepts to third graders and have sixth and seventh graders play a sexuality matching game with terms like "bisexual," "gay," "lesbian," and "homophobia."[32]

Programs like Planned Parenthood's "Get Real" curriculum for middle school students are replete with same-sex examples, like this role-playing scenario for seventh graders:[33]

Brittany's girlfriend wants to have oral sex with her. Brittany really likes her girlfriend, and her friends say that having oral sex will bring them closer together. But Brittany's mom thinks she should wait until she is older. Brittany agrees with her mom, but she is scared of hurting her girlfriend's feelings. What should she do?

California law instructs public school teachers to emphasize homosexual relationships: "Teachers should ... actively use examples of

31. Pullmann, "6 Crazy School District Responses."
32. Jeff Johnston, "Austin School District Approves Sexualizing Children over Parents' Protests," *Daily Citizen*, November 8, 2019, https://dailycitizen.focusonthefamily.com/austin-school-district-approves-sexualizing-children-over-parents-protests/.
33. "Learn More: Comprehensive Sex Education for Middle and High Schools," Get Real, accessed February 27, 2020, https://www.getrealeducation.org/learn-more.

same-sex couples in class discussions."[34] Can you define "consensual non-monogamy" or use "polyamory" in a sentence? Your children might soon be able to.

Officials in California are insisting that sex ed lessons for students be inclusive of *sexual relationships with multiple partners*.[35] The California State Health Department instructs teachers to talk to children as young as 12 about sex "partners" and to avoid terms like "boyfriend" and "girlfriend" because "some students may be non-monogamous."[36]

Have you heard of PrEP? Most parents haven't, but it is being promoted to children in public schools today. Pre-exposure prophylaxis, or PrEP, is a prescription drug taken daily to reduce the risk of contracting HIV.[37] It was designed for a particular high-risk population: men who have "unprotected" anal sex with multiple/anonymous sex partners of unknown HIV status. PrEP is controversial even in the community for which it was designed. Michael Weinstein, the founder and director of the AIDs Healthcare Foundation, has called it a "party drug" and says it "will cause a 'public health catastrophe' by triggering a dangerous increase in risky sex."[38]

Why would a school board decide to promote a controversial daily sex pill designed for men who have anonymous sex with men? Is this really the expectation that schools have for their students? Apparently so. The Fairfax County school board voted to promote the daily sex drug to its high schoolers every year,[39] even when the drug was not legal for use by minors.[40]

34. "Chapter 6: Grades Nine through Twelve," California Department of Education, May 2019, https://www.cde.ca.gov/ci/he/cf/documents/hefwch6gr9 -12.docx.

35. Cathy Ruse, "Polyamory Is for Pre-Teens in Public Schools. Oh, Really?," The Stream, July 15, 2019, https://stream.org/polyamory-pre-teens-public-schools-not/.

36. "Chapter 5: Grades Seven and Eight," California Department of Education, May 2019, https://www.cde.ca.gov/ci/he/cf/documents/hefwch5gr7-8.docx.

37. "PrEP," Centers for Disease Control and Prevention, accessed February 27, 2020, https://www.cdc.gov/hiv/basics/prep.html.

38. Christopher Glazek, "The C.E.O. of H.I.V.," *New York Times Magazine*, April 26, 2017, https://www.nytimes.com/2017/04/26/magazine/the-ceo-of-hiv.html.

39. Angela Woolsey, "FCPS Curriculum Takes 'Biological Gender' Out of Its Official Language," *Fairfax County Times*, June 22, 2018, http://www.fairfaxtimes.com/articles/fairfax_county/fcps-curriculum-takes-biological-gender-out-of-its-official-language/article_8fe1fd5c-763d-11e8-b0e2-4b85ebdb3813.html.

40. "FDA Approves Truvada for PrEP in Teenagers," Healio, May 16, 2018, https://www.healio.com/pediatrics/hiv-aids/news/online/%7Be5c06d0c-0e13-4a40-b0e0-2e9367aa5d42%7D/fda-approves-truvada-for-prep-in-teenagers.

Born in the Wrong Body?

Many public schools are beginning to teach the radical, anti-science proposition that biological sex is meaningless, that some kids are born in the wrong body, and that some girls have penises, too. The American College of Pediatricians rightly calls this psychological child abuse.[41]

Fairfax County, Virginia, recently scrubbed its sex education materials of the concept that human beings have a biologically determined sex of male or female and replaced it with "sex assigned at birth."[42] "Sex assigned at birth" is transgender "newspeak" to support the idea that a person's sex can change; that a male-bodied person can have a female brain. In Fairfax, sex ed lessons present transgenderism as a healthy sexual identity, without any mention of the health and medical risks associated with so-called sex transition.[43] In fact, curriculum drafters voted twelve times to exclude health risk information from student lessons.[44]

What would you call a program that asks teachers to avoid using the words "mom" and "dad" to describe parents? You might call it radical, like the new curriculum adopted in Austin, Texas, in the face of overwhelming community opposition.[45] "It is important to avoid

41. Michelle Cretella, "I'm a Pediatrician. How Transgender Ideology Has Infiltrated My Field and Produced Large-Scale Child Abuse," *Daily Signal*, July 3, 2017, https://www.daily signal.com/2017/07/03/im-pediatrician-transgender-ideology-infiltrated-field-pro-duced -large-scale-child-abuse/.

42. Austin Ruse and Cathy Ruse, "Fairfax County Votes to Tell Boys They Might Be Girls," The Stream, June 15, 2018, https://stream.org/fairfax-county-votes-tell-boys-might-girls/.

43. "Hormonal transition" involves giving children as young as 10 years old monthly injections of Lupron, a "puberty-blocking" intervention. "Cross-sex hormones" force bodies to develop secondary sex characteristics, like beards on females. Puberty blockers for "sex transition" have never been tested and are not approved by the US Food and Drug Administration. When they are combined with cross-sex hormones, they can stunt growth, cause bone fractures, impair memory, and will cause lifelong sterility. The next step in transition is "sex change" surgery, now called "surgical affirmation"—the surgical removal of healthy organs and grafting of tissue and muscle to impersonate opposite-sex organs.

44. "Family Life Education Curriculum Advisory Committee Recommendations to the School Board—2017–2018," Fairfax County Public Schools, June 14, 2018, https://go.board docs.com/vsba/fairfax/Board.nsf/files/AYKU7H699ED9/$file/FLECAC%20Annual%20 Recommendations%20Report%202017_18_051018g.pdf.

45. James Wesolek, "Austin ISD Adopts Radical Sex Education, Opens Government Up to Legal Attacks," Texas Values, October 29, 2019, https://txvalues.org/2019/10/29/austin-isd -adopts-radical-sex-education-opens-government-up-to-legal-attacks/.

terms which refer only to 'male' and 'female' identities when speaking with young children," the teacher instructions say. "Try not to only use terms like 'mom' or 'dad.'"[46] This curriculum teaches middle school children that doctors assign a sex to babies based on their genitalia but that "sex does NOT always match with their gender identity." Do not "assume that people with a penis are boys" because "someone with a penis might identify as a girl."[47]

Teachers in North Carolina receive comprehensive training on how to introduce transgender concepts into the minds of very young children, courtesy of the "Welcoming Schools" curriculum, created by the Human Rights Campaign, the nation's largest LGBTQ lobby.[48]

According to leading parent advocacy group N.C. Values Coalition, the curriculum uses psychological reconditioning techniques to cause children to question their sex through strategies such as role-playing, games, videos, and affirmation statements like "I used to think, but now I know." Differences of opinion are not welcome; the curriculum demands conformity.

Does Your School's Curriculum Include Any of These?

Family Watch International has compiled this helpful list of fifteen harmful elements typically found in Comprehensive Sexuality Education curricula,[49] any one of which is cause for concern. Check your school's curriculum today!

1. *Sexualizes Children.* A curriculum that normalizes child sex or desensitizes children to sexual things may give examples of children having sex or imply many of their peers are sexually active. It may

---

46. "Austin ISD Sex-Ed Curriculum," Texas Values, accessed April 27, 2022, https://txvalues.org/wp-content/uploads/2014/04/AISD-Sex-Ed-Curriculum-Presentation-final.pdf.

47. "Planned Parenthood Sex-Ed Not Radical Enough, AISD Proposes Canadian Curriculum to Indoctrinate Children," Texas Values, September 24, 2019, https://txvalues.org/2019/09/24/planned-parenthood-sex-ed-not-radical-enough-aisd-proposes-canadian-curriculum-to-indoctrinate-children/.

48. "How Are Teachers Trained?," N.C. Values Coalition, accessed February 27, 2020, https://www.ncvalues.org/how_are_teachers_trained.

49. "15 Harmful Elements of CSE," Family Watch International, accessed April 27, 2022, https://www.comprehensivesexualityeducation.org/15-harmful-elements-of-cse/.

glamorize sex, use graphic materials, teach explicit sexual vocabulary, or encourage discussion of sexual experiences, attractions, fantasies, or desires.

2. *Teaches Children to Consent to Sex.* Another harmful element is teaching children how to negotiate sexual encounters or how to ask for or get "consent" from other children to engage in sexual acts with them. Note: "Consent" is often taught under the banner of sexual abuse prevention. While this may be appropriate for adults, children of minor age should never be encouraged to "consent" to sex.

3. *Normalizes Anal and Oral Sex.* Some curricula normalize these high-risk sexual behaviors and may omit vital medical facts, such as their extremely high rates of sexually transmitted infections (including HIV and HPV) and of oral and anal cancers.

4. *Promotes Homosexual/Bisexual Behavior.* The curriculum may normalize or promote acceptance or exploration of diverse sexual orientations, sometimes in violation of state education laws. It may omit vital health information and/or may provide medically inaccurate information about homosexuality or homosexual sex.

5. *Promotes Sexual Pleasure.* Beware of curricula that teach children they are entitled to or have a "right" to sexual pleasure or encourage children to seek out sexual pleasure. They may fail to present data on the multiple negative potential outcomes for sexually active children.

6. *Promotes Solo and/or Mutual Masturbation.* Also troubling is any curriculum that encourages masturbation at young ages, which may make children more vulnerable to pornography use, sexual addictions, or sexual exploitation. Such a curriculum may instruct children on how to masturbate or encourage children to engage in mutual masturbation.

7. *Promotes Condom Use in Inappropriate Ways.* Some curricula inappropriately eroticize condom use (e.g., emphasizing sexual pleasure or "fun" with condoms) or use sexually explicit methods (i.e., penis and vagina models, seductive role plays, etc.) to promote condom use to children. They may provide medically inaccurate information on condom effectiveness and omit or deemphasize failure rates. They may erroneously imply that condoms will provide complete protection against pregnancy or STIs.

8. *Promotes Early Sexual Autonomy.* Another harmful practice is teaching children they can choose to have sex when they feel they are ready or when they find a trusted partner. The school may fail to provide data about the well-documented negative consequences of early sexual debut, or to encourage sexually active children to return to abstinence.

9. *Fails to Establish Abstinence as the Expected Standard.* Any program that fails to establish abstinence (or a return to abstinence) as the expected standard for all school-age children is concerning. Such a program may mention abstinence only in passing, or teach children that all sexual activity—other than "unprotected" vaginal and oral sex—is acceptable and even healthy. Also concerning is any effort to present abstinence and "protected" sex as equally good options for children.

10. *Promotes Transgender Ideology.* Many sex ed curricula today promote affirmation and/or exploration of diverse gender identities. They may teach children they can change their gender or identify as multiple genders, or they may present other unscientific and medically inaccurate theories. Not taught is the fact that most gender-confused children resolve their confusion by adulthood and that extreme gender confusion is a mental health disorder (gender dysphoria) that can be helped with mental health intervention.

11. *Promotes Contraception/Abortion to Children.* An additionally harmful element is presenting abortion as a safe or positive option while omitting data on the many potential negative physical and mental health consequences. The school may teach children they have a right to abortion and refer them to abortion providers. It also may encourage the use of contraceptives, while failing to present failure rates or side effects.

12. *Promotes Peer-to-Peer Sex Ed or Sexual Rights Advocacy.* The curriculum may train children to teach other children about sex or sexual pleasure, through peer-to-peer initiatives. It may even recruit children as spokespeople to advocate for controversial sexual rights (including a right to CSE itself) or to promote abortion.

13. *Undermines Traditional Values and Beliefs.* Any sex ed curriculum that encourages children to question their parents' beliefs or their

cultural or religious values regarding early sex, sexual orientation, or gender identity should be concerning.

14. *Undermines Parents or Parental Rights.* Another troubling trend is for the school to instruct children they have rights to confidentiality and privacy from their parents. It may teach children about accessing sexual commodities or services, including abortion, without parental consent. It also may instruct children not to tell their parents what they are being taught about sex in school.

15. *Refers Children to Harmful Resources.* Beware of any program that refers children to harmful websites, materials, or outside entities. Such programs may specifically refer children to Planned Parenthood or their affiliates or partners for their lucrative services or commodities (i.e., sexual counseling, condoms, contraceptives, gender hormones, STI testing and treatment, abortions, etc.). Note: A conflict of interest exists whenever an entity that profits from sexualizing children is involved in creating or implementing sex education programs.

Sex Politics in the Halls, in History Class, on the Calendar, in the Library

Even if parents identify problematic lessons in sex ed and manage to opt their kids out, that won't protect them from sex propaganda elsewhere in school, sometimes where they least expect it. In health class—really in any class—students might be encouraged to attend "Pride" parades or to become an LGBTQ "ally."[50] They may receive lessons on how to denounce "homophobia" and "challenge" others who do not agree.

They might encounter posters like one by the powerful National Education Association that states:

This is a safe and affirming space for: Lesbian, Gay, Bisexual, Transgender and Questioning Students and Their Allies. Bully Free It Starts With Me.

50. Jeff Johnston, "Austin School District Approves Sexualizing Children over Parents' Protests," *Daily Citizen*, November 8, 2019, https://dailycitizen.focusonthefamily.com/austin -school-district-approves-sexualizing-children-over-parents-protests/.

The message is crystal clear: Affirm the lie that some children are born in the wrong body, or you are a bully.

The New "Transgender Normal" in Public Schools

Meanwhile, public schools are opening girls' bathrooms to biological male students who identify as girls. Can't they just use the teachers' bathroom? Nope. Transgender activists call that "bullying."

Well-funded pressure groups like the Human Rights Campaign and GLSEN (Gay, Lesbian, Straight Education Network) target school nondiscrimination policies and demand policy changes they claim are necessary to prevent harassment and to ensure a "safe" environment.

These policies demand total conformity from the entire school community. Authors Mary Hasson and Theresa Farnan have written a bracing and deeply researched new book, *Get Out Now: Why You Should Pull Your Child from Public School Before It's Too Late*.[51] The result of these sweeping changes is what they call the "new transgender normal."

Model transgender school policies[52] can include:

1. School-wide affirmation of a student's transgender identity.
2. Forced use of false pronouns.
3. Opening of private spaces and sports teams to the opposite sex.
4. Adding "born in the wrong body" lessons to sex ed.

Much can be written about how each of these policy changes is problematic. The most fundamental problem is they ignore the fact that the vast majority of children who experience sex confusion grow out of it.[53] Will system-wide affirmation of a child's false gender im-

51. Mary Rice Hasson, J.D. and Theresa Farnan, Ph.D., *Get Out Now: Why You Should Pull Your Child from Public School Before It's Too Late* (Southlake, TX: Gateway, 2018).

52. "Model School District Policy on Transgender and Gender Nonconforming Students," GLSEN and the National Center for Transgender Equality, September 2018, https://transequality.org/sites/default/files/images/resources/trans_school_district_model_policy_FINAL.pdf.

53. "Gender Ideology Harms Children," American College of Pediatricians, accessed

pede that natural resolution? Will it sow confusion in other children, who did not question their sex? The consequences in either case are potentially devastating. Children should never be pushed down the path that can lead to irreversible chemical and surgical mutilation of their bodies.

Pediatrician Michelle Cretella, president of the American College of Pediatricians, tells the story of a phone call she received from a distraught mom. Her daughter had gotten out of the bathtub, looked at her long hair slicked back, and burst into tears, thinking she was turning into a boy. The mom discovered that the little girl had been subjected to a male classmate's "coming out" ceremony as a "trans girl," orchestrated by the teacher without parents' knowledge.

The pronoun issue is serious. Propaganda expert Stella Morabito says coercive speech practices have historically been used as a form of psychological manipulation.[54] In public schools today, it is about enforcing conformity—conformity of feelings, attitudes, emotions, speech, beliefs, and behavior. Nonconformity carries the threat of social isolation—a terrifying notion to any child in school.

Transgender activists demand that biological males have access to girls' private spaces in school. Not only bathrooms—but also dressing rooms and showers. If girls are anxious about sharing these intimate spaces with males, if they feel intimidated or uncomfortable, what recourse do they have? None. To object is to be labeled a bigot.

What about girls who may have been sexually victimized—a population that far, far exceeds the population of boys who want to identify as female? These were their safe spaces. Now they're being taken away *in the name of inclusion and compassion*. But there is no compassion for these girls.

Who's going to win the sports trophies and the scholarships, if taller, stronger males are allowed to compete against females? Three high

May 11, 2020, https://www.acpeds.org/the-college-speaks/position-statements/gender-ideology-harms-children, citing *Diagnostic and Statistical Manual of Mental Disorders*, 5th ed. (Arlington, VA: American Psychiatric Association, 2013), 451–59.

54. Stella Morabito, "13 Ways Public Schools Incubate Mental Instability in Kids," The Federalist, February 21, 2018, https://thefederalist.com/2018/02/21/13-ways-public-schools-incubate-mental-instability-kids/. See also Stella Morabito, "Transgenderism, Children, Cognitive Chaos," *Human Life Review* 44, no. 2 (Spring 2018): https://www.humanlifereview.com/wp-content/uploads/2018/06/2018-spring.pdf.

school girls who have been forced to compete against biological males in track and field have filed a lawsuit against the Connecticut Inter-scholastic Athletic Conference. "Girls deserve to compete on a level playing field," their attorney says. "Forcing them to compete against boys isn't fair, shatters their dreams, and destroys their athletic opportunities."[55]

School Assemblies

Who would suspect that an assembly on suicide would be used to promote the LGBTQ agenda? In West Virginia, students were shown a popular anti-suicide video set to music by rap artist Logic.[56] The video, with high production values and award-winning, recognizable actors, features a teen boy exploring a new same-sex relationship. One day his father comes home to discover his son in bed with another boy. The video shows scenes of the son being bullied at school, in anguish, contemplating suicide. Eventually, the son wins over his father, and the video ends with gauzy footage of the son's gay wedding and the father's embrace of the couple's adopted baby. After one screening of this video, a teacher told students not to tell parents about it. Wouldn't a true anti-suicide message encourage students to talk with their parents?

A public school in Arlington, Virginia, held a school-wide assembly featuring *Washington Post* reporter Amy Ellis Nutt on her book *Becoming Nicole*, about a boy who took puberty-suppressing drugs and then at age 17 had his sexual organs surgically removed.[57] Nutt told the students that, thanks to cross-sex hormones, Nicole was able to "make the puberty that all girls do." That is obviously impossible without ovaries or a uterus. At the end, Nutt told the students Nicole was now "physically and biologically a girl." Wrong. Every cell in Ni-

55. Valerie Richardson, "Three Female Students File Lawsuit against Connecticut Trans-gender-Athlete Policy," *Washington Times*, February 12, 2020, https://www.washingtontimes.com/news/2020/feb/12/three-female-students-file-lawsuit-against-connect/.

56. "Logic: 1-800-273-8255 ft. Alessia Cara, Khalid," YouTube video, August 17, 2017, https://www.youtube.com/watch?v=Kb24RrHIbFk.

57. Cathy Ruse, "Public School Assembly Tells Kids Sex Changes Are Perfectly Normal," *Daily Signal*, January 18, 2018, https://www.dailysignal.com/2018/01/18/public-school-assembly-tells-kids-sex-changes-perfectly-normal/.

cole's body contains male sex chromosomes, and a lifetime of male-suppressing hormones will never change that fact.

Was attendance optional? That's not clear. In her presentation, Nutt quipped, "Thank you for coming, although I know you're probably required to be here." What does seem clear is that this public school will not hold another school-wide assembly correcting Nutt's falsehoods or featuring other views on the issue. Just a little propaganda for the children, paid for by Arlington taxpayers.

"Queer America" History

Some school districts are beginning to teach LGBTQ history, thanks to the Southern Poverty Law Center (SPLC). The SPLC, the discredited, anti-Christian "hate" profiteer, has created a campaign for public schools called "Teaching Tolerance," which instructs history teachers in how to put a "queer" spin on nearly every major event in American history.[58]

All public schools in California,[59] New Jersey,[60] and Illinois[61] are now required to teach children LGBTQ history. In Illinois, schools are not even allowed to purchase history textbooks that fail to include an LGBTQ angle.

School districts are considering denying the right of parents to opt their children out of LGBTQ sexuality-based lessons. One Illinois school district has already implemented a no-opt-out policy. The school board president defended his action this way: "The District 65 Board of Education does not support allowing students to opt out of this or any curriculum that seeks to include a more complete account of the role of historically marginalized people in our society."[62]

58. "Welcome to Queer America," Teaching Tolerance, accessed April 28, 2022, https://www.tolerance.org/podcasts/queer-america/welcome-to-queer-america.

59. Stacy Teicher Khadaroo, "California Becomes First State to Mandate Gay History in Curriculum," Christian Science Monitor, July 14, 2011, https://www.csmonitor.com/USA/Education/2011/0714/California-becomes-first-state-to-mandate-gay-history-in-curriculum.

60. Dan Alexander, "These 12 Schools Will Be First in NJ to Teach LGBTQ Curriculum," New Jersey 101.5, January 7, 2020, https://nj1015.com/these-12-schools-will-be-first-in-nj-to-teach-lgbtq-curriculum/.

61. Pullmann, "How Illinois Schools Teach."

62. Ibid.

What does a gay history lesson look like? Here is how one California mom describes a lesson for second-grade children.[63] Students are taught about Jose Julio Sarria, a California man who ran for office in the 1960s. They are asked to read this passage about Sarria in their textbook:

He decided to be honest. He told people he was gay and that sometimes he dressed as a woman. He was the first person to do this when running for office. He did not win. But he made people know they had to pay attention to the gay community.[64]

Then the children are prompted to write their own essay about how Sarria's honesty was inspirational to others.

Propaganda on the School Calendar

Every October, the public schools in Evanston, Illinois, go all out for LGBTQ Equity Week. Kindergarten children get story time with books like *My Princess Boy* and *I Am Jazz*, about Jazz Jennings, breakout star of the transgender movement. First graders are tasked with making "pride" flags and practicing gender-fluid pronouns. Sixth graders learn about various LGBTQ activists and their strategies.[65]

Consider an Equity Week student mural featured on the school district's website, with various flags labeled with the following words: Bisexual Flag, Gender Queer Flag, Transgender Flag, Pan Sexual Flag, Poly Sexual Flag. What do children think when making such a mural? What are they told?

Mission America has researched the various celebrations that public schools now place on their calendars and found fifteen that involved sexual propaganda for the 2019–20 school year.[66] (Dates may vary depending on the year.)

63. "New Law Being Used to Spread LGBT Gender Identity Ideology into CA Public Schools," California Family Council, October 6, 2017, https://californiafamily.org/2017/new-law-being-used-to-spread-lgbt-gender-identity-ideology-into-ca-public-schools/.

64. Savvas (formerly Pearson's K–12 Learning), *myWorld Interactive 2* (Paramas, NJ: Savvas, 2022), chap. 5.

65. "What Is LGBTQ+ Equity Week?," District 65 GSEA, accessed April 13, 2020, https://gsea65.weebly.com/lgbtq-equity-week.html.

66. "School Corruption and Propaganda Calendar," Mission: America, September 29, 2019, https://missionamerica.com/article/school-corruption-propaganda-calendar/.

1. No Name-Calling Week (January 20–27)[67]

2. Transgender Day of Visibility (March 31)[68]

3. Day of Silence (April 24)[69]

4. International Day against Homophobia, Transphobia, and Biphobia (May 17)[70]

5. Harvey Milk Day (May 22)[71]

6. LGBTQ Pride Month (June)[72]

7. Banned Books Week (September 22–28).[73] This event includes books that have never been banned but have been the subject of parental concern because of age-inappropriate sexual content.

8. Ally Week (September 23–27).[74] Pressures students to declare themselves "allies" of students or teachers who identify as LGBTQ.

9. Bisexual Awareness Week (September 16–23)[75]

10. LGBTQ History Month (October).[76] Labels historical figures as LGBTQ, even when they never identified as such.

11. National Coming Out Day (October 11)[77]

12. International Pronouns Day (October 16).[78] Ignores the fact that forced declaration of one's own pronouns, or false pronouns for others, violates one's rights to free speech and religious freedom.

67. "No Name-Calling Week," GLSEN, accessed February 28, 2020, https://www.glsen.org/no-name-calling-week.

68. "International Transgender Day of Visibility," Human Rights Campaign, accessed February 28, 2020, https://www.hrc.org/resources/international-transgender-day-of-visibility.

69. "Day of Silence," GLSEN, accessed February 28, 2020, https://www.glsen.org/day-of-silence.

70. "International Day against Homophobia, Transphobia and Biphobia," accessed February 28, 2020, https://may17.org/about/.

71. "Resources—Harvey Milk Day," GSA Network, accessed February 28, 2020, https://gsanetwork.org/resources/harvey-milk-day/.

72. "LGBTQ Pride Month Guide for Educators," GLSEN, accessed February 28, 2020, https://www.glsen.org/activity/lgbtq-pride-month-guide-educators.

73. "Banned Books Week (September 27–October 3, 2020)," Banned and Challenged Books, accessed February 28, 2020, http://www.ala.org/advocacy/ bbooks/banned.

74. "Ally Week," GLSEN, accessed February 28, 2020, https://www.glsen.org/ally-week.

75. "#BiWeek 2019: Celebrate Bisexuality+," GLAAD, accessed February 28, 2020, https://www.glaad.org/biweek2019.

76. "October Is LGBT History Month," LGBT History Month, accessed February 28, 2020, https://lgbthistorymonth.com/.

77. "Celebrate National Coming Out Day with HRC!," Human Rights Campaign, accessed February 28, 2020, https://www.hrc.org/resources/national-coming-out-day.

78. "International Pronouns Day—October 21, 2020," International Pronouns Day, accessed February 28, 2020, https://pronounsday.org/.

13. Spirit Day (October 17).[79] Encourages students and teachers to wear purple, and highlights LGBTQ bullying, where even polite dissent can be characterized as such.

14. Transgender Awareness Week (November 12–19)[80]

15. Transgender Day of Remembrance (November 20)[81]

School Libraries: Safe Spaces for LGBTQ Indoctrination

Read Across America Day is an annual event promoted by the National Education Association to celebrate the joy of reading. Recently, the NEA joined with the Human Rights Campaign, the nation's largest LGBTQ lobby, to co-sponsor the event.[82] With cameras flashing, kindergarten children sat on the library floor listening to HRC spokesman Sarah McBride, a man who identifies as a woman, read transgender-themed books and tell them he is really a woman. Parents in this Arlington, Virginia, public school learned the details after the fact, but the school made no apologies.

In Loudoun County, Virginia, moms and dads were horrified to learn that the #BigGayBookDrive had brought hundreds of controversial titles to their schools.[83] The school system did not notify families that on offer to their kids are lesbian love stories like *Georgia Peaches and Other Forbidden Fruit* and books with "steamy lines describing the unbuttoning of clothes," erections, orgasms, threesomes, and masturbation.[84]

79. "#SPIRITDAY," GLAAD, accessed February 28, 2020, https://www.glaad.org/spirit day#intro.

80. "Trans Awareness Week," GLAAD, accessed February 28, 2020, https://www.glaa .org/transweek.

81. "Transgender Day of Remembrance," GLAAD, accessed February 28, 2020, https:// www.glaad.org/tdor.

82. Debbie Truong, "In a Virginia School, a Celebration of Transgender Students in a Kindergarten Class," *Washington Post*, March 3, 2019, https://www.washingtonpost.com/ local/education/in-a-virginia-school-a-celebration-of-transgender-students-in-a-kindergarten -class/2019/03/03/10fc9f90-3b7e-11e9-a06c-3ec8ed509d15_story.html.

83. Samantha Schmidt, "Angry Parents Protest LGBTQ Books in Virginia Classrooms," *Washington Post*, November 10, 2019, https://www.washingtonpost.com/local/social-issues/ perversity-angry-parents-protest-lgbtq-books-in-loudoun-classrooms/2019/11/10/6dbe0024 -01b3-11ea-9518-1e76abc088b6_story.html.

84. John Battiston, "Diverse Classroom Libraries Spark Debate in Loudoun County,"

Included in the new school library collection is the notorious book *Beyond Magenta: Transgender Teens Speak Out*, in which a teen describes how he enjoyed performing oral sex on neighborhood boys when he was 6 years old.[85]

So far, none of the books has been removed.

Who Has Replaced Parents?

Parents have given over the task of teaching children about sex to the local schoolteachers they know and trust. But those teachers are often not the people crafting or delivering the lessons on this extremely important and complex topic. Organizations with a mission to undermine the family have taken advantage of trusting parents and underfunded schools.

Who are they?

SIECUS (siecus.org) is one of the oldest and most established "authorities" on sex education for children. Founded by a Planned Parenthood medical director, with roots in child sex abuser Alfred Kinsey, SIECUS promotes sex education "as a powerful vehicle for social change." SIECUS is regarded as a pioneer of Comprehensive Sex Education.

GLSEN (glsen.org), the Gay, Lesbian and Straight Education Network, has fifty state chapters that push LGBTQ policies on public schools. A focus of this group is the establishment of Gender and Sexuality Alliance (GSA) clubs in public schools. GSA clubs can be ground zero for recruitment of kids. One mom of a middle school child in Virginia asked to attend a meeting of the GSA club, which her daughter had recently joined; the mother was only allowed to attend with the school principal as an escort. In 2018, GLSEN boasted to the *Washington Post* that California and Northern Virginia schools

---

Loudoun Times-Mirror, October 11, 2019, https://www.loudountimes.com/news/diverse-class room-libraries-spark-debate-in-loudoun-county/article_62e8671c-eaa6-11e9-ac15-4f7856694f30 .html.

85. "Transgender Book Describes Oral Sex by a 6 Year-Old," Binary, August 16, 2019, https://www.binary.org.au/transgender_book_describes_oral_sex_by_a_6_year_old.

are their "laboratories" for LGBTQ policies.[86] What does that make students? The lab rats.

Planned Parenthood (plannedparenthood.org) claims to be the nation's largest sex education provider.[87] It teaches sex education to at least 221,000 students in thirty-one states, according to CBS News.[88] For Planned Parenthood, promiscuity is a healthy lifestyle choice for students: "There's nothing bad or unhealthy about having a big number of sexual partners," it tells students on its Tumblr page.[89] Planned Parenthood's booklet for HIV-positive youth, "Healthy, Happy and Hot," also tells young people that it is their "human right" to not tell their partner they have HIV.[90] Planned Parenthood's "Get Real" curriculum teaches 12- and 13-year-olds how to use grocery store saran wrap as a dental dam for oral and anal sex[91] and recommends to 11-year-olds a book with pornographic illustrations of teenagers masturbating.[92]

Human Rights Campaign (hrc.org) created "Welcoming Schools," which started out as a PDF offered to public schools after the Obama administration's "Dear Colleague" letter in 2015 formally endorsed the transgender free-for-all in schools across the country. (President Obama threatened to hold federal funds hostage unless schools opened girls' bathrooms and locker rooms to boys, and vice versa.)

86. Debbie Truong, "In Fairfax, a Lesson on Why Words Matter, Especially in Sexual Health Class," *Washington Post*, June 23, 2018, https://www.washingtonpost.com/local/education/in-fairfax-a-lesson-on-why-words-matter-especially-in-sexual-health-class/2018/06/23/bc705114-6ef6-11e8-afd5-778aca903bbe_story.html.

87. "What Is Sex Education?," Planned Parenthood, accessed February 28, 2020, https://www.plannedparenthood.org/learn/for-educators/what-sex-education.

88. "N.C. School District Votes to End Widely Used Sex Education Program amid Outcry," CBS News, February 14, 2018, https://www.cbsnews.com/news/debate-over-planned-parenthood-sex-education-program-north-carolina/.

89. "Planned Parenthood," Tumblr, accessed February 28, 2020, https://plannedparenthood.tumblr.com/post/60220544819/someone-asked-us-is-promiscuity-a-bad-thing.

90. "Healthy, Happy and Hot," International Planned Parenthood Federation, https://www.ippf.org/sites/default/files/healthy_happy_hot.pdf.

91. "Protection Methods Chart," Planned Parenthood League of Massachusetts, accessed April 28, 2022, https://www.mafamily.org/wp-content/uploads/2015/06/GetReal_Curriculum_DD.pdf.

92. Mary Ellen Siegler, "Do not open all the pictures in this post with your child close by," Facebook, October 24, 2019, https://www.facebook.com/groups/691040948079576/permalink/709447136238957/.

From that original "Welcoming Schools" PDF and the influx of millions of dollars in contributions and corporate grants, a whole new organization was spawned, dedicated to providing resources and training to public elementary school educators regarding transgenderism.

Teaching Tolerance (splcenter.org/teaching-tolerance) is the education arm of the Southern Poverty Law Center, the discredited, anti-Christian "hate" profiteer. Teaching Tolerance's website has seemingly endless free information for teachers and schools with their spin on LGBTQ rights, race and ethnicity, immigration, and beyond. SPLC's "LGBTQ Best Practices Guide" has been mailed to every school principal in the nation. The guide covers everything you can imagine and more: how to make sure your prom is LGBTQ inclusive, how to have a queer school culture, and how to adopt policies for schools that allow the school to affirm a child's sexuality or transgenderism without notifying parents. In fact, the material in these resources promotes the idea that LGBTQ youth may not be safe at home with their parents, suggesting the school as a place of refuge.

Advocates for Youth (advocatesforyouth.org) works in collaboration with national, state, and local groups on Comprehensive Sex Education with a focus on ending what they consider to be "homophobia" and "transphobia" against youth.

All together, these groups raise close to $1 billion a year, with nearly $1 billion in reserves. Some of this money comes to them in the form of grants from the Department of Health and Human Services and USAID. They not only raise money; they get taxpayer dollars, too.[93]

Parents, Protect Your Children— And Your Rights!

What can parents do to counter this onslaught? Here are some things to consider.

93. "Health and Human Services Funding for Abstinence Education, Education for Teen Pregnancy and HIV/STD Prevention, and Other Programs That Address Adolescent Sexual Activity," US Department of Health and Human Services, accessed April 28, 2022, https://aspe.hhs.gov/system/files/pdf/75581/report.pdf; "How Sex Education Gets Funding," Planned Parenthood, accessed February 28, 2020, https://www.plannedparenthoodaction.org/issues/sex-education/how-sex-education-funded.

Ground Your Children in the Truth about Human Sexuality

Institutionalized, politicized sex education can never replace a healthy dialogue between mother, father, and child about the goodness and beauty of married love. Parents know their children best. If they pray together, worship together, and take courage, God will equip them to explain these timeless facts of life to their children. Christians should take courage in the fact that God reveals his love and care in all things, including our sexual nature. This is indeed part of the Good News that we are called to share.

Every human person is made in God's image and likeness, unique and unrepeatable. In all of Creation, only humans are given the gift of a sexuality that is more than a biological reproductive drive. Animals go into "season" or "heat" when it's time to reproduce, but human sexual union has a more complex and beautiful purpose, by God's design. Men and women are created by God for each other. Marriage is the union of one man and one woman who give themselves to each other completely, and the sexual union of husband and wife in marriage is a physical sign and expression of their love and commitment. And marriage is a great good for all of mankind because marriage produces strong families that are the building blocks of society.

The sexual component of marriage is what distinguishes this relationship from all others in the human experience. God values this union so much that he ordered Creation to allow us to cooperate in giving life. Human love is so powerful that it can result in another human being—because God ordained it so.

Parents must never tire of teaching these truths to their children. They must always resist cultural efforts to demean or warp or diminish them. They must help their children understand that the family is attacked not because it is weak, old fashioned, or out of style, but because it is a powerful and protective force for human good, by God's design.

Be Present, Be Watchful, Make Demands

Here are some practical, proactive ideas for parents to let their school know they are informed, they are watching, and they are prepared to act:

1. Help your child *organize a club* that will have a positive impact on the school, like a Bible Study Club, a Pure Fashion Club, or a Biology Club. How about a Kindness Club? Parents cannot let the Gender Sexuality Alliance club dominate the school culture. Give the students alternatives.

2. Be the squeaky wheel! Did you know that in most states, parents have the right to *ask to see instructional material* that will be used in the classroom? Even just asking for lesson plans will put the school on notice that you are present and watching.

3. Invite a group of trusted parents to *review your school's sex ed lessons*. Create a summary of your findings, and post it for other parents to see. A group of concerned parents in Fairfax County did just that in creating parentandchild.org, and they are happy to have others use their model. Remember to read the *actual* lessons, watch the videos, and visit the recommended websites—do not settle for summaries provided by the school.

4. No one has the time, but you must find the time to *attend school board meetings*. Learn what the board is planning, and tell your friends. Find out who the good guys are on the board and introduce yourself.[94] When the board faces tough votes, have friendly faces in the auditorium to show your support. Sign up to speak at meetings. You are the expert on your own family, and it is powerful when moms and dads stand up and say their children, and all children, deserve better.

Leave Nothing to Chance

Beyond the opt-out mechanism provided by schools for sex ed classes, parents may opt their children out of this material *whenever and wherever it may crop up*—in lessons, school events, assemblies, classes,

94. Cathy Ruse, "School Board Sex Politics with Students in Fairfax County," The Stream, October 19, 2019, https://stream.org/playing-sex-politics-students-fairfax-county/.

or any activities that violate their families' beliefs. They can let their school know, in writing, every year, that they do not consent to their child's participation in inappropriate sex-related lessons or activities.

The Family Research Council has produced a "Universal Model Opt-Out" letter that parents can file every year with their schools. (For the electronic version, go to frc.org/optout.) This letter notifies the school that you do not give consent for your child to be exposed to these issues in any class. It cites US Supreme Court cases on the constitutional right of parents to direct the education and upbringing of their children. And it puts schools on notice that parents intend to pursue every legal avenue available to them if their instructions are not honored. A few letters from parents can make a big impact on a school.

Consider Education Alternatives

Millions of parents already have pulled their children out of public school. Authors Mary Hasson and Theresa Farnan predict the new transgender mandates will be the "game changer" that will cause even more families to do so.[95]

Private schools are being founded by smart parents with a vision for providing better education than what is on offer in their area. Homeschooling continues to be a growing trend in America,[96] and with it the wonderful homeschool co-ops that can make homeschool doable for families.

There has never been a better time to consider alternatives to public school, and parent resource groups are forming to help families make the transition.[97] "Hybrid homeschooling" is a new option for families who find the cost or time demands of homeschooling too difficult.[98] In hybrid homeschooling, children spend part of their school

95. See Hasson and Farnan, *Get Out Now*.

96. National Center for Education Statistics, 2018 Digest, https://nces.ed.gov/programs/digest/d18/tables/dt/18_206.10.asp?refer+schoolchoice.

97. "Reimagine Education Conference," accessed May 11, 2020, https://reimagineeducationconference.com/.

98. Mike McShane, "Is Hybrid Homeschooling the Wave of the Future?" *Forbes*, May 21, 2018, https://www.forbes.com/sites/mikemcshane/2018/05/21/is-hybrid-homeschooling-the-wave-of-the-future/#1d5b06ae6bf7.

time at home and part of it in a more traditional school setting with other students.

One example of a growing hybrid homeschool program currently in eleven states is Regina Caeli, which describes itself as providing "classical hybrid education in the Catholic tradition."[99] Children learn at home two days a week and wear uniforms to class with other students three days a week. Hybrid homeschool programs like this one are attracting impressive and experienced teachers who seek a more flexible schedule, and the tuition is a fraction of what private schools charge.

But Don't Stop Working for Better Public Schools

Even if we do pull our kids out of public school, we cannot stop working for change. Almost 90 percent of America's children attend public schools.[100] While the number of families who homeschool their children doubled during the COVID-19 pandemic, that shift barely moved the needle in overall numbers.

The reality is, public schools will continue to be the training grounds for the vast majority of our future teachers, sheriffs, college professors, governors, and other public officials. A quote often attributed to Abraham Lincoln is apt: "The philosophy of the schoolroom in one generation will become the philosophy of the government in the next."

Public schools will continue to be one of the major forces that shape the next generation. Why give the sex ed radicals a monopoly on how that generation will be shaped? Besides, we are paying for all of it. In many areas of the country, the majority of property taxes each homeowner pays goes to the school board. That means we all have a stake in what happens there, even if we don't have children in the system. It is not an overstatement to say that the very future of our country depends on what's happening right down the street at our local public schools.

99. "Regina Caeli," accessed May 11, 2020, https://www.rcahybrid.org/.
100. "Back to School Statistics," National Center for Education Statistics, accessed April 13, 2020, https://nces.ed.gov/fastfacts/display.asp?id=372.

9

In Defense of Homeschooling

A Response to Critics of Parents' Rights to Educate Their Children

JAMES R. MASON

Timing is everything—in comedy and in law review articles. Just ask Harvard law professor Elizabeth Bartholet, who, by publishing the latter, unwittingly engaged in the former.

By the middle of April 2020, the whole world was considering homeschooling as public schools began closing due to COVID-19. Just then, *Harvard Magazine* profiled Professor Bartholet's newly released eighty-page law review article, titled "Homeschooling: Parent Rights Absolutism versus Child Rights to Education and Protection."[1] And

Portions of this chapter are reprinted by permission from *Homeschool Freedom: How It Works and Why We Must Protect It* (Purcellville, VA: Home School Legal Defense Association, 2020). This version updates and adds to that paper.

1. Erin O'Donnell, "The Risks of Homeschooling," *Harvard Magazine* (May 2020): https://harvardmagazine.com/2020/05/right-now-risks-homeschooling; Elizabeth Bartholet, "Homeschooling: Parent Rights Absolutism vs. Child Rights to Education and Protection," *Arizona Law Review* 62, no. 1 (2020): https://arizonalawreview.org/pdf/62-1/62arizlrev1.pdf.

in it she recommended *banning* homeschooling in all but a tiny set of special cases.

Talk about bad timing.

We at the Home School Legal Defense Association knew about the article months before the magazine profile because it had been released many months earlier in draft form, long before the word "coronavirus" made its way into our daily vocabulary.[2] We even planned to write a rebuttal to it.

When Professor Bartholet and others announced in February 2020 that they would be holding an invitation-only "homeschooling summit" at Harvard, called the "Risks of Homeschooling," her speaker bio referred to the law review article. We informed our members and friends about the summit in what became one of our most shared pre-pandemic Facebook posts.[3]

Even then, however, the law review article itself did not make much of a public splash. Law review articles of this sort have popped up for decades, and they rarely get much attention outside of a small cadre of academics and activists. Ask yourself, How many other law review articles have you even heard of—much less cared about?

Harvard Magazine Goes Viral

I learned about the *Harvard Magazine* article as I was heading to bed on that fateful Saturday night in the middle of April. As I reached the top of the stairs, my 17-year-old daughter, Abby, thrust her phone into my face and indignantly said something like, "Can you even believe this?"

Her indignation escalated as she scrolled down the article, quoting such gems as, "Bartholet notes that some of these parents are 'extreme religious ideologues' who question science and promote female subservience and white supremacy." Religious we Masons may be, but the Taliban we are not.[4] Thanks to the Internet's accelerant properties,

2. Bartholet, "Homeschooling."

3. Darren Jones, "Harvard Summit to Discuss Regulating Homeschooling," HSLDA, March 27, 2020, https://hslda.org/post/harvard-summit-to-discuss-regulating-homeschooling.

4. See James R. Mason, "California: Don't Punish All Home-Schoolers for One Abuse

the *Harvard Magazine* article spread like wildfire. In keeping with its unfortunate timing, one might even say it went viral.

Just about everybody who cared about homeschooling reacted to the article—mostly negatively. In light of the publication of the magazine, the underlying law review article itself suddenly came under immediate scholarly scrutiny. One prominent group of social scientists who study education and homeschooling wrote the following just days later:

> We expected it to be rigorous and fact-based but were sadly disappointed … Upon reviewing Professor Bartholet's article, we conclude that it suffers from contradictions, factual errors, statements of stereotyping, and a failure seriously to consider that the alternative to homeschooling—public schooling—shares the problems that she attributes to home education.[5]

Dozens of homeschooled Harvard University and Harvard Law students, past and present,[6] also wrote to protest the article's sloppy portrayal of them and against its shoddy reasoning in support of a ban.[7]

Case," *Sacramento Bee*, January 24, 2018, https://www.sacbee.com/article196473769.html. In this special column that I wrote during the Turpin case, I proposed a simple word problem: "This parent who claims to be home schooling has committed unspeakable acts. Therefore, we need to treat all parents who claim to be home schooling with suspicion and make them submit to periodic government inspections of their homes and children. Now substitute 'parent who claims to be home schooling' with 'Muslim.' This Muslim has committed unspeakable acts. Therefore, we need to treat all Muslims with suspicion and make them submit to periodic government inspections of their homes and children. If this makes you uncomfortable, it should. It would be wrong to treat Muslims or any other group of people this way."

5. Patrick J. Wolf, Matthew H. Lee, and Angela R. Watson, "Harvard Law Professor's Attack on Homeschooling Is a Flawed Failure. And Terribly Timed, Too," *Education Next*, May 5, 2020, https://www.educationnext.org/harvard-law-professors-attack-on-homeschooling-flawed-failure-terribly-timed. "We are empirical social scientists who have studied and written about homeschooling along with other education policy topics.… We seek here to move the discussion beyond the 1,000-word *Harvard Magazine* article that sparked such opprobrium by carefully considering Bartholet's 80-page Arizona Law Review article that inspired the story. We expected it to be rigorous and fact-based but were sadly disappointed.… Upon reviewing Professor Bartholet's article, we conclude that it suffers from contradictions, factual errors, statements of stereotyping, and a failure seriously to consider that the alternative to homeschooling–public schooling–shares the problems that she attributes to home education."

6. "Cambridge 02138," *Harvard Magazine* (July–August 2020): https://harvard magazine .com/2020/07/letters-cambridge-02138. "First, and unsurprisingly, 'The Risks of Homeschooling' (May–June, page 10) attracted *many* comments, mostly critical. We publish a sample in the letters columns. Many were much longer than the article itself; we could not nearly print them all *and* accommodate diverse perspectives, so we refer you to the online issue to sample more, at length."

7. See also Dan Beasley, "Don't Ban Homeschooling Based on Stereotypes," HSLDA, June 8, 2020, https://hslda.org/post/do-not-ban-homeschooling-based-on-stereotypes.

The Home School Legal Defense Association Responds

According to my fancy word-search tool, Professor Bartholet mentioned "Home School Legal Defense Association" 113 times in her eighty-page article. And she made a pretty good case that HSLDA is an especially effective advocacy organization. To be fair, she casts our effectiveness in darker terms than we would. If her portrayal of HSLDA had been a political ad, we would appear in a grainy black-and-white photo, and as ominous bad-guy music plays, the sinister voiceover would say, "HSLDA—brutal, extremely aggressive, extraordinarily powerful, unreasonable religious ideologues."[8]

One of the most insidious advocacy tactics that our allied state homeschooling organizations, who are the backbone of homeschooling freedom, have frequently used goes by various names—but my favorite is "apple pie day." On those days, homeschool families from across the state gather on the steps of the state house. There, the state organization holds an old-fashioned rally, often featuring bad-guy HSLDA lawyers as keynote speakers. State legislators, some who were homeschooled themselves, make an enthusiastic appearance, thrilling the crowd. After the hoopla is over, the families, children in tow, visit their representative's office to chat and deliver a piece of homemade apple pie.

The fiends.

We at HSLDA responded to Professor Bartholet with a series of essays, many of which were written by our attorneys, who were homeschooled themselves. We responded not because of Professor Bartholet's jaundiced view of our organization, but because we love homeschooling. We have devoted our professional lives to advancing the cause of homeschool freedom because "our belief—our worldview if you will—leads us to conclude that a system where parents have wide latitude in raising their children, while not perfect, is far better for

8. Bartholet, "Homeschooling," 43, 56.

many more children than a system where the raising of children is highly regulated, restricted, and in some cases, dictated by the state."[9]

In pursuit of that goal, HSLDA has unapologetically used every legitimate tool of public advocacy—including moms and apple pie—to roll back the barriers to homeschooling. As homeschoolers ourselves, we have stood with other homeschoolers for homeschool freedom, in the courts, in the state houses, and in the media. We have done so because we believe that homeschool freedom is a just cause, a civic virtue, and is good for kids.[10]

Clashing Worldviews

Our disagreement with Professor Bartholet is probably best described as a clash of worldviews. We at HSLDA do what we do because we sincerely believe that raising, nurturing, and educating children is best left to loving parents. We also believe that the best interests of children are furthered when the state respects a diversity of approaches to child-rearing and education, while recognizing that parents sometimes fail in ways that require state intervention.

Beginning with the title of her article, Professor Bartholet describes our view as "parent rights absolutism." That is, of course, a straw man.[11] Our view of the correct relationship of the state to the family is that parents have *fundamental* rights, not absolute rights. A fundamental right means that the state should only intervene for compelling reasons, and then only in a limited fashion.[12]

9. James R. Mason, "Who We Are, What We Do, and Why We Do It," *Home School Court Report* 33, no. 2 (2017): 10–15, https://www.nxtbook.com/nxtbooks/hslda/2017q2/index.php?startid=11#/p/10.

10. James R. Mason, "The Civic Virtue of Private Home Education or How I Learned to Stop Worrying and Oppose So-Called Education Savings Accounts for Homeschoolers," *Home School Court Report* 34, no. 4 (2018): http://read.nxtbook.com/hslda/the_home_school_court_report/fourth_quarter_2018_vol34_no4/the_civic_virtue_of_private_h.html.

11. Bartholet, "Homeschooling," 44. Ironically, she even quotes from our mission statement, in which we say our mission is to "preserve and advance the fundamental, God-given, constitutional right of parents and others legally responsible for their children to direct their education."

12. See Michael J. Smith, "HSLDA to Harvard Prof: Homeschooling Is a Fundamental Right," HSLDA, May 12, 2020, https://hslda.org/post/no-homeschoolers-don-t-assert-an-absolute-right. President Smith's column provides a more detailed discussion of the subject.

This legal distinction between absolute and fundamental rights is not complicated—even Harvard law professors can figure it out. In her article, Professor Bartholet juxtaposes those of us she incorrectly paints as being parents' rights absolutists with her argument that the courts should start recognizing that children have a *fundamental* right to public education.[13] By this, she means public education compelled by the state, even if the child's otherwise-fit parents prefer homeschooling. That view turns the traditional relationships between the state, parents, and children upside down.

Parents or the State?

According to Professor Bartholet's worldview, the state has a prior and superior interest—above that of parents—in the raising of children, which authorizes the state to compel parents to behave in certain ways against their wishes, in the name of children's rights. This is especially true, she argues, through compulsory public education and an ever-expanding and evermore-intrusive child protective apparatus.

Her ideological companion and summit co-organizer, law professor James Dwyer, has said, "The reason the parent-child relationships *exist* is because the *state* confers legal parenthood."[14] And here I thought my wife and I played an important role in birthing seven parent-child relationships.

Professor Bartholet would prefer for the state to step in to make major educational decisions for children—decisions she happens to agree with—and for parents to be compelled out of their traditional role. Professors Bartholet and Dwyer think this is no big deal. Here's what they say:

Parents would retain enormous control over children, even if children were required to attend regular school throughout the period of compulsory education. Parents could still raise these children at home with total control over their lives from infancy until kindergarten. They could still dominate the lives

13. Bartholet, "Homeschooling," 71.
14. "Law Professor Attacks Parental Rights," YouTube video, October 11, 2017, https://www.youtube.com/watch?v=5Dxf-HeMovw&feature=emb_logo.

of children enrolled full-time in school, with total control during a huge proportion of their waking hours.[15]

The unstated assumption animating the ideas behind the above paragraph is that homeschooling parents cannot be trusted to raise their children to grow up to be self-sufficient, curious, engaged citizens. Mandating these seven hours per day is to ensure those children are exposed to ideas different from their parents.

Here is what Professor Bartholet claims: "a very large proportion of homeschooling parents are ideologically committed to isolating their children from the majority culture and indoctrinating them in views and values that are in serious conflict with that culture."[16] Based on this assumption about homeschooling parents, she builds the "total control" straw man, in the apparent belief that the compelled seven hours per day is not a form of "domination."

As a homeschooling parent of seven children myself, I can honestly say I never had total control, even if I had wanted it—which I did not. Faith, reason, and hard, cold experience taught me early on that my children were autonomous beings with minds of their own. I came to see it as "my job to prepare them for their life to come—both temporal and eternal—not to live it for them."[17] Based on my personal experience with the homeschooling community for almost thirty years, my wife and I are not unusual in this regard. And after being a homeschool advocate for more than twenty years, that observation has not changed.

Homeschooled Students Are More Tolerant

It is ironic that, in the name of exposing children to different views, Professor Bartholet has worked so hard to stamp out a tiny group of nonconformists. Especially when compelling social science research strongly suggests that "those [college students] with more exposure to homeschooling relative to public schooling tend to be more politically

15. Bartholet, "Homeschooling," 77.
16. Bartholet, "Homeschooling," 5.
17. Mason, "Who We Are," 15.

tolerant." The author of this study, Albert Cheng of the University of Arkansas, also wrote that there are

two theories for why homeschooling may cause an increase in political tolerance ... First, students who are homeschooled may attain a greater degree of self-actualization because homeschooling is highly conducive to personalized instruction and enables students to be taught a consistent worldview. Second, the religious values taught in a homeschooling environment as well as in many religious private schools are consistent with political tolerance and other values necessary for a liberal democracy.[18]

Professor Bartholet does not cite Professor Cheng's study in her law review article.[19]

She Really Means to Ban Homeschooling

Make no mistake, the stated goal of Professor Bartholet in her law review article is not to nibble around the edges to adopt "reasonable" regulations.[20] Given her druthers—based *not* on empirical evidence but on what is, at bottom, a competing worldview—homeschooling as we know it today would be outlawed. Professor Bartholet should be commended for forthrightly stating her preferred policy goal of banning homeschooling, notwithstanding her feeble attempt to walk it back later in the face of intense criticism.[21]

For almost forty years, motivated by a traditional worldview, which is in turn animated by our understanding of Christian teaching, HSLDA has worked to remove legal barriers to allow *all* parents the freedom to make responsible choices for their children. Further, "we don't ask you to share our worldview or its religious underpinnings to re-

18. Albert Cheng, "Does Homeschooling or Private Schooling Promote Political Intolerance? Evidence from a Christian University," *Journal of School Choice* 8, no. 1 (2014): 49–68, https://doi.org/10.1080/15582159.2014.875411.

19. See also Patrick J. Wolf, "Civics Exam," *Education Next* 22, no. 2 (2007): https://www.educationnext.org/civics-exam/.

20. Scott Woodruff, "Here's Why Good People Oppose 'Reasonable' Homeschool Regulation," HSLDA, August 4, 2020, https://hslda.org/post/here-is-why-good-people-oppose-reasonable-homeschool-regulation.

21. James R. Mason, "Bartholet: A Change of Heart?," HSLDA, July 14, 2020, https://hslda.org/post/bartholet-a-change-of-heart.

ceive our help. If you are a parent of a child, we want you to enjoy the same liberty we want for ourselves. For the sake of *your* children."[22]

Agree or disagree, we put our money where our mouth is. All our attorneys who have children have homeschooled them, and five of them—which is now over half—were homeschooled themselves growing up.

Professor Bartholet, however, would compel all parents to send their children to public schools, even though she has admitted since the *Harvard Magazine* article was published "having sent her kids to private school."[23] We assume the private school she chose for her own children was to her liking and was not forced on her by those with a competing worldview.

The Way We Were

In *Land of Hope*, historian Wilfred M. McClay begins the chapter about events leading up to the Civil War with this reminder:

When we look back to a moment in the past, it is hard not to read into it nearly everything that we know is to come after it. We can't help but see it as something carrying along with itself a future that we already know about, an awareness that gives us a perspective very different from that of the participants in that past moment.[24]

Looking back at the birth of the modern homeschooling movement, it is easy to forget that what may seem inevitable in hindsight was far from certain back then.

In the 1980s, prosecutors in Iowa, Michigan, North Dakota, Texas, and other states charged parents with crimes for homeschooling without a state teaching license. And across the country, parents faced considerable peril when they navigated the kind of bureaucratic "regime" that Professor Bartholet would have us return to.

22. Mason, "Who We Are," 14.

23. Martin Bürger, "Harvard Prof: Homeschoolers Should Be Required to Attend Some Public School Classes," LifeSite, June 9, 2020, https://www.lifesitenews.com/news/harvard -prof-homeschoolers-should-be-required-to-attend-some-public-school-classes.

24. Wilfred M. McClay, "Gathering Storm," in *Land of Hope* (New York: Encounter Books, 2019), 151.

The peril was real. The outcome was uncertain. Yet early homeschoolers endured.

HSLDA participated in state supreme court cases in each of the states mentioned above. And we have worked hard with state and local allies across the country to help parents roll back the old anti-homeschooling regime. The fact that homeschooling today is unquestionably legal, mainstream, and widely accessible was never a foregone conclusion.

The Way We Are

Homeschooling today, however, *is* unquestionably legal, mainstream, and widely accessible. Also, since the public schools were put into unexpected disarray due to COVID-19, homeschooling provides millions of families with real choices to address the education of their children.

Homeschooling is not just a legal question about education. An important quality of homeschooling involves its place as one of the most dynamic social movements in modern American history. While Mark Zuckerberg may have created a virtual social network, homeschoolers have formed a vast array of actual social networks—yes, often complemented by Facebook—based on religion, sports, Latin instruction, debate, drama, spelling, ages of children, needs of parents, self-directed learning, and a host of other reasons people choose to voluntarily associate with each other. And this vast array of lawful, innovative, voluntary associations is strong, vibrant, and active in seeking to meet the needs of struggling families during the current crisis.

So, we at HSLDA quickly shifted our focus—but not our vigilant attention—away from the anti-homeschooling naysayers like Professor B. Families today do not need a bunch of grumpy Old Sneeps sucking on lemons to stop the band from playing.[25] (That's a Robert McCloskey reference from his children's book *Lentil*.)

Parents new to homeschooling need help getting started and help enduring; they need solutions, not barriers; they need mentors like experienced homeschool moms and dads; they need co-ops and pods

---

25. See Robert McCloskey, *Lentil* (New York: Puffin, 1978). I didn't just make this up.

and micro-schools; and they need all the good things we have built together over these past forty years. And we at HSLDA aim to do everything in our power to help.

Looking Ahead

As I reflect on the last year and a half since Professor Bartholet's article created such a stir—and look ahead to the coming years—one thought keeps percolating to the top: *Homeschool freedom exists for such a time as this.*

Fifty years ago, if you had asked education officials of all fifty states whether it was legal for parents without teacher certifications to educate their own children at home, the near-unanimous chorus would have been: "Don't be ridiculous—no!" Today, the answer would be a resounding, unanimous, "Don't be ridiculous—of course homeschooling is legal!"

Homeschooling's progress from a perceived fringe to a mainstream option has been one of the most dramatic "wins" of my lifetime. HSLDA founder Mike Farris calls it a "generational win." Getting from there to here was never a foregone conclusion. Parents in the 1960s, '70s, and '80s risked legal peril and social stigma to do what homeschoolers take for granted today.

Yet homeschooling steadily grew, as more moms and dads just like you and me took the plunge. And as the movement removed more and more legal, social, and practical barriers, together we created a dizzying array of networks, co-ops, and state and local organizations—the rich mosaic we know as homeschooling today.

Entrepreneurs created homeschool curricula and tools. Technology created amazing new opportunities for connecting and learning scarcely imagined at the dawn of the movement. And the number of children being homeschooled grew slowly but steadily for decades. Then the world shut down, and homeschooling exploded

All the decades of preparation—unwitting though it may have been—created a new dynamic. We in the movement have fervently hoped it would grow more quickly, but we never anticipated what just happened. By some estimates, the number of children being homeschooled has doubled and maybe even tripled since the spring of 2020. Many parents who were forced by circumstance to see their children's public school experience through a Zoom window discovered at least two things: (1) they didn't like what they saw, and (2) having their children at home was actually fun and good for their family.

A September 16, 2021, news report from Loudoun County, Virginia, where our office is located, and which has become the focus of national attention for a host of education-related reasons, none of them good, provides a fitting example. The local school officials expected 88,000 students to enroll in the fall of 2021, but only 81,000 enrolled.

Now, those 7,000 students didn't just disappear into thin air. They chose other options. According to the local paper, school officials cited a lack of virtual learning options, continuing COVID safety concerns, and the high-profile battles over equity and other social issues.[26] At $17,000 per pupil, that's a loss of $119 million dollars out of a $1.4 billion dollar budget.[27] A sudden, unexpected 8.5 percent budget hit will not go unnoticed.

The same article quotes a local social worker who noticed that her phones were quieter, and fewer parents were calling for her services for their high school-aged children. Here's what she had to say: "For some kids, whose anxiety was high, it actually was a help to be home. Being home allowed them to have a calmer, less anxiety-provoking situation." According to her, "Families who would not consider homeschooling prior to the pandemic, because of COVID, they saw how their child did and that they actually still could learn quite well, they are now moving to homeschool, because for their child it was actually better ... For them, it was a Godsend."

This discovery was not confined to public schools. A young father I know exemplifies the significance of what is now happening. Before the pandemic, he and his wife had considered homeschooling but de-

26. "School Enrollment Again Declines," *LoudounNow* 6, no. 43 (September 16, 2021).

27. "Loudoun County Public Schools FY 2022 Budget," Loudoun County Public Schools, January 7, 2021, https://www.lcps.org/cms/lib/VA01000195/Centricity/Domain/64/FY%20 22%20Budget/02-08-21%20fy22_sb_adopted_%20exec_summary/Executive_Summary_ FY22%20SB_Adopted.pdf.

cided to send their children to a private Christian school, a school they liked and had no issues with. When that school closed to in-person learning and homeschooling became the family's only option, they experienced the joy of teaching their own kids. As many parents know, there is no substitute for being the one to see a child's eyes light up with discovery. And homeschooling makes possible particularly rich, fulfilling relationships between parents and children and among siblings. This dad told me they have continued homeschooling because of their firsthand experience of these and other benefits. Stories like this are exemplative of why I think that many families who started homeschooling because of COVID-19 will continue out of joy.

COVID-19 is not the only factor in the current shakeup of educational norms, however. Public schools are becoming more engaged in ideological indoctrination that many parents cannot go along with. On issues ranging from sexuality to race to whether our American story should be celebrated (warts and all) or should be a source of shame, the public schools appear bent on taking sides, based on diktats from on high rather than grassroots demand. In response, parents all over the country are speaking up to school boards and education departments, taking a stand for the traditional role of schools and against an imposed orthodoxy with which they disagree.

In response to this renewed civic vigor, the US Department of Justice is launching an investigation into whether these parents should be treated as domestic terrorists under the Patriot Act. Not something I thought I'd ever say, but it's true.

Whether those newly involved public school parents prevail remains to be seen. When COVID-19 broke the public school monopoly on education, however, millions of moms and dads learned that homeschooling is a real, viable choice. Whether the challenge to their children's education comes from COVID-19 or from public schools refusing to answer to parents, homeschooling is a choice that works, is available to almost any family, and is one that helps children thrive.

And today, everybody knows it.

Tipping Point

Which brings me to a vital question for the future. The future of education, yes, but perhaps the future of liberty more generally conceived.

Merriam-Webster defines "tipping point" as "the critical point in a situation, process, or system beyond which a significant and often unstoppable effect or change takes place." Is it possible that homeschooling has reached a tipping point?

The pandemic has been an unbelievably difficult challenge. Out of something devastating, however, something good is sweeping across our country.

Right now, we have a once-in-a-lifetime opportunity to triple or perhaps quadruple the size of the homeschooling movement. What if, together, we can help expand homeschooling to even more families— enough to reach the tipping point? Enough to cause an *unstoppable change*. Enough to permanently shift education of children from so-called experts back to families and organically grown local communities. What would such a tectonic shift do to preserve and promote liberty for future generations?

A large-scale educational shift such as this would allow even more parents to provide what they know is best for their unique children in a safe learning environment. For many Christians, this means having the opportunity to raise their children in the nurture and admonition of the Lord, which in turn could bring revival to our land.

Together, we can grasp key opportunities to make homeschooling possible for more and more families and be alert to the challenges that could well come our way if—or, more likely, when—the empire strikes back. Together, we can make homeschooling possible for many more parents.

Here's what HSLDA has been doing to inspire and equip parents interested in trying homeschooling since the early days of COVID-19 school closures, to grow the homeschooling movement: (1) We've hosted almost fifty how-to-homeschool webinars, answering parents' most-asked questions and turning them into a library of on-demand recordings. (2) We've worked with the VELA Education Fund to provide hundreds of thousands of dollars in grants to homeschooling groups to assist them in launching innovative approaches to homeschooling, especially to serve the new homeschoolers. (3) We've provided more than a thousand low-income families the ability to afford curriculum and other resources through Compassion Grants. (4) We've created easy-to-use tools to connect new homeschoolers to their state and local homeschool organizations—groups that play an irreplaceable role in keeping homeschooling free by monitoring legislation and by forming supportive communities for families. (5) We've produced a winsome video called *Make the World Your Classroom*, to inspire parents looking for a public school alternative, and to direct them to important resources for newcomers—to help grow the movement.

Throughout this time, HSLDA's core mission has remained the same: to provide quality legal assistance to homeschool families, keeping homeschooling free for all of us. We've continued to field hundreds of calls every day from homeschoolers with specific legal questions or those who are navigating sometimes-distressing encounters with local officials. This has been especially important for those new to homeschooling.

Despite the uncertainty all around us, together we can chart an exciting path for the future of homeschooling and America's families, which in turn could expand liberty for all. The unstoppable change brought about by unforeseen events, exacerbated by the growing overreach of the education establishment, and the ameliorating maturity of the homeschooling movement to capture the moment by providing a safe haven for families all work together to offer real choice and hope to more and more parents.

Unstoppable change—I like the sound of that.

Closing Thought

I am reminded of the last sentence of the last chapter of the Book of Malachi in the Old Testament. There, the prophet Malachi says, "And he will turn the hearts of the fathers to their children, and the hearts of the children to their fathers."[28]

---

28. Malachi 4:6 (ESV).

It is our prayer that this present adversity will make us all stronger and more caring, and that, hard as it is, it will become a blessing for you and for many. We hope that you and yours will be safe and well, and that your hearts will turn to each other, as we hope the same for ourselves.

10

The Weakening of the American Family and How It Has Undermined Parental Rights

ALLAN C. CARLSON

In 1929, US President Herbert Hoover—a Republican—launched an unprecedented investigation by "eminent scientists" into private American life. Their assigned task was "to help all of us see where social stresses are occurring and where major efforts should be undertaken to deal with them constructively." The result was a massive, two-volume, 1,568-page report titled *Recent Social Trends*. It had one recurrent, and perhaps surprising, theme: The American family was in irreversible institutional decline.

As the committee of scientists summarized, "the factory [has] displaced the family as the chief unit of economic production." Meanwhile, most "educational and protective functions" of the family had also been transferred "to the state or to industry." Americans, they elaborated, had "sometimes forgotten" the degree to which the family in preindustrial times had been the chief economic, schooling, and security institution of society: "the home was, in short, a factory"; in marriages, men and women sought "not only a mate and companion, but a business partner"; children were not only "objects of affection" but also "productive agents"; each family "furnished protection to its own members"; and the family was a center for religious and recreational acts.

By 1930, though, the average family produced little food, clothing, or much else, while "the teaching function" had shifted to schools. Meanwhile, the practice of family prayer was in apparent decline, and recreation moved to dance halls, movie houses, and ballparks. What was left were merely the "personality functions of the family," whereby each family member adapted himself or herself to the outside world. The committee agreed with the popular judgment that "some homes are merely 'parking places' for parents and children who spend their active hours elsewhere."[1]

Tellingly, the research committee emphasized that children were diminishing in number, as well. Fertility and average family size were falling. In 1930, for the first time in American history, the US Census counted fewer children under age 5 than in the prior census. Meanwhile, as families shed their historic functions, children were "individualized," meaning that a child "is now regarded more as an individual and less as a bearer of the family name." Fathers and husbands had largely surrendered their role as arbiters of interfamily disputes. Wives, meanwhile, faced a crisis of identity. With their productive tasks—such as sewing, food preservation, and cooking—now surrendered to industry and with fewer children being born, they contributed "proportionately less to family support." Indeed, the rise of factories had "obviously" reduced "the economic importance of the woman in the home." One result was a surge in the entry of women into outside occupations during the 1920s.[2]

As Americans no longer made things in their homes, the scientists continued, "the efforts of family members are focused instead on buying a living." The "resulting proliferation of consumer goods" soared

1. *Recent Social Trends in the United States: Report of the President's Research Committee on Social Trends* (New York: McGraw-Hill, 1933), v, xliii–xlv, 661–62.

2. *Recent Social Trends*, xliv, 662–63, 666.

during the 1920s. New practices of advertising pushed this along, involving "commercial stimulation on the greatest scale yet attempted." Between 1909 and 1929, the value of advertising in magazines rose six-fold, reaching $320 million; in newspapers, from $149 million to $792 million (to translate these sums into current dollars, multiply by 30). These advertisers openly sought "to break down consumer resistance; to create consumer acceptance; [and] to create consumer demand" and succeeded in astonishing fashion. Housing patterns changed, as structures built during the nineteenth century and fitted to many children and home production gave way to smaller units without functional intent. Even family structure changed to conform to this commercialism. These new expenditures made the family less of a consumption unit. Rather, new ideas "as to equality of marriage partners and in parent-child relationships" *individualized* the purchase of goods and services, distributing "the family's spending money more generally" through individual members.[3]

This loss of family functions and the individualization of social life also meant a sharp decline in the authority of parents. As Hoover's committee summarized, "the government is assuming a larger protective role with its policing forces, its enormously expanded schools, its courts and its social legislation." More specifically, "compulsory education laws ... represent an assumption of family functions by government agencies," while the public school teacher "may be viewed as a substitute parent in regard to the function of training the child." These teachers were "reaching into the home" ever earlier and so "taking the child at a younger age." As "homes and families" failed in fulfilling other responsibilities, additional "social welfare" agencies moved in "as equivalent to the task of social reconstruction."[4] In such a context, alas, "parental rights" went unmentioned because they were irrelevant, backward looking, and even dangerous. According to the nation's leading experts, America's future lay in the consummation of these social trends, leaving "the family" gone in all but name, and "parental rights"—appropriately—but a memory.

3. *Recent Social Trends*, 857, 866, 871, 873.
4. *Recent Social Trends* , 662, 674, 676, 709.

The force of analysis in *Recent Social Trends* bears the stamp of inevitability. But this hallmark in large part arose from the influence of William F. Ogburn, professor of sociology at the University of Chicago and "director of research" for this project. Ogburn held to a form of soft or academic Marxist analysis, arguing that technological change drove all else, from economic relations to social structure to ideas and culture. "Cultural lag"—a term that he popularized—commonly followed, with the remnant and fairly pathetic "American family" as a prime example.

Truth, however, is more complex. A closer analysis of change in three areas discussed in *Recent Social Trends*—the meaning of home, fertility decline, and advertising—reveals a very different story and possible future.

On the Meaning of "Home"

Why has the fundamental transformation of the family home and its functions attracted so little attention? One scholar suggests that the preindustrial system of "family morality and production" has been little described "precisely because it was so all-embracing. It was not *a* morality, it was *the* morality, and hence commonsensical and unremarkable."[5] All the same, artifacts of this social order survive in the historical record, such as this description of a fairly typical family home from a nineteenth-century New England diary: "My farm gave me and my whole family a good living on the produce of it and left me, one year with another, one hundred and fifty silver dollars, for I never spent more than ten dollars a year, which was for salt, nails, and the like. Nothing to eat, drink, or wear was bought, as my farm produced it all."[6]

In that time, the English/Germanic word "home" still bore meanings reaching back more than a millennium. From the Viking era in my paternal grandfather's ancestral Oestergoettland (eastern Sweden) came this legal sense of sanctuary: "you may not arrest a killer

---

5. John C. Caldwell, *Theory of Fertility Decline* (London: Academic Press, 1982), 326.
6. In Lawrence K. Frank, "Social Change and the Family," *Annals of the American Academy of Political and Social Science* 160 (March 1932): 95.

at his home." More edifying definitions of *heimen* (Middle German), *ham* (Old English), and *heimr* (Old Scandinavian) included "village," "dwelling," "one's farm," "peace for every man," "love," "beloved," "marry," "to bring to bed," "to have sexual intercourse," "to lie down," "to return," and "where things are as they should be." *Home* represented material shelter, safe territory, sustenance, and a setting for family life, especially the presence of children. Home also served as an expression of identity, "after the body itself ... as the most powerful extension of the psyche."[7]

The press to industrialize the whole of human life launched two assaults on this concept of home. The first was to sever "work" from "home," to eliminate the functionality of the family dwelling and environs. At the intellectual level, this meant breaking the close connection of home to marriage and children. One historian has noted with seeming delight that not only had "marriage and the family home ... been challenged but also discarded by a large portion of the population of industrialized countries."[8] As the authors of *Recent Social Trends* correctly observed, American houses built after 1900 ceded most functions to the factories and schools, bringing a shift in design. As the official history of housing by the quasi-governmental Federal National Mortgage Association ("Fannie Mae") explained, "the family was no longer the basic economic as well as the social unit." This meant the disappearance of loom rooms, sewing rooms, work rooms, pantries, carpentry shops, storage cellars, sheds, chicken and pigeon coops, attics, and large kitchens, as productive activities now took place elsewhere. Housing design featuring "open" (and materially useless) space remained, to promote the "personality adjustments" endorsed by the experts.[9]

7. Stefan Brink, "Home: The Term and the Concept from a Linguistic and Settlement Historical Viewpoint," in *The Home: Words, Interpretation, Meanings, and Environments*, ed. David N. Benjamin (Aldershot, UK: Avebury, 1995), 17–22; and Lorna Fox, "The Meaning of Home: A Chimerical Concept or a Legal Challenge," *Journal of Law and Society* 29 (December 2002): 589–90, 600.

8. Roderick J. Lawrence, "Deciphering Home: An Integrative Historical Perspective," in Benjamin, *The Home*, 53.

9. Gertrude Sipperly Fish, ed., *The Story of Housing: Sponsored by the Federal National Mortgage Association* (New York: Macmillan, 1979), 476–78.

The second assault was monetary. Again, prior to the industrializing of human life, home carried a special legal understanding, where the house and property sheltering a family held preferred status. That ended in the early twentieth century. In Great Britain, a 1925 law designed to encourage the sale and transfer of land turned the family home into "a mere piece of capital." As legal scholar Lorna Fox elaborates, property law so embraced "the rhetoric of land [and home] as investment, and the assimilation of land with other forms of capital."[10] The same change occurred in the United States, one also consummated in the first half of the twentieth century. Instead of protections for home, all valuable parcels of land and structures should be allocated to individuals ready to pay the highest price on the free market. The "family home" so became just another thing for sale. Legal historian Lawrence M. Friedman summarizes, "Land transfers shifted from status to contract, land rights were no longer matters of family, birth, and tradition; rather, land was a commodity, traded on the open market."[11]

The Fannie Mae history concurs. By the 1970s, housing in America ceased to serve primarily as a place for shelter and the nurture of children. Rather, houses had now become more important as a form of investment, forced savings, and hedge against inflation. Americans increasingly purchased houses with "re-salability" rather than "livability" in mind. Experts explained that there was no longer a "standard family" of mom, dad, and kids to guide housing demand. Indeed, the old problem of providing shelter to large families in urban settings had vanished, since such families no longer formed. Hence the "safe, sound, sanitary provisions of the prior generation" were no longer relevant.[12]

10. Fox, "Meaning of Home," 582–83.

11. Lawrence Friedman, *A History of American Law* (New York: Simon and Schuster, 1985), 63. See also Emery N. Castle, *Why Land Matters* (Madison: Land Tenure Center, University of Wisconsin, 1995).

12. Fish, *Story of Housing*, 484–85; and George Sternlieb and James W. Hughes, *America's Housing: Prospects and Problems* (New Brunswick, NJ: Center for Urban Research, Rutgers University, 1980), 100, 156.

Fertility Decline

Human fertility in America has had episodes of serious decline: from 1890 to 1930, from 1965 to 1990, and again since 2009. Demographic determinists such as Willian Ogburn continue to point to human adjustment to industrialization as the cause. Does this hold up?

A better explanation comes from the Australian demographer John C. Caldwell. He builds his argument on a careful analysis of population trends in both the developed (Australia, North America, Western Europe) and developing (Africa) worlds, which gives his approach added depth. His conclusion is unambiguous: "the primary determinant" of fertility decline "is the effect of mass [state] education on the family economy." Compulsory state schools change the "direction of wealth flow" and authority structures between generations. More specifically, family-based production of the preindustrial sort rests on "a framework of *family morality*, which enjoins children to work hard, demand little, and respect the authority of the old." Caldwell insists that this morality system can survive within a competitive, capitalist economy, partly owing to continued support by "public religion and private adage" and partly because parents can contrive ways to create and maintain family businesses that involve forms of domestic production and control. But "What the family morality cannot survive and is ultimately supplanted by is a new, community morality that is eventually necessary for fully developed non-family production (whether described as capitalist or socialist) and *that is taught ... by national educational systems.*" Mass state schools trample out family bonds and economies, children change from assets into expensive liabilities, and fertility falls—with no clear ending point, except zero.[13]

How does this work? First, Caldwell shows how compulsory state schooling reduces "the child's potential for work inside and outside the home." Children must be in school for most of the day and then do homework and are quickly alienated from their traditional chores: "Parents may feel that the child should retain all its energies for succeeding at school." Second, state schooling increases the expense of

13. Caldwell, *Theory of Fertility Decline*, 301–2.

rearing children. Beyond fees, uniforms, and notebooks, "school children demand more of their parents," such as better clothing. Indeed, the children's "authority is the new authority of the school, and their guides are the non-traditional ways of life that have been revealed." Third, mass state education upends parental rights: "it becomes clear that the society regards the child as [its] future … and that it expects the family to protect the society's investment in the child for the future." Caldwell notes that strong "child protection" laws commonly appear during the early years of universal governmental schools. Fourth, state schooling "speeds up cultural change and creates new cultures." In African societies the schools suppress traditional ways in favor of corporate friendly behaviors. (While unmentioned by Caldwell, in Western Europe and North America the latest "new" culture teaches lesbian, gay, bisexual, trans, and queer behaviors.) And fifth, state schools denigrate and crush local customs and economies in favor of a globalized economic order.[14] As educational historian Joel Spring puts it, around the globe "the promise of school graduation is a high income for a good shopping experience."[15]

More broadly, Caldwell's theory shows how compulsory school attendance is part of a massive shift in the social and legal treatment of children, where they are lifted out of families and treated as individuals with distinctive needs and claims.[16] He writes: "Governments have always been in competition with the family for loyalty." Textbooks show how states see their schools as the "chief instruments for teaching citizenship—for going over the heads of patriarchs [read 'parents'] and appealing directly to the children." As to the consequences for fertility, Caldwell is blunt: no society "can sustain stable high fertility beyond two generations of mass schooling."[17]

14. Caldwell, *Theory of Fertility Decline*, 303–5.

15. Joel Spring, *Global Impacts of the Western School Model: Corporatization, Alienation, Consumerism* (New York: Routledge, 2019), 102.

16. On this point, he cites D. B. Tyack, "Ways of Seeing: An Essay on the History of Compulsory Education," *Harvard Educational Review* 46 (1976): 363.

17. Caldwell, *Theory of Fertility Decline*, 305, 311, 325.

Advertising

As it took form after 1900, commercial advertising was an intentional and direct assault on the confidence and authority of parents. In order to sell ever more goods and services, the productive family had to be torn down and left helpless except for the largesse provided by the industrial order. Ads were the vehicles for this radical change. And yet it needed to be done cleverly. The new advertisements commonly spoke "with reverence for the family," while subtly and steadily undermining its control over children.

Fathers were a clear target, with ads serving—in historian Stuart Ewen's words—as "propaganda to replace the father's authority." Writing in 1931, marketing consultant Edward Filene wrote that since most men in the industrialized milieu no longer controlled significant economic activities in their homes, and as women and children discovered that their economic well-being now came from industry, fathers "must be relieved of many ancient responsibilities and therefore of many of [their] prerogatives." This decline of a "materially based patriarchal authority" left the male in crisis. As sociologist Lawrence Frank observed, the young man who wanted to "fulfill the older conception of a competent male, ambitious, enterprising, prepared to support a wife and family," actually faced "a most perplexing situation," for he was no longer relevant. Real or potential fathers found themselves stripped of social power, except as their wages supported consumption by family members. In 1929 the popular home economist Christina Frederick summarized the situation this way: "our [industrial] civilization is lush soil for the feminine, but barren soil for the masculine characteristics."[18]

Conversely, women as *mothers* found that the advertisers worked to strip them of authority. Ad men were fully aware of the competition between new manufactured goods and the older skills, wisdom, and commonsense of home keepers. Again, striking a delicate balance, the

18. Stuart Ewen, *Captains of Consciousness: Advertising and the Social Roots of the Consumer Culture* (New York: McGraw-Hill, 1976), 131; Edward A. Filene, *Successful Living in the Machine Age* (New York: Simon and Schuster, 1931), 96; Frank, "Social Change and the Family," 98; and Christine Frederick, *Selling Mrs. Consumer* (New York: Business Course, 1929), 14.

advertisers simultaneously "educated" women into using more biscuits while ridiculing baking at home. Instead, motherhood had become a task defined by female spending; the former home-based creator had become a buyer. As Columbia University "household economist" Benjamin Andrews explained, "the home woman as purchasing agent is [now] essential to present well-being and to social progress." He continued: "The world in which the typical family lives is the world built for it by the woman who spends."[19]

Christine Frederick was more blunt. The modern housewife, she proudly reported, "is no longer a cook; she is a can-opener." Just as remarkably, Frederick presented to industrialists a "pledge" to do all in their power to crush any lingering female domestic skills: "I affirm that the manufacturer's real success is measured by the degree of thoroughness with which the owner or operator of the appliance has been able to adapt herself to a transformation from a hand and craft technique over into a machine process."[20]

At the same time, the ad men worked relentlessly to pulverize women's self-confidence as mothers. Everywhere in the home, the latter read, dangers lurked—with solutions provided by the business sector. Sample messages from *Ladies Home Journal* during the 1920s included claims like Hygenia bottles did not carry germs to the baby and so were "safe"; Fly-Tex bug killer was the best way to protect the "defenseless" child; Lysol was necessary because even "the doorknobs" threatened children with disease; and Pepsodent ensured that children would not "suffer as you did from film on teeth."[21]

More insidiously, the advertisers twisted female sexuality into another splendid marketing opportunity. In one notorious episode, business psychologist A. A. Brill explained how women might be turned into smokers. "Some women regard cigarettes as symbols of freedom," he wrote. "Smoking is a sublimation of oral eroticism." Meanwhile,

19. Benjamin A. Andrews, "The Home Woman as Buyer and Controller of Consumption," *Annals of the American Academy of Political and Social Science* 143 (May 1929): 41.

20. Frederick, *Selling Mrs. Consumer*, 181.

21. Sample advertisements gathered in Ewen, *Captains of Consciousness*, 169–70. See also Bryce Christensen, "Sell Out: Advertising's Assault on the Family," *Family in America* 4 (February 1990): 3.

the legal and cultural emancipation of women had "suppressed many of the feminine desires." Accordingly, cigarettes might be sold as "torches of freedom." Ad man Edward Bernay proceeded to place in New York's 1929 Easter Parade a contingent of young women lighting up their "torches of freedom," gaining front page stories across the country.[22] Meanwhile, a 1928 ad for Palmolive soap employed blatant Freudian/Oedipal imagery to undercut again the confidence of women. It showed an attractive young mother, in Ewen's words, "submitting to her boy-child's scrutiny and pleasure," where the use of Palmolive would maintain her as "His First Love."[23]

From another angle, the ad men directly sought to break the parent-child bond, the better to sell. Where parents would have more "prejudices" to overcome, children were "blank slates," innocently open to consumer messaging. As advertising psychologist Alfred Poffenberger put it, "the great difficulty that one meets in breaking habits among parents" highlighted the "importance of introducing innovations by way of the young."[24] The advent of television enhanced the opportunities here. S. M. Dworetz shows how broadcasters "deliberately and effectively" worked to undercut parental influence. They designed programming to repel adults while tantalizing children. The goal, largely achieved, was to transform the parent from guardian and teacher into "simply a purchasing agent for the child."[25]

In the end, the "consuming family" was still there: Mom, Dad, and the kids enjoying a cornucopia of material goods. But in truth this family model was a "parody of the old." Real, tangible bonds had diminished or even vanished. The "nuclear" family had actually gone "atomic," scattered into the consuming wind. In the regime of advertising the former natural linkages between parents and their children were "thoroughly externalized," driven only by "their common involvement with the time-space dictates of business."[26]

22. Edward Bernays, *Biography of an Idea: Memoirs of a Public Relations Counsel* (New York: Simon and Schuster, 1965), 386–87.

23. Ewen, *Captains of Consciousness*, 182.

24. Albert T. Poffenberger, *Psychology in Advertising* (Chicago: A. W. Shaw, 1925), 35.

25. S. M. Dworetz, "Before the Age of Reason: Liberalism and the Media Socialization of Children," *Social Theory and Practice* 13 (1987): 187–218.

26. Ewen, *Captains of Consciousness*, 184.

Inevitable?

As this more detailed recounting of developments in the meaning of home, fertility decline, and advertising affirms, the corrosion in legal and cultural "parental rights" during the last one hundred years was accompanied by, and often preceded by, the evisceration of the natural family. Family decay, evident as early as 1930, had consequences, with parents and their claims as the consistent losers.

Was this inevitable? Did technological and economic innovations relentlessly drive family change in a distinctive and necessary way?

No. As these three examples also show, ideological pressure—the politics of ideas—and choices in the making of laws and regulations and in the exercise of consumer spending occurred at every stage. Other options existed, and still do.

Consider, for instance, the supposed inevitable separation of workplace from home. A curious essay, "Sustaining a Sense of Home and Personal Identity," appeared in 1995. It sought to explain the strange persistence of paid work in some of the homes of Great Britain. In the spirit of William Ogburn, the authors agreed that within the context of the necessary "split between home and work," the practice of homework could be viewed "as exceptional, or abnormal, in some cases deviant": a drastic case of cultural lag. While mentioning in passing some recent attempts at computerized "teleworking," the essay reported that the vast majority of homeworkers were a remnant "source of cheap, unregulated labor" and corrupt franchising, women who had small children or similar domestic care duties, a few persons self-employed, and those from minority ethnic groups seeking to escape racism in the industrial workplace. At the same time the writers acknowledged that homeworkers often identified a desire to be "a more integral part of home and family life" as their chief motivation. And they redesigned their dwellings to create separate work rooms in an extra bedroom, a converted garage, a shed, or a hut of some kind.[27]

Almost needless to say, the year 2020 showed such homeworkers

27. Marjorie Bulos and Waheed Chaker, "Sustaining a Sense of Home and Personal Identity," in Benjamin, *The Home*, 227–35.

to be not a struggling remnant but the avant-garde of a workplace revolution, and not only in Britain, but also in the United States and globally. COVID-19 restrictions turned perhaps 2 billion persons into homeworkers, most for more than a year. A frantic search for productive workspace in dwellings once deliberately stripped of them brought back the twenty-first-century equivalents of sewing rooms and family workshops. A related surge in home gardening and home cooking buoyed demand for pantries and large kitchens. Many homeworking employees found pleasure in a new freedom from the commute and a reintegration of work and family. Employers discovered the vast waste of time and emotional energy in the industrialized workplace, a truth already (and delightfully) exposed in long-running television series, *The Office*. The demand for new dwellings with defined and efficiently built workrooms soared. While the post-COVID order will see some return of old ways, this undoing of the industrial revolution will predictably have a lasting, major legacy.

Relative to fertility decline, there is also no record of inevitability. As already noted, John Caldwell implies that a "family morality system" and relatively high fertility can survive under industrial capitalism—in the *absence of compulsory mass state schools*. He is more specific. Caldwell notes that in seventeenth- and eighteenth-century America, literacy was nearly universal in New England, among women and men, girls and boys alike. And yet fertility was high, reaching an average of nine live births per woman.[28] In Australia, he traces the considerably higher mid-twentieth-century birth rate found among Irish Catholics to "denominational schools," which "almost certainly taught ... the need for more traditional ... family relationships than did the state educational system." Caldwell also finds in Europe, prior to 1880, a "persistence of high fertility ... among those classes ... that habitually educated their children" in their homes. Evident especially among the wealthy employing tutors, these homeschools exhibited "a strong family morality that placed family interests first" and were

---

28. Caldwell, *Theory of Fertility Decline*, 305. On fertility in colonial New England, see Allan C. Carlson, *Family Cycles: Strength, Decline, and Renewal in American Domestic Life, 1630 to 2000* (New Brunswick, NJ: Transaction, 2016), chaps. 1 and 3.

spaces in which family members "helped each other." As late as 1900, a fifth of those entering England's Cambridge University were homeschooled. Finally, he shows that a "classical education" along the ancient model (quadrivium) did not "provide much fuel ... to upset a traditional family morality system."[29] In short, religious schools confidently teaching a family morality, homeschools framed by family interests, and classical schools using ancient models do not produce the demographic woes caused by mass state schooling.

On advertising, the contemporary ambiguities are greater. Vast sums continue to be spent by corporations seeking to sell their wares, with home production of any sort still the primary target. The authority of fathers and mothers continues to be undermined, both subtly and directly. And yet, at least until now, the consumption of advertisements remains a voluntary act. The one exception—outdoor messaging—is relatively insignificant. Meanwhile, the ad men of Madison Avenue now face their own crisis. Revenues from advertisements in both magazines and newspapers are plummeting, a hundred years after the great surge began. Meanwhile, in television, commercial stations are steadily losing ground to streaming services that do not employ advertising. True, computer sites are awash in little ads, both still and animated. Yet these strangely resemble that sort seen in newspapers prior to 1900, more like postings on notice boards than the sophisticated corruptions that came later. And even these pale shadows can often be avoided ("Skip Ad").

Advertising has been called "a kind of cross between poetry and adultery."[30] Perhaps the wages of sin here have grown too unwieldy. And perhaps family morality systems—complete with respect for parental rights—are on the cusp of cultural and legal renewal.

29. Caldwell, *Theory of Fertility Decline*, 312–13.
30. Christensen, "Sell Out," 7.

11

Immutable Traits

Blackness, Poverty, and Child Protective Services

ALLISON FOLMAR

The only remedy to racist discrimination is antiracist discrimination.
—Ibram X. Kendi

Racism—race prejudice—in American life and institutions is real. It exists and endures despite all the progress we've made in our society. It disrupts Black families.[1] It seeps into all aspects of civic and *private* life.[2] Our US Constitution promises to protect every citizen from op-

---

Epigraph. Ibram X. Kendi, *How to Be an Antiracist* (N.Y.: Random House, 2019), 19.

1. See, e.g., Barbara Bennett Woodhouse, "Keynote: Race, Culture, Class and the Myth of Crisis: An Ecogenerist Perspective on Child Welfare," *St. John's Law Review* 81 (2007): 519, 524: "Our child welfare programs and priorities are distorted by ideologies about race, class, and individual responsibility that have nothing to do with children's safety or well-being." Tanya A. Cooper, "Racial Bias in American Foster Care: The National Debate," *Marquette Law Review* 97 (2013): 233–34.

2. See, e.g., Charles R. Lawrence III, "The Id, the Ego, and Equal Protection: Reckoning with Unconscious Racism," *Stanford Law Review* 39 (1987): 317, 322–23 (noting the historic and

pressive state power. For Black and brown families, however, the Constitution's promises of "due process" and "equal protection of the law" are not honored in our child welfare system.

The history of the American child welfare system is one of historic discrimination[3] against poor Black families. Race and class keep poor Black families under the state's watchful eye. Race discrimination tilts the scales toward family separation, foster care, and termination of parental rights. According to the American Bar Association, "race and socioeconomic status often impact decisions in every stage of the child welfare system from reporting, to foster care placements, to termination of parental rights decisions."[4] As legal scholar Dorothy Roberts noted:

The racial disparity is also caused by a fundamental flaw in the system's conception. The child welfare system is designed not as a way to for government to assist parents in taking care of their children, but as a means to punish parents for their failures by threatening to take their children away.[5]

The child welfare system is pervasive, as administrative agencies across the country seek poor, unprotected children to justify the need

---

ongoing patterns of racial discrimination and economic injustice that continue to affect African American families). See also Roy L. Brooks, "Critical Race Theory: A Proposed Structure and Application to Federal Pleading," *Harvard Blackletter Law Journal* 11 (1994): 85, 90: "All [of] our institutions of education and information—political and civic, religious and creative—either knowingly or unknowingly provide the public rationale to justify, explain, legitimize, or tolerate racism" (alteration in original). Here Brooks quotes Derrick Bell, *And We Are Not Saved: The Elusive Quest for Racial Justice* (N.Y.: Basic Books, 1987), 156 discussing Professor Manning Marabel's "ideological hegemony" of white racism.

3. Black families are investigated more often for allegations of abuse. See John D. Fluke et al., "Disproportionate Representation of Race and Ethnicity in Child Maltreatment: Investigation and Victimization," *Child and Youth Services Reviews* 25 (2003): 359, 364–65, 367. See also Alicia Summers et al., National Council of Juvenile and Family Court Judges Juvenile Law Program, *Disproportionality Rates for Children of Color in Foster Care*, Technical Assistance Bulletin 1 (2013), who found that "While disproportionality rates increased between 2000 and 2004, African American/Black disproportionality has now decreased to 2.0 from 2.5 nationally." http://www.ncjfcj.org/sites/default/files/Disproportionality%20Rates%20for%20 Children%20of%20Color%20in%20Fo ster%20Care%202013.pdf.

4. Krista Ellis, "Race and Poverty Bias in the Child Welfare System: Strategies for Child Welfare Practitioners," last visited July 30, 2021, https://www.americanbar.org/groups/public_interest/child_law/resources...019/race-and-poverty-bias-in-the-child- system---strategies-f/.

5. Dorothy E. Roberts, "Child Welfare and Civil Rights," *University of Illinois Law Review* 1 (2003): 171, 176.

for social services that most Black families just do not receive. Most Black families that encounter the child welfare system come to know it as an instrumentality of *family separation*. The Government Accountability Office notes:

Each year, hundreds of thousands of the nation's most vulnerable children are removed from their homes and placed in foster care. While states are primarily responsible for providing safe and stable out-of-home care for these children, Title IV-E of the Social Security Act provides federal financial support. The Administration for Children and Families (ACF) in the Department of Health and Human Services (HHS) is responsible for administering and overseeing federal funding for Foster Care.[6]

Systemic racism creates two Americas:[7] one just, the other unjust. Too often, systemic racism intersects with poverty.[8] As the Supreme Court determined in *Smith v. Organization of Foster Families*, "foster care has been condemned as a class-based intrusion into the family life of the poor."[9] Too often, a family's race and class are outcome-determinative[10] in child protective services proceedings. Studies show that "children from families with annual incomes below $15,000 were 22 times more likely to experience harm"[11] from the child welfare system. Resourceless Black families find that Child Protective Services (CPS) is no respecter of the poor—especially poor *Black* fam-

6. US Government Accountability Office, *Foster Care Program: Improved Processes Needed to Estimate Improper Payments and Evaluate Related Corrective Actions*, GAO-12-312 (Washington, DC: US Government Accountability Office, 2012), App. II, 41–42, http://gao.gov/assets/590/589114.pdf.

7. See, e.g., *Smith v. Org. of Foster Families*, 431 U.S. 816, 835 n.35 (1977), which noted that "systems of foster-care funding ... encourage agencies to keep the child in foster care."

8. "Poverty has had a persistently strong relation to minority status in the United States." John Fluke, Brenda Jones Harden, Molly Jenkins, and Ashleigh Ruehrdanz, "A Research Synthesis on Child Welfare Disproportionality and Disparities," in *Disparities and Disproportionality in Child Welfare: Analysis of the Research* (Washington, DC: Alliance for Racial Equality in Child Welfare, December 2011), 11. See also Roberts, "Child Welfare and Civil Rights": "Poverty is key to explaining why almost any child gets in the system. It is the dominant explanation of researchers in the field for the inequitable representation of black children." See also Mark Courtney et al., "Race and Child Welfare Services: Past Research and Future Directions," *Child Welfare* 75 (1998): 99, 101–7.

9. *Smith v. Org. of Foster Families*, 431 U.S. 816, 833 (1977).

10. "Race also influences child welfare decision making through strong and deeply embedded stereotypes about black family dysfunction." Roberts, "Child Welfare and Civil Rights."

11. Alliance for Racial Equality in Child Welfare, *Disparities and Disproportionality*.

ilies. Those families soon discover that there are no presumptions of humanity, or civility, with CPS. In a Philadelphia hospital study, Black and Hispanic toddlers with bone fractures "were more than five times more likely to be evaluated for child abuse, and more than three times more likely to be reported to child protective services, than white children with comparable injuries."[12] These immutable traits—Blackness and poverty—tell us the types of services CPS will (or won't) provide; these immutable traits also predetermine the lengths CPS will (or won't) go to reunify Black families. The point of this paper is this: *Black children are overrepresented*[13] *in our juvenile courts and child welfare institutions.* "Black children remain in foster care longer, are moved more often, receive fewer services, and are less likely to be either returned home or adopted than any other children."[14] Moreover, "excessive state interference in Black family life damages Black people's sense of personal and community identity."[15] As a result, Black families become "passive, voiceless subjects of the [system's] paternalistic directives, [not] active participants in the determination of their own destinies."[16]

As Ibram X. Kendi notes, "one of racism's harms is the way it falls on the unexceptional black person who is asked to be extraordinary

12. Dorothy E. Roberts, "Race and Class in the Child Welfare System," Frontline, accessed July 30, 2021, https://www.pbs.org/wgbh/pages/frontline/shows/fostercare/caseworker/roberts.html.

13. "The criminalization of poor black and brown mothers' parenting practices is a well-documented phenomenon dubbed 'Jane Crow.'" Rachelle Hampton, "The Devonte Hart Case Highlights a Profound Racial Disparity in the Treatment of Child Abuse," Slate.com, April 3, 2018, https://slate.com/human-interest/2018/04/devonte-hart-and-siblings-death-shows-racial-disparity-in-child-abuse-investigations.html.

14. Roberts, "Child Welfare and Civil Rights"; see also Edward V. Mech, "Public Social Service to Minority Children and Their Families," in *Children in Need of Roots*, ed. R. O. Washington and Joan Boros-Van Hull (1985), 133, 161; Loring P. Jones, "Social Class, Ethnicity, and Child Welfare," *Journal of Multicultural Social Work* 6 (1997): 123, 130. A 2017 Washington State report found African American children were 2.2 times more likely to be removed from their homes than their white counterparts. "Child Welfare Data at a Glance," Partners for Our Children, accessed July 30, 2021, https://partnersforour children.org/data/quickfacts.

15. Roberts, "Child Welfare and Civil Rights"; Jones, "Social Class, Ethnicity, and Child Welfare."

16. Tanya Asim Cooper, "Race Is Evidence of Parenting in America: Another Civil Rights Story," in *Civil Rights in American Law, History, and Politics*, ed. Austin Sarat (Cambridge: Cambridge University Press, 2014), 103.

just to survive."[17] We can only measure our pursuit of justice by protecting the *unexceptional* citizen. The unexceptional citizen is most at risk of government oppression, without the ability to access the government's protections, privileges, and promises. As one scholar noted, "addressing the overrepresentation of children and families of color in our juvenile courts requires careful consideration and reform of the policies and practices that drive bias and structural racism."[18] We must do everything in our power to right this obvious yet enduring wrong.

Race Prejudice, "The Child Savers," and the Dawn of the American Child Welfare System

"Americans have long been trained to see the deficiencies of people rather than policy."[19] Racist ideas are policy deficiencies in our society. And that is not some novel concept. Similar to crime, civics, and places of accommodation, racist ideas infected the American child welfare system at its outset.[20] The movement for juvenile courts began during the America's Progressive Era, near the turn of the twentieth century. Organizations such as the Child Savers pushed for social reforms in American courts.[21] Some of those reforms were based on bias, eugenics, and racist ideas.[22] In 1899, Illinois passed the Juvenile Court Act, which created courts for delinquent neglected children under 16 years old. Jurists such as Julian Mack envisioned these courts

17. Kendi, *How to Be an Antiracist*, 93.
18. Ellis, "Race and Poverty Bias."
19. Kendi, *How to Be an Antiracist*, 28.
20. Dorothy E. Roberts, "Criminal Justice and Black Families: The Collateral Damage of Over-Enforcement," *University of California, Davis, Law Review* 34 (2001): 1005, 1020–27.
21. Cheryl Nelson Butler, "Blackness as Delinquency," *Washington Law Review* 90 (2013): 1335, 1346; see also Michael Willrich, *City of Courts: Socializing Justice in Progressive Era Chicago* (New York: Cambridge University Press, 2003), 229–30.
22. Butler, "Blackness as Delinquency"; see also Anthony M. Platt, *The Child Savers: The Invention of Delinquency*, 2nd ed. (Chicago: University of Chicago Press, 1977), xxiii–xxvi. Kendi says in *How to Be an Antiracist* (20), "A racist idea is any idea that suggests one racial group is inferior or superior to another racial group in any way" and "Racist ideas argue that the inferiorities and superiorities of racial groups explain racial inequities in society." As far as eugenics is concerned, it is a bundle of racist ideas cloaked as progressive theory.

as a place of "social rehabilitation" and "a revolution in the attitude of the state toward its offending children." This burst of progressivism, however, was not without its biases—especially for Black children. At the turn of the twentieth century, many of these organizers considered Black children "degenerate from birth."[23]

Chicago is the birthplace of our juvenile court system. As the juvenile court system began to take shape, civil rights activist Ida B. Wells grew concerned that these nascent courts were falling short of true justice.[24] Wells's concerns weren't heeded, however. According to a modern legal scholar, the juvenile court system "promised to protect the child in cases where the family or neighborhood had failed him."[25] One of the early promisors was Chicago's Judge Julian Mack, considered a founding father of the juvenile justice system. Judge Mack envisioned the juvenile court to be a place where young people would come before a "wise and merciful father" and be reformed.[26] In Mack's view the system would be a forum of "social rehabilitation,"[27] staffed with benevolent, Platonian philosopher-kings: "probation officer acts as a parent, and does in each case what seems wisest and best for him to do, having the authority and sanction of the court to fall back upon."[28] These high ideas never took off the ground for poor people of color, however.

Over time, Judge Mack's dreams[29] of the child welfare system as

23. Butler, "Blackness as Delinquency," 1335, 1346; see also Jane Addams Talks: Addresses Club Women on Democracy and Social Ethics Chicago Inter-Ocean (Nov. 18, 1900) available at http://tigger.uic.edu/htbin/cgiwrap/bin/urbaneexp/main.cgi?file=new/show_doc.ptt&doc =154&chap=83.

24. Ida B. Wells, *Crusade for Justice*, ed. Alfreda M. Duster (Chicago: University of Chicago Press, 1970), 70; Butler, "Blackness as Delinquency."

25. Butler, "Blackness as Delinquency," 1335.

26. Julian Mack, "The Juvenile Court," *Harvard Law Review* 23 (1909): 104, 107; Butler, "Blackness as Delinquency"; Daniel M. Miller and Austin E. Smith, "The New Rehabilitation, as Delinquency," *Iowa Law Review* 90 (2006): 951, 957–58.

27. Butler, "Blackness as Delinquency," 1335.

28. Richard S. Tuthill, "Illinois: History of the Children's Court in Chicago," in *Children's Courts in the United States: Their Origin, Development and Results* (Washington, DC: US Government Printing Office, 1904), 1, 4.

29. "In theory, the court was to ensure fair and humane treatment of all children; the promise would, in Judge Mack's words, 'apply with equal force to the son of the pauper and the son of a millionaire.' . . . [But] the court's idealistic pronouncements about protecting children masked class and ethnic biases; a child's social class blatantly determined the disposition of his

a "wise and merciful father" gave way to the realities of race and class inequities in our country. In the 1950s, child welfare institutionaliza-tion replaced segregation as the looming horror for poor Black fam-ilies.[30] Today, "child protective agencies are far more likely to place black children in foster care instead of offering their families less trau-matic assistance."[31] According to the Department of Health and Hu-man Services, "minority children, and in particular African American children, are more likely to be in foster care placement than receive in-home services, even when they have the same problems and char-acteristics as white children."[32] In fact, "Black children make up more than two-fifths of the foster care population."[33] Data from the Child Welfare Information Gateway show "the average stay in foster care for White children at the end of FY 2003 was approximately 24 months," but "the average length of stay for African-American children at the same time was more than 40 months."[34] In Chicago, the birthplace of the benevolent idea of the juvenile justice system, Black children make up approximately 95 percent the city's foster children.[35] In summary, our laws do not do enough to help the powerless and the oppressed.

Legal doctrines, such as the best interest of the child, "[allow] fos-

---

case. Middle class children from 'thoroughly good' families were given a warning, while chil-dren from lower class homes were often considered 'morally defective' and institutionalized." Butler, "Blackness as Delinquency."

30. Leroy H. Pelton, *For Reasons of Poverty: A Critical Analysis of the Public Child Welfare System in the United States* (Westport, CT: Praeger, 1989), 20.

31. Roberts, "Child Welfare and Civil Rights."

32. Admin for Children and Families, US Department of Health and Human Services, *Child Maltreatment 1998: Reports from the States to the National Child Abuse and Neglect Data System* (Washington, DC: US Government Printing Office, 2000).

33. Roberts, "Child Welfare and Civil Rights."

34. Child Welfare Information Gateway, US Department of Health and Human Services, *Addressing Racial Disproportionality in Child Welfare* (Washington, DC: Government Printing Office, 2011), 4 (citing a memorandum from Emilie Stoltzfus, Specialist in Soc. Legislation, Cong. Research Serv., to Hon. Charles Rangel, on Race/Ethnicity and Child Welfare, August 25, 2005): "Some of this disparity may be attributed to the trend for African-American children to spend more time in foster care with relatives, but that practice does not account for the enormity of the gap."

35. Natalie Pardo, "Losing Their Children," *Chicago Reporter* 28 (1999): 1, 7. In Chicago, "al-most all child protection cases are clustered in two zip code areas, which are almost exclusive-ly African American." Chicago, however, is not alone. See Roberts, "Child Welfare and Civil Rights," 171, 172: "The racial imbalance in New York City's foster system is truly mind boggling: out of 42,000 children in the system at the end of 1997, only 1,300 were white."

ter care professionals and even judges to substitute their own judgment about what is in a child's best interest and allows unintended biases to permeate decision-making."[36] The Supreme Court called the "best interest of the child" standard "imprecise and open to the subjective values of the judge."[37] In fact, "the best interests of the child standard has been criticized almost since adoption because its indeterminacy invites the use of cognitive shortcuts; these shortcuts include stereotypes and biases as well as the scripts and models left behind by metaphors and stories."[38] In *Parent Representation in Child Welfare: A Child Advocate's Journey*, author and family lawyer Tracy Green argues, "The system's laws and policies ... are fundamentally biased against parents in their application and practice. The bias is deeply rooted in our society's disdain for the poor or ignorance regarding the [e]ffects of poverty. This bias is so extreme, that it obfuscates the glaring harm that foster care imposes upon the very children the system seeks to protect. It is, therefore, through primarily the zealous, diligent, and effective advocacy of the parent's attorney in child welfare proceedings that the negative consequences imposed on children by foster care can be combated and averted."[39]

The Way Forward: Remedies for Racism in the Child Welfare System

More must be done to erase the inequities we see in the child welfare system. Like Ida B. Wells a century ago, many citizens remain com-

36. Robert H. Mnookin, "Child-Custody Adjudication: Judicial Functions in the Face of Indeterminacy," *Law and Contemporary Problems* 39 (1975): 226, 229; Tanya A. Cooper, "Racial Bias in American Foster Care: The National Debate," *Marquette Law Review* 97 (2013): 245.

37. *Lassiter v. Department of Social Services*, 452 U.S. 18, 45 (1981) (Blackmun, J. dissenting); see also *Smith v. Org. of Foster Families*, 431 U.S. at 835 n.36 (1977), which notes that "judges too may find it difficult, in utilizing vague standard like 'the best interest of the child,' to avoid decisions resting on subjective values."

38. Linda L. Berger, "How Embedded Knowledge Structures Affect Judicial Decision Making: A Rhetorical Analysis of Metaphor, Narrative, and Imagination in Child Custody Disputes," *Southern California Interdisciplinary Law Journal* 18 (2009) 259, 298.

39. Tracy Green, "Parent Representation in Child Welfare: A Child Advocate's Journey," *Michigan Child Welfare Law Journal* 13 (2009): 16, http://chanceatchildhood.msu.edu/pdf/CWLJ _fa09.pdf.

mitted to bridge the justice gap between families of color and others. Organizations such as Child Welfare Information Gateway propose a community-centered approach, otherwise known as Family Group Decision-Making (FGDM): "The use of FGDM reflects the traditional values of kinship and community seen, for example, in African cultures, as well as Native American Tribal culture. It may also help promote a community-based approach to addressing disproportionality. FGDM can also help the community at large view child welfare workers and agencies in a more positive light."[40] Likewise, organizations like the American Bar Association publish guidance on identifying implicit bias for social workers and other government agents who encounter families in the child welfare system.[41]

Conclusion

Systems can be dismantled. While systemic racism is ever present in our society, so are policies, practices, and *people* committed to reform. FGDM, along with other restorative justice concepts, can move us away from bias and bring us closer to the spirit of our child welfare laws: *rehabilitation, family support, mercy, justice, and fair play.* As Professor Martha Minow aptly notes, "Forgiveness offers something that punishing cannot give ... Restorative justice aspires to integrate forgiveness within the judicial process, rather than simply correct its excesses, and it seeks to engage victims, offenders, and community members in efforts to make right in the present and the future."

40. Martha Minow, *When Should the Law Forgive* (New York: W. W. Norton, 2019), 5, 11. Despite our history—and the statistics—we possess the power to change, to remedy what is wrong in our communities. The law is not a dead letter. The law *lives.* And when we chose to act—to right that which is wrong—we reaffirm our American story, our true creed: *equal justice for all.*

41. Child Welfare Information Gateway, *Addressing Racial Disproportionality in Child Welfare*, 12.

12

False Child Abuse Allegations, the Child Protective System, and the Threat to Parental Rights

STEPHEN M. KRASON

US public policy on child abuse and neglect and the formation of what we now call Child Protective Services (CPS) was shaped by landmark legislation passed by Congress and signed into law by President Richard M. Nixon in 1974 called the Child Abuse Prevention and Treatment Act (CAPTA), or the Mondale Act, after its prime sponsor, Senator and later Vice President Walter F. Mondale. The act made federal funds available to the states for child abuse prevention and research programs on the condition that they passed laws that mandated the following: reporting by certain professionals (such as physicians) of even *suspected* cases of child abuse and neglect; the setting up of specialized child protective agencies, usually housed within state and corresponding county public social service or child welfare agencies, to deal with abuse and neglect; the granting of complete immunity from criminal prosecution or civil liability for the mandated reporters and

CPS investigators, regardless of their actions and even if the allegations are grossly erroneous; the ensuring of confidentiality of records and proceedings in each case; and the providing for appointment of a guardian *ad litem* in judicial proceedings for children alleged to have been abused or neglected.[1] Effectively, CAPTA transformed public policy with respect to child abuse and neglect by means of a new federal grant-in-aid program to the states, the way in which public policy in so many different areas from the early twentieth century onward has been reshaped.[2] CAPTA's mandates encompassed all kinds of known and suspected child maltreatment, including physical abuse, sexual abuse, physical neglect, and psychological and emotional maltreatment. CAPTA never defined these terms, however, and there has not been and is not today any widely accepted definition of them even among professionals working in the field.[3] (This problem of definition has been a major reason for an ongoing explosion of false abuse/ neglect reports.) CAPTA further required the US secretary of health, education, and welfare (later health and human services) to establish a National Center on Child Abuse and Neglect to act as "a clearinghouse for the development of information and dissemination of information about child protective research and programs." The grants that were made through the center became the basis for shaping child abuse/ neglect policy across the country because to get the grants, states had to put in place the practices that we now associate with CPS.[4]

States had adopted some of the above sorts of changes even before being motivated to do so by CAPTA, and some even went beyond what CAPTA required, for example, by mandating *every citizen* to re-

1. See Douglas J. Besharov, "'Doing Something' about Child Abuse: The Need to Narrow the Grounds for State Intervention," *Harvard Journal of Law and Public Policy* 8 (Summer 1985): 543–44, quoting 42 U.S.C. §§5101–5106 (Supp. V 1975) (CAPTA). CAPTA has subsequently been amended—there were some important changes in 2003—but its basic features remain largely unchanged.

2. On the latter point, see Stephen M. Krason, *The Transformation of the American Democratic Republic* (Piscataway, NJ: Transaction Publishers, 2012), 418.

3. Besharov, "'Doing Something,'" 545; Stephen M. Krason, "Child Abuse: Pseudo-Crisis, Dangerous Bureaucrats, Destroyed Families," in *Parental Rights: The Contemporary Assault on Traditional Liberties*, ed. Stephen M. Krason and Robert J. D'Agostino (Front Royal, VA: Christendom College Press, 1988), 167–73.

4. Besharov, "'Doing Something,'" 543.

port known or suspected abuse/neglect and providing both criminal and civil immunity for false reporting, even if willful. In 1963, at the time that the first generation of (limited) reporting laws were being put into place, there were 150,000 reports of abuse and neglect nationwide. By 1972, just prior to the passage of CAPTA, there were 610,000. In 1982, there were 1.3 million.[5] In 1984, ten years after passage, the number had climbed to 1.5 million.[6] By 1991, the number was 2.7 million reports annually,[7] by 1993 it was 2,936,000,[8] and by 1997 it rose to 3 million.[9] The trend continued in the first decade of the twenty-first century. In 2009, it was 3.3 million.[10] In 2018, it was over 3.5 million.[11] This meant that there was an astounding increase in reports of *2,233 percent* in the more than fifty-five years since the first reporting laws! It must be kept in mind that these figures merely tell us about the increase in reports; they do *not* verify that an expanding epidemic of actual child abuse and neglect occurred over this time, as they are often cited to supposedly prove.

All the evidence indicates that the number of reports are grossly out of line with the actual number of cases of abuse and neglect. In Ohio in 1994 the state Department of Human Services, under pressure from the American Civil Liberties Union and other organizations, purged 471,000 names—mostly of parents—from its Central Registry on Child Abuse primarily because the allegations were unsubstantiated[12] (registries are publicly available state listings of people who have been investigated by the CPS as possible abusers). This

5. Besharov, "'Doing Something,'" 545.

6. Douglas J. Besharov, "Unfounded Allegations—A New Child Abuse Problem," *Public Interest* 83 (1986): 19.

7. Trevor Armbrister, "When Parents Become Victims," *Reader's Digest* (April 1993): 101.

8. Brenda Scott, *Out of Control: Who's Watching Our Child Protection Agencies?* (Lafayette, LA: Huntington House, 1994), 29, citing statistics compiled by the American Humane Association.

9. Douglas J. Besharov, "Symposium: Violence in the Family, Child Abuse Realities, Over-Reporting and Poverty," *Virginia Journal of Social Policy and the Law* 8 (Fall 2000): 176.

10. "Childhelp," http://www.childhelp.org/pages/statistics; Internet (accessed 28 Dec., 2011).

11. Children's Bureau, Administration on Children, Youth, and Families, U.S. Dept. of Health and Human Services, *Child Maltreatment 2018*, ii, https://www.acf.hhs.gov/sites/default /files/cb/cm2018.pdf; Internet (accessed 9 Aug., 2020).

12. *Washington Times*, June 4, 1993, A6.

was an astonishing 78.5 percent of the names in the registry! Things have not been much different since then. Nearly twenty years ago, a federal court in Illinois performed a review and reversed 74.5 percent of indicated findings of abuse or neglect in that state.[13] In the same decade in Pennsylvania the substantiation rate kept steadily dropping, from 18 percent in 2006, to 17 percent in 2007, to 16 percent in 2008, to 15.5 percent in 2009, to 14.8 percent in 2010.[14] This has been the case all over the country since not long after the passage of CAPTA. One national study in the late 1970s showed that 65 percent of allegations—which involved 750,000 children—were "unfounded."[15] Another in the mid-1980s concluded that about 80 percent of child sexual abuse complaints were unfounded;[16] another at that time showed that 60 percent of abuse complaints in general were unfounded.[17] Douglas Besharov is a longtime authority on the child abuse question who played an important role in shaping our current national policy and initially served in the federal government to help implement it, but he later became one of its harshest critics. According to Besharov, in the mid-1980s, 65 percent of abuse/neglect reports nationwide "prove[d] to be unfounded," and "over 500,000 families [annually] are put through investigations of unfounded reports."[18] By 2000 the percentage of false reports was still about 65–66, and the number of innocent families investigated annually had increased to about 700,000.[19] In one representative year (1997), unfounded reports in-

13. Diane L. Redleaf, "Center Wins Three Important Appellate Victories Advancing Family Rights," *Family Defender* 5 (Winter 2012): 12. For Illinois, the article cites *Dupuy v. McDonald*, 141 F. Supp. 2d 1090 (N. D. Ill. 2001), aff'd in relevant part, 397 F. 3d 493 (7th Cir. 2005).

1414. Jonathon N. Fazzola, "I'm a Reporter, You're a Reporter, Everyone's a Reporter: The Hidden Harms of Recent Legislative Responses to the Penn State Child Abuse Scandal," *Family Defender* 5 (Winter 2012): 13.

15. Besharov, "'Doing Something,'" 556, citing US National Center on Child Abuse and Neglect, *National Analysis of Child Neglect and Abuse Reporting* (Washington, DC: National Center on Child Abuse and Neglect, 1978), 36.

16. William D. Slicker, "Child Sex Abuse: The Innocent Accused," *Case and Comment* 91, no. 6 (1986): 14, citing Scott Kraft, *Kansas City Times*, February 11, 1985.

17. Slicker, citing *Wall Street Journal*, October 10, 1985, which reported on a paper given by Dr. Diana Schetsky and Howard Boverman at the 1985 Annual Meeting of the American Academy of Psychiatry and the Law.

18. Douglas J. Besharov, "Afterword," in Lawrence D. Spiegel, *A Question of Innocence: A True Story of False Accusation* (Parsippany, NJ: Unicorn Publishing, 1986), 265, 268.

19. Besharov, "Child Abuse Realities," 176, 179, 190.

volved 2,046,000 children.[20] According to Department of Health and Human Services data (known as NCANDS, the National Child Abuse and Neglect Data System), of the 3.3 million reports in 2009, less than 15 percent were substantiated.[21] In 2016, 83 percent of reports leading to CPS investigations were unfounded.[22] Even among substantiated cases, the number of cases of *serious* maltreatment of children (e.g., involving death, life-threatening situations, or serious injury) is small;[23] most "substantiated" cases of abuse or neglect involve "minor situations," such as slapping and poor housekeeping.[24] Besharov concludes that "the high level of unwarranted [state] intervention" has led to a condition in which the child protective "system is overburdened with cases of insubstantial or unproven risk."[25] In 1994 the US Department of Health and Human Services published a study that found 1,227,223 false reports of child abuse in 1992 alone.[26] Fast-forwarding to Fiscal Year 2017, its annual report indicated that there were 2,826,000 reports that were false or not substantiated.[27] All this means

20. Besharov, "Child Abuse Realities," calculated from the chart he provides at 182. This was a large increase in the total number of children (750,000) who were the subject of unfounded reports in 1978, the data for which he provides in one of his earlier articles (see Besharov, "'Doing Something,'" 556). The near-two-thirds figure of unsubstantiated reports, in his estimation, remained the same (see "Child Abuse Realities," 179–80), so there were obviously many more total reports. This does not mean that there were more *actual cases* of abuse and neglect, however, since the CPS could have been using looser criteria for what is "substantiated," or the number of unsubstantiated complaints could already have been much higher than two-thirds (which clearly was the case within a decade).

21. Fazzola, *Family Defender* 5 (Winter 2012), 12, citing the Health and Human Services data that appears at http://www.acf.hhs.gov/programs/cb/pubs/cm09/pdf.

22. Children's Bureau, *Child Maltreatment 2016* (Washington, DC: US Department of Health and Human Services, Administration for Children and Families, Administration on Children, Youth and Families, 2018), https://www.acf.hhs.gov/cb/research-data-technology/statistics-research/child-maltreatment, cited at https://parentalrightsfoundation.org/learn/parental-rights-and-child-abuse-prevention/#_ftn1.

23. Besharov, "Child Abuse Realities," 171–72. Most children in substantiated cases of physical abuse suffered what is called "moderate" injuries or impairments: bruises, depression, or emotional distress that persisted longer than two days.

24. Besharov, "'Doing Something,'" 578.

25. Besharov, "'Doing Something,'" 540.

26. Cited in Paul Craig Roberts, "Parents in the Pillory?," *Washington Times*, April 29, 1996, A20.

27. US Department of Health and Human Services, Administration for Children and Families, "Child Abuse, Neglect Data Released," January 28, 2019, https://www.acf.hhs.gov/media/press/2019/child-abuse-neglect-data-released.

that while for more than three decades the number of unfounded reports apparently was between 60 and 66 percent, now it has shot up to
80 percent or more.[28]

We now have a situation where a massive state bureaucracy with
sweeping coercive power is pouring millions upon millions of dollars
into the problem each year even though more than 80 percent of its
actions are completely unnecessary.[29] We have been told for several
decades that there is a "crisis" of child abuse in the United States. In
reality, the evidence is that child abuse and neglect had been declining.
Analyzing NCANDS and National Incidence Study (NIS) data—NIS-4
is the most recent of the periodic congressional-mandated studies of
child abuse data around the country—David Finkelhor, Lisa Jones,
and Anne Shattuck of the Crimes against Children Center at the University of New Hampshire assert—even in the context of the prevailing
loose definition of terms, both in law and in CPS understanding (as
discussed below)—that in the period 1992–2009, sexual abuse against
children declined by 61 percent, and physical abuse declined 55 percent.[30]

28. Prevent Child Abuse America, "Frequently Asked Questions," accessed February 8,
2012, http://www.preventchildabuse.org/about_us/faqs.shtml#indicated. See also "About Child
Abuse: Frequently Asked Questions," National Exchange Club Foundation, accessed February 8,
2012, http://preventchildabuse.com/abuse.shtml. Some people also try to draw a distinction
between "false" or "unfounded" and "unsubstantiated" reports. I think that there is no true
distinction. If we are to be true to our eminently sensible tradition of Anglo-American law that
holds that one is innocent until proven guilty, and that there has to be some evidence to find a
person guilty, I do not see how a distinction between these terms is valid. I believe that some
who have made the distinction—and are also ready to distinguish "substantiated" from what
the CPS calls "indicated" cases (see n. 28 below)—are just unwilling to accept the fact that the
incidence of child abuse/neglect is not as great as the conventional wisdom—which has never
been based on hard facts, anyhow—holds.

29. By the way, the term "substantiated" in the CPS lexicon generally means that it is established that child maltreatment occurred—though, as mentioned and further discussed below,
it is questionable that many of the parental behaviors that fit the CPS categories of "abuse" or
"neglect" really constitute that in the minds of the average person—whereas the term "indicated" means that there is no proof that maltreatment occurred, but "there is reason to suspect"
that it did, or even that it "could happen." This seems like a bit of a verbal sleight of hand and it
is not clear what it means. Sometimes an "indicated" determination of abuse is simply treated
as though it occurred, and in fact some states do not distinguish between the terms. This can
easily have the effect of inflating the supposed number of cases of actual abuse.

30. David Finkelhor, Lisa Jones, and Anne Shattuck, "Updated Trends in Child Maltreatment, 2009," short publication of the Crimes Against Children Research Center, 2. They say
that there is "no consensus in the child maltreatment field about why sexual abuse and physical

The experience of facing false charges—perhaps it is better to call it an ordeal—can happen to any parent, merely by a stranger picking up the telephone and anonymously calling a well-publicized hotline number or the local children's services or child-welfare agency to say, without any evidence, that a parent maltreated his or her child. The result of this can be a disruption of family life, legal troubles, and financial difficulties growing out of parents having to defend themselves, and forcibly removing children from their homes and separating them from their parents, perhaps for months or even years. While parents can do things to protect their children and families from many of the threats the current culture poses to them (e.g., controlling their associations with bad playmates or peers, limiting television use, installing computer screening software to stop the invasion of immoral influences, or homeschooling them to circumvent the negative influences found in schools), it is almost impossible to fully insulate one's family from the threat of a system that on little pretense can simply reach into the home and take away one's offspring. The massive incidence of false abuse/neglect allegations shows that the current law and public policy and the routine actions of the CPS are a major threat to the American family today.

The first serious problem, indicated above, about the current abuse and neglect statutes is that they in no way provide a precise definition of what constitutes the offense. This is summed up by an oft-quoted passage from Jeanne M. Giovannoni and Rosina M. Becerra's late 1970s book *Defining Child Abuse*: "Many assume that since child abuse and neglect are against the law, somewhere there are statutes that make clear distinctions between what is and what is not child abuse and neglect, but this is not the case. Nowhere are there clear-cut definitions of what is encompassed by the terms."[31] Nothing has changed since then. Writing in 2000, Besharov states, "confusion about reporting is largely

---

abuse have declined so substantially over the longer term" (3). They also note that from 1992 to 2009, child neglect declined much less, only 10 percent (2). If most of the neglect cases are really poverty cases, as Wexler says, this much lesser increase is not surprising. This publication was posted at www.unh.edu/ccrc/pdf.

31. Jeanne M. Giovannoni and Rosina M. Becerra, *Defining Child Abuse* (New York: Macmillan [Free Press], 1979), 2.

caused by the vagueness of reporting laws." Such laws are "often vague and overbroad."[32] This problem of lack of clarity of definition traces itself back to the early state reporting laws and CAPTA itself. Lawyers and legislators are well aware of the need for statutes to meet the basic, traditional constitutional tests of vagueness and overbreadth. The vagueness doctrine in constitutional law holds that a statute or regulation cannot impose penalties without giving a clear idea of the sort of conduct that is prohibited; the overbreadth doctrine says that activity cannot be proscribed or restricted that is beyond the legitimate reach of government, and that government cannot forbid or inhibit conduct that is constitutionally protected, and it cannot reach beyond conduct that is illegal to restrain conduct that is legal.[33] In fact, it is an ancient principle of the Anglo-American legal tradition that a law has to make clear what it demands. One is prompted to think that if this were any other area of law than child abuse/neglect, many of the statutes long since would have been struck down, in whole or in part, as unconstitutionally vague or overbroad. Efforts to declare state statutes in the child abuse/neglect area unconstitutional on these grounds have had limited success in state courts, and apparently no federal court has intervened on these grounds.[34]

32. Besharov, "Child Abuse Realities," 195, 196.

33. Craig R. Ducat and Harold W. Chase, eds., *Constitutional Interpretation*, 5th ed. (St. Paul, MN: West, 1992), G10, G6; Steven H. Gifis, *Law Dictionary* (Woodbury, NY: Barron's Educational Series, 1975), 145.

34. We can note a number of state judicial decisions that rejected such vagueness and/or overbreadth claims: In 1989 the Minnesota Supreme Court held that the state's child abuse/neglect statute, which subjects certain professionals to criminal misdemeanor liability if they fail to file a report, is *not* unconstitutionally vague or overbroad (*State v. Grover*, 437 N.W. 2d 60 [1989]). In 1990 the Nebraska Supreme Court rejected a vagueness challenge to that state's child abuse statute (*State v. Crowdell*, 451 N.W.2d 695). In 2002 the Florida Supreme Court held that the provision of that state's criminal child abuse statute referring to "mental injury" was not unconstitutionally vague (*DuFresne v. State*, 826 So.2d 272). In 2008 the Massachusetts Supreme Judicial Court brushed aside a challenge to that state's child endangerment statute on vagueness grounds (*Commonwealth v. Hendricks*, 452 Mass. 97). In 2011 the North Dakota Supreme Court held that that state's child abuse statute was not unconstitutionally vague (*Simons v. State*, 803 N.W.2d 587). A lower-level appellate court in Virginia did declare a portion of that state's child endangerment law unconstitutional vague in 1995 (*Commonwealth v. Carter*, 462 S.E.2d 582). In 1977 the Florida Supreme Court held part of that state's criminal child neglect statute to be unconstitutionally vague and overbroad (*State v. Winters*, 346 So. 2d 991), and it struck down the statute as unconstitutionally vague (*State v. Mincey*, 672 So.2d). What should be pointed out, however, is that these were criminal statutes. Most child abuse/neglect investigations by

Regarding neglect, consider the Ohio statute (it is typical of state statutes on this subject): a "neglected child" is defined, *inter alia*, as one "who lacks proper care because of the faults or habits of his parents, guardian, or custodian," or "whose parents [et al.] neglect or refuse to provide him with proper or necessary subsistence, education, medical or surgical care, or other care necessary for the child's health, morals or well-being," or "whose parents [et al.] neglect or refuse to provide the special care made necessary by the child's mental condition."[35] There are two other sections of the Ohio child abuse/neglect statute that deal with a "dependent child" and a "child without proper parental care" (these are additional dimensions of the matter of neglect). A dependent child is defined, *inter alia*, as one who is "homeless or destitute," or one "who lacks adequate parental care by reason of the mental or physical condition of the child's parents [et al.]," or one "whose condition or environment is such as to warrant the state, in the interests of the child, in assuming the child's guardianship."[36] A "child without proper parental care" is defined as one "whose home is filthy and unsanitary; whose parents, stepparents, guardian, or custodian permit him to become dependent, neglected, abused, or delinquent; whose parents [et al.], when able, refuse or neglect to provide him with necessary care, support, medical attention, and educational facilities; or ... fail to subject such child to necessary discipline."[37]

These provisions present many questions. What is "proper" parental care? What is meant by "faults or habits" of the parents et al.? Could these include behavior that while traditionally thought virtuous might now in the minds of some be viewed as unacceptable? Are parents' faults or habits enough to deprive them of their offspring? What is "proper or necessary subsistence"? Too much sugar in the child's diet? Too little? Would designer jeans have to be bought for the child? "Appropriate medical care" often becomes one physician's opinion, or viewpoint, about what may be harmful to a child. Often this in-

---

CPAs do not involve criminal matters. As is pointed out in this article, they involve a certain area of civil law.

35. Ohio Rev. Code Annotated, Sec. 2151.03.
36. Ohio Rev. Code Annotated, Sec. 2151.04.
37. Ohio Rev. Code Annotated, Sec. 2151.05.

volves mere speculative harm, or else may be a point that physicians or other medical authorities disagree about.[38] Recently, we have seen some hospitals employ what they call child abuse pediatricians—a new subspecialty—and seems to have resulted in finding even more questionable cases of child abuse.[39] What is "proper or necessary education"? Does it exclude homeschooling, since this is outside the academic norm and disliked by educational professionals, even while homeschooled pupils are on average excelling academically and even outstripping many pupils in institutionalized schools?[40] What is considered neglect regarding required special care for certain mental conditions? One problem is that there is much, much disagreement about what constitutes a "mental condition" that requires special attention. For example, the eagerness to push children into some kind of medical or psychological treatment for hyperactivity, attention deficit disorder, and the like is controversial. Are parents who balk at these diagnoses and recommended treatments neglectful? Would taking a "special needs" child out of a public school to teach him at home because he didn't make progress and the school failed to protect him from bullies—as happened in a case in Virginia—constitute neglect under the Ohio statute, as Virginia authorities intimated it was in that state?[41]

If the statutes are vague as to what child abuse and neglect are, the agencies charged with enforcing them are no better. As Besharov states, "Existing standards set no limits on intervention and provide no guidelines for decision-making."[42] It is up to CPS social workers to decide what is meant by "abuse" and "neglect."

38. See Stephen M. Krason, "Parental Rights and Minor Children's Health Care Decisions," *Ethics and Medics* 19, no. 7 (July 1994): 3–4.

39. See, e.g., Mike Hixenbaugh, "An ER Doctor Was Charged with Abusing His Baby, but 15 Medical Experts Say There Is No Proof," NBC News, January 27, 2020, https://www.nbcnews.com/news/us-news/er-doctor-was-charged-abusing-his-baby-15-medical-experts-n1123756.

40. On the academic excellence of homeschooled pupils, see the reports about standardized test results in the following issues of the *Home School Court Report*: 8, no. 6 (November–December 1992): 19, 26; 10, no. 4 (July–August 1994): 11–12; 10, no. 5 (September–October 1994): 17; 10, no. 6 (Winter 1994–1995). Volume 10, no. 5 (18) also reports on a study of learning-disabled pupils that showed that those who were being homeschooled were progressing better than those in public schools.

41. Joseph Sobran, "Reminding Parents Who's in Charge," *Washington Times*, February 4, 1995, A13.

42. Besharov, "'Doing Something,'" 570.

In her book *Out of Control: Who's Watching Our Child Protection Agencies?*, Brenda Scott relates what the National Committee for the Prevention of Child Abuse, a leading advocacy organization, regards as signs of possible abuse: the child has a chronically unkempt appearance; the child is overly neat or a girl is dressed in an overly feminine way; the child is too loud or too talkative; the child exhibits shyness; low self-esteem is apparent from the child's actions or words; the child uses aggressive or passive behavior; the child is reluctant to participate in sports; there are noticeable signs of fractures, burns, bruises, cuts, welts, or bite marks; the child has sexual knowledge inappropriate for his/her age or acts out above maturity level; the child complains of pain or itching, or unusual bleeding or bruises are noticed in or around the genital area; the child seems constantly hungry or fatigued; there is a noticeable lack of supervision; there is delayed physical, emotional, or intellectual behavior; the parent is chronically late for meetings, picking up the child, and the like; the child exhibits chronic health problems; the parent fails to promptly repair a child's broken eyeglasses; there is a noticeable need for dental work; the loss of a parent due to death or illness (the remaining parent may become physically or sexually abusive as a result of the stress); the presence in the home of a stepfather; the child lives in an untidy home; the child is pulled out of school to be taught at home; the parent appears to suffer depression, apathy, or hopelessness; and there are reports from the child about occasionally sleeping in a parent's bed.[43] The committee even says that how parents talk to their children can be a form of abuse.[44]

While certain of these could be indications of abuse, most of course would have nothing to do with it. In fact, Besharov and Mary Pride—who wrote one of the earliest critical books of CPS, titled *The Child Abuse Industry*—both cite studies that show that social workers and others employed in child protective agencies (CPAs) do not even agree among themselves about what is or is not child abuse or neglect.[45]

---

43. Scott, *Out of Control*, 52–53.

44. See "Words Hurt," YouTube video, January 4, 2018, https://www.youtube.com/watch?v = 4YO3duf7omw.

45. Mary Pride, *The Child Abuse Industry* (Westchester, IL: Crossway Books, 1986), 230; Besharov, "'Doing Something,'" 569–70.

Despite the uncertainty among CPA personnel about what is abuse and neglect, many examples could be cited to show that the agencies interpret these vague and unclear laws decisively against parents, that parents are often not given the least benefit of the doubt. The very fact of the existence of such vague and unclear laws (which have been so substantially shaped by childrearing "experts" and those working in the child protection field) and the application of these laws in such an anti-parent fashion in so many cases—in fact, routinely—betrays a CPS attitude of hostility to the family—or at least one showing a complete lack of awareness of what it really means to be a parent or what family life really involves. Pride speaks about how so many social workers are either older, Caucasian females who have had a poor personal home life (divorced, etc.) and carry with them all the related emotional "baggage," or are young, Caucasian, middle- or upper-middle-class females, never married, and fresh out of college, with no experience or significant training in dealing with children.[46] Scott concurs with these findings and indicates that one additional group, which has not been known for its affection for the family, is now increasingly represented among agency social workers: homosexuals.[47] She wrote about this fact in the mid-1990s, and it is likely that this is even more the case today.

Apart from the question of hostility to the family, just how ignorant the shapers of child abuse/neglect policy and the operatives in CPS often are to the complexities and dynamics of family life and the nature of children—indeed, the naiveté with which they often approach these matters—is seen in the very generalizations they are so well known for making. To be sure, this was observed above in the whole, unrealistic range of supposed conditions and "symptoms" that they believe indicate maltreatment—which are more typically seen in perfectly normal situations. It also is seen in their use of such "tools of the trade" as risk assessment forms, in which caseworkers give numerical rankings to how well parents measure up in various categories on the forms and then add up the total to supposedly determine how

46. Pride, *Child Abuse Industry*, 241.
47. Scott, *Out of Control*, 58.

great a risk a child faces in his home.[48] Besides being completely subjective (Scott relates that while some agencies have guidelines of what
conditions render a child "at risk," the assessments basically are left to
the discretion of the individual caseworker[49]), it should not have to
be pointed out that family life, with its uncertainties, difficulties, and
burdens, is not something that can be easily and instantaneously reduced to a number on a sheet. Such an attempt to quantify a difficult
problem that is not so intrinsically subject to quantification is a typical bureaucratic approach. It is probably supposed to act as a kind of
check on agency discretion or a means of helping to ensure competent
judgment and accountability by the bureaucracy. In reality, it creates
surrealism about the entire subject of abuse/neglect and easily leads to
false and unjust conclusions.

Pride speaks about CPS adhering to what she calls "the doctrine
of total depravity," which holds that all parents are actual or potential
abusers, and that all home environments are abusive. Thus all state
interventions are justifiable. In actuality, it is not *all* parents who are
the likely abusers. Abuse—*genuine* abuse—is uncommon in intact
families, especially in the absence of such factors as alcohol or drug
abuse. Abuse disproportionately occurs in cases of single parentage,
foster parentage, "live-in" boyfriends, and the like.[50] It is also much
more likely to occur in poor families than those that are better off
economically.[51]

The same confusion about what abuse and neglect are, which char-
acterizes CPS social workers, is shared by physicians and judges. The

48. Armbrister, "When Parents Become Victims," 105.

49. Scott, *Out of Control*, 55. She writes that on one of the standard risk assessment forms
used by many agencies, produced by Norman Polansky and associates, the items range from
the trivial (e.g., whether meals have courses that "go together") to those embodying ideological
preferences (e.g., whether the toys in the home have a traditional gender orientation—dolls for
girls, trucks for boys). Apparently, on the latter, if the parents have not had their consciousness
sufficiently raised by feminism to break away from such traditional practices, their children
will be concluded to be "at risk."

50. Pride, *Child Abuse Industry*, 11, 33, 236. One of her sources is a study reported in the
St. Louis Post-Dispatch, October 30, 1985; another is Pamela D. Mayhall and Katherine East-
lack Norgard, *Child Abuse and Neglect: Sharing Responsibility* (New York: John Wiley & Sons,
1983), 11.

51. Richard Wexler, "Invasion of the Child Savers," *The Progressive* 49, no. 3 (September
1985): 22.

same study involving social workers cited by Besharov above showed that an even higher percentage of physicians than the former were unclear about what constituted "child maltreatment."[52] Besharov also notes that the same survey, as well as a review of various court opinions, leads to the same conclusion about judges. They seem to decide cases of abuse and neglect that come before them on the basis of the context of the circumstances. Besharov says that they "are saying that, although they cannot define child maltreatment, they know it when they see it."[53] (He wrote this even before the onslaught of child abuse pediatricians.)

Three other factors that contribute substantially to the great number of false abuse/neglect allegations and the ensuing CPS intrusion into families are the ease of making reports to agencies, the legal pressures placed on various professionals and other occupational groups that encourage them to report in doubtful cases to protect themselves, and the blanket legal immunity given to the CPAs and their personnel.

Regarding the ease of making reports, it was noted that hotlines have been set up in many communities to take reports. These are publicized in the local media and elsewhere, with the phone numbers frequently given. People are encouraged to report any suspected cases of abuse (without, of course, being provided a definition of what it is). If there is no hotline in a particular area, the local CPA's number is readily available, and reports are encouraged. Reports can be made anonymously, and on hotlines they generally are.[54] All that is usually need-

52. Besharov, "'Doing Something,'" 570, citing R. Nagi, "Child Abuse and Neglect Programs: A National Overview," *Children Today* 13, no. 17 (1975). A study reported by United Press International in January 1994, which had been conducted by Ohio State University at Children's Hospital in Columbus, Ohio, and published in the *Journal of Child Abuse and Neglect*, likewise discovered a great deal of disagreement among physicians about what medical neglect is and when it should be reported to authorities. The study also reported that there were no guidelines for physicians to follow in determining what is neglect. *Home School Court Report* 10, no. 1 (January–February 1994): 21, 23.

53. Besharov, "'Doing Something,'" 568–69. The court cases that he cites as examples of this view being expressed are *In re Stilley*, 363 N.E.2d 873 (Ill., 1977) and *In Interest of Nitz*, 368 N.E.2d 1111 (Ill., 1977).

54. Organizations like Parentalrights.org have been trying to get CAPTA changed to require that people making reports to CPAs via hotlines or otherwise give their names, even though their names would not be disclosed. So far, such a reform of CAPTA has not been made.

ed to trigger an agency investigation is an anonymous report. Hotline calls may or may not be screened, and no attempt necessarily needs to be made to determine whether there is any validity to a report, nor is any threshold of probable cause generally required by law before an investigation is undertaken or even (generally) additional action taken, including removal of children.[55] In 2004 the Home School Legal Defense Association stated that only sixteen states specified any standard in their child welfare laws that "comes even close to the constitutional requirement for 'probable cause.'"[56] The result is that, in effect, anonymous reporters—not even the CPAs themselves—are often deciding what the vague laws on child abuse/neglect actually mean. If their reports automatically give rise to investigations and CPS interventions into families, they essentially become the arbiters of child protection policy.[57] Most state statutes or the regulations issued pursuant to

55. As defined by Gifis, "probable cause" is "a requisite element of a valid search and seizure or arrest, which consists of the existence of facts and circumstances within one's knowledge and of which one has reasonably trustworthy information, which are sufficient in themselves to warrant a man of reasonable caution in the belief that a crime has been committed" (Gifis, *Law Dictionary*, 162). Applied to noncriminal allegations of child abuse/neglect, what it essentially would mean is that there must be a reasonable belief that a deliberate action or omission by a parent had occurred that would warrant a CPS investigation.

56. *Home School Court Report* 20, no. 4 (July–August 2004): 10.

57. There is some dispute about the actual percentage of reports that are anonymous. The Home School Legal Defense Association (HSLDA), which does much litigating on false abuse/neglect reports, told this writer that they believe that 60–70 percent of reports are from anonymous sources, though they acknowledge that this figure is not based on a systematic study but from anecdotal information such as the experiences of their members and others who they have defended and discussions with social workers (pers. comm., July 30, 2004). The Children's Bureau of HHS claims that about 10 percent are anonymous. See Children's Bureau, US Department of Health and Human Services, *Child Maltreatment 2002* (Washington, DC: US Government Printing Office, 2004), 6. One of my former university colleagues who worked in a CPA in Ohio for a time found that perhaps 50 percent of the reports to his county agency were anonymous, although one cannot know if this is typical. My own years of research and gathering of anecdotal information indicate to me that the HHS figure is definitely much too low. There is some problem with duplicate reporting, and it is also likely that the organization of their data puts what are essentially anonymous reports into other categories of sources of reports that are perhaps based only on the reporter's stating some relationship to or association with the person he is accusing without actually identifying himself (which is typically done when reporters contact CPAs). Thus in its 2002 report, HHS says 8 percent of reports are from another relative other than a parent (the latter would probably mostly be noncustodial parents during custody disputes), and about 6 percent are from friends or neighbors. Among "nonprofessional sources" of reports, HHS lists almost another 18 percent in the category of "other" or "unknown or missing." Thus if we assumed that virtually all of the reports

them mandate the investigation of all reports of even *suspected* abuse or neglect (though there may be some screening). Since the passage of CAPTA, there have been large-scale media and outreach campaigns, carried on by CPS, law enforcement agencies, and different organizations, to "educate" the public about child abuse. These campaigns have sought to convince people of the "epidemic" of abuse and about the need to look out for and report it, but little has been done to *truly* educate the public about what abuse is (which, as we have said, CPS, judges, professionals, and lawmakers are not sure of themselves). The laws respecting mandated reporters also encourage false allegations because they typically state that if such reporters fail to report even suspected abuse/neglect, they can be criminally prosecuted.

If the secrecy of the child protective system has helped prompt its abusive practices, the immunity its institutions and agents possess from either criminal prosecution or civil liability has made it ever more likely (this is in addition to the immunity which mandated reporters possess). This is typically a blanket statutory immunity, even when the agents have acted in bad faith or maliciously.[58]

So, there is what Mary Pride calls the "one-sided liability." Social workers and/or state agencies can be sued or even criminally prosecuted for *not* removing a child from his home who afterwards is harmed or killed, but they are generally immune from suit when they wrongly remove a child, even without grounds and regardless of how much

in these additional categories came from people who did not specifically identify themselves (my knowledge of the issue suggests to me that this is a reasonable assumption), this would be 42 percent. It is also fair to assume that there are a not insignificant number of reports made from two of the categories of "professional sources" listed—educational personnel and medical personnel (which together make up 32 percent of the overall number of reports)—without the person specifically identifying himself (e.g., a nurse simply calls a local CPA saying she is a staff member at the emergency room of a local hospital). Let's assume it is 5 percent, which is probably low. This would bring the overall total of what are in effect anonymous reports to 47 percent, which is close to the percentage mentioned by my former colleague. It is at least reasonable to conclude that a sizable minority of reports are anonymous. Actually, the percentage of anonymous reports is almost certainly higher than even 50 percent. The HHS data indicate that the categorization of referrals is compiled only from referrals that have not been "screened out." HHS's numbers show that fully 32 percent were screened out. It is likely that the screened-out reports were overwhelmingly from nonprofessional sources and also likely that most of these were anonymous (which according to any rational screening procedure would make reports less reliable).

58. Children's Bureau, *Child Maltreatment 2002*.

damage is done to the child or the parent-child relationship. So, they err on the side of excessive caution to protect themselves.

The juvenile courts are not a significant check upon CPS. First, most CPS contacts with a family do not end up in juvenile court.[59] Second, as Professor Paul Chill of the University of Connecticut Law School has written, there are substantial obstacles faced by parents when confronting CPS in juvenile court. He writes that in legal proceedings after a removal (generally in juvenile court), CPS has tilted the legal "playing field" decisively against the parents, as the burden is shifted entirely to them to show that they are fit instead of on the CPS to justify its continued control of the child.[60] Like the CPS operatives covering themselves, juvenile court judges often engage in a kind of "defensive judging." For example, they will issue an order to permit a child to be removed from a home or will uphold an "emergency" removal on the basis of weak evidence with the thought that it is better to err in the direction of excessive intervention, because to do otherwise is more likely "to come back to haunt them."[61]

Chill tells us that the passage of the federal Adoption and Safe Families Act of 1997, while supposedly aimed at the good purpose of giving children who have been in the unstable and even dangerous (see below) foster care system for extended periods the chance for the permanency of adoption, has in practice made it easier for CPS and juvenile courts to terminate the rights of the natural parents, even if unjustifiable. The act created an incentive to do that because to qualify for federal funds, the states are generally required to seek a termination of parental rights for any child who remains in foster care for fifteen out of twenty-two consecutive months.[62] Thus there is now a financial incentive for the child welfare system to secure adoptions for children in foster care—even if they were wrongfully put there—just as there has been a financial incentive to put them in foster care in

---

59. Even fewer involve criminal charges, where parents allegedly run afoul of criminal child maltreatment laws.

60. See Paul Chill, "Burden of Proof Begone: The Pernicious Effect of Emergency Removal in Child Protective Proceedings," *Family Court Review* 41 (October 2003): 459, http://web.lexis-nexis.com/universe/document?.

61. Chill, "Burden of Proof Begone," 461.

62. Chill, "Burden of Proof Begone," 463.

the first place, since programs to keep families intact generally cannot qualify for the same amount of federal funding as foster care programs do.[63]

Pride compiled data about the civil rights of those accused of child abuse in each of the fifty states. She considered which states guarantee five basic due process rights generally given in criminal cases: the right to be informed of the charge while under investigation, the right to trial by jury, the right to access to records being kept about a person, the right to have an unsubstantiated record removed or not to have a record kept on file until after a hearing, and the right to challenge information kept on file about a person. Persons accused of noncriminal child abuse or neglect—most of whom are parents—had none of these rights in thirty-one states. Some states guaranteed one or more of these rights; none protected all of them. When she wrote in the mid-1980s, none of the fifty states required that the accused be told of the charges. Court decisions were handed down later that required CPS operatives to tell parents about the reason they are being investigated when they show up at their door. As is mentioned below, later changes to CAPTA also required CPAs to inform people why they are being investigated. Pride pointed out that only one state permitted a person to request a jury trial, although in noncriminal matters, that would not be irregular. Sixteen states permitted access to records under at least some conditions, while only fourteen protected against unsubstantiated records being kept in the file at least as a general rule, and only fourteen permitted challenges to the record.[64] Another aspect of due process that also is not found in child abuse proceedings is the right to appeal, provided in state statues for both criminal and civil matters.[65] As Pride writes, even if on paper one has a right to appeal civil matters such as decisions in child abuse proceedings, he may not be able to effectively pursue that appeal. Appellate courts seldom make their

63. Armbrister, "When Parents Become Victims," 106.

64. Pride, *Child Abuse Industry*, 169.

65. We are aware that state statutes do not necessarily guarantee the right to appeal—or at least not the right to have an appeal taken up—but they establish the procedures and mechanics for it. In criminal matters, at least, there is a liberal view about allowing appeals to be filed and even heard.

own findings of fact; normally, they accept the facts as determined at a trial court or hearing (in child abuse or neglect matters, it is usually a civil hearing) and will just consider questions of law. The rub here is that in child abuse/neglect proceedings, one has no right to review the record in most states, as has been noted, and in fact, no evidence upon which to base an appeal may even have been presented at the hearing. Recall that state agencies really do not need evidence to conclude that abuse or neglect has occurred or to take away children or impose other sanctions, and hearing judges are generally not required to solicit it.[66]

A further fact about the constitutional rights of those accused of noncriminal child abuse or neglect was the view of CPS and even law enforcement officials that the guarantee of the Fourth Amendment against unreasonable searches and seizures did not necessarily apply. CPS operatives have generally had wide latitude in removing children from their homes even without evidence of abuse or neglect; this in itself is a "search and seizure." In some states, when accompanied by a police officer, social workers have been able to force entry into a private dwelling. Often, however, social workers secure entry even when not entitled to by threats or deception (i.e., saying they have a right to enter without a warrant when they do not) or simply because parents do not know that they have a right to refuse. Also, once let into a home, a social worker has virtually carte blanche to look around for anything upon which to build a case against parents. They can even do a strip search of a child to find evidence of sexual abuse.[67] The statutes do not require a warrant for any of this. They also usually permit authorities to circumvent judicial approval for their actions or for taking custody of a child if they believe the child to be imminently in danger (generally, without defining what this means).[68] After initially not being willing, courts have begun to respond positively to Fourth Amendment challenges to warrantless CPS entries into the homes of families.[69] A seminal case was *Calabretta v. Floyd* in the Ninth US

66. Pride, *Child Abuse Industry*, 229.
67. Pride, *Child Abuse Industry*, 160–61, 228–29.
68. Chill, "Burden of Proof Begone," 458.
69. For example, in 1985, a US district court decision in Illinois held that searches of a family's home without a warrant by that state's Department of Children and Family Services

Circuit Court of Appeals in 1999, which was brought by Home School Legal Defense Association. In this case, the court ruled that CPS social workers—who in this case, accompanied by police, conducted a warrantless search of a home, including strip-searching the children—are bound by the Fourth Amendment and can be sued for federal civil rights violations if they do not uphold it.[70]

Another constitutional right that is basically denied is the right to confront one's accuser. The right to confront is denied to parents, first of all, by the fact that so many complaints are made anonymously, so the identity of the complainants is not even known. If the complainant is, say, a child's physician and the parents thus know his identity, they are still not generally afforded the right to confront him in a legal proceeding. Indeed, even in criminal child abuse cases, the law has been changed in some states to remove the right of the accused to confront a child witness in court for fear of the child being traumatized. The US Supreme Court, after some initial hesitancy, held that this is not a violation of the Sixth Amendment. Other legal innovations, which have changed traditional criminal law practices, have involved the abolition of both minimum age provisions in the law, below which children are presumed incompetent to testify, and the need for corroboration for a child's testimony to stand, as well as a greater willingness to allow hearsay testimony to be introduced in court. The latter includes not just out-of-courtroom testimony (i.e., videotaped testimony by child victims), but also statements by third parties to whom children supposedly confided tales of their abuse.[71]

---

did not violate the Fourth Amendment (Pride, *Child Abuse Industry*, 228, citing Stephen Chapman's op-ed column in the *St. Louis Post-Dispatch*, March 28, 1985, and the *Jefferson City [Mo.] Post-Tribune*, April 5, 1985). We see contrary later rulings following in the text.

70. See *Calabretta v. Floyd*, 199 F3d 808.

71. In *White v. Illinois*, 502 U.S. 346 (1992) the Supreme Court upheld the admission of hearsay testimony from third parties in child abuse trials. On the subject of admitting hearsay evidence, Armbrister discusses one Washington State case in which a Christian husband and wife were convicted of sexually abusing their 3-year-old daughter. The child and her friend supposedly confided the story of her abuse to a day care worker. The day care worker and her supervisor became the chief witnesses against the parents. There was no corroboration of any kind of the two day care center employees' testimony, nor was any physical evidence entered into the record that showed that any sexual molestation had occurred. A physical examination after the trial showed that the child almost certainly could not have been raped (this is what the parents were alleged to have done; they were convicted of statutory rape). The CPA

Scott speaks about parents being subjected to something like double jeopardy because even if parents are exonerated by a criminal court (if a case goes there), agency actions and proceedings against them in juvenile and civil courts may often still go ahead. American law has traditionally permitted such situations and not considered them double jeopardy per se. Still, it gives one pause to wonder whether this legal interpretation does not promote injustice, and so such a traditional approach to double jeopardy should perhaps be reevaluated. Parenthetically, criminal exoneration is no guarantee they will get their children back if they have been taken away from them.

On the question of being innocent until proven guilty, the attitude that views parents as guilty as soon as an accusation is made, even without any evidence, and then expecting them to bear the (sometimes overwhelming) burden of proving themselves innocent, is one of the major injustices of CPS.[72] American law has provided the means for this to occur because it does not seek to apply the standards of criminal courts to juvenile law matters. Nevertheless, the injustice of this is evident from the mountain of cases of false accusation (I related some especially egregious ones in previous articles on this topic, as have other authors).

There is also the problem of eliminating statute of limitations protection in this area. Normally, if one is to be criminally charged or if someone is to be subject to being sued civilly, it must be done within a stated period, usually a few years, after the alleged action occurred.

---

suppressed the examination. The day care worker who first came forth with the allegations claimed in a posttrial interview that she had been herself abused for more than twenty years, saying that almost anyone who came near her abused her. She also said that most people were "sex perverts" and that every other house in her neighborhood had abuse going on inside it. She said she had on numerous other occasions tried to turn in supposed sex offenders and hated men. Besides such seeming paranoia, she admitted that she was a daily drug user. The trial judge refused to permit any effort to impeach this witness's character. A Harvard Law School evidence professor, Charles Nesson, examined the case and later filed an *amicus curiae* brief in the appeal to the Ninth US Circuit Court of Appeals in support of the parents in which he wrote that the case was "the most extreme example of erosion of the confrontation clause of which I am aware" (Armbrister, "When Parents Become Victims," 101–3). Nevertheless, the Ninth Circuit sustained the convictions (*Swan v. Peterson*, 6 F.3d 1373 [1993]).

72. A grand jury in San Diego County, California, specifically charged that its CPS had shifted the burden of proof in sexual abuse cases from the state to the alleged perpetrator (Scott, *Out of Control*, 84).

Eliminating the statute of limitations has resulted in parents and others being threatened with both criminal and noncriminal allegations indefinitely. A CPA, for example, can commence an investigation and take action against parents, in many cases, for alleged acts happening years earlier. Civil suits and criminal charges can be filed against parents or others for alleged abuse occurring decades before. The latter became an issue especially as a result of "repressed memory syndrome," in which putative acts of abuse committed years earlier and allegedly repressed by the person because of their dreadful nature are supposedly brought back into a person's consciousness with the help of therapy, hypnosis, and the like. The validity of the entire matter of repressed memory syndrome has come under considerable criticism from within the discipline of psychology itself.[73] Certain federal appeals courts have overturned criminal convictions that were based on repressed memory.[74]

There have been legal developments regarding parents' right to be told up front the nature of the allegations against them. The CAPTA amendments of 2003 require social workers to tell parents of the nature of the accusations against them on first contact.[75] These amendments also require that CPS operatives be trained about the constitutional and other legal rights of families.[76] States, however, have not had a history of acting quickly to implement such changes in CAPTA, and the federal government has not sufficiently leaned on them to do so.

The question is, Why have we had this denial of basic constitutional guarantees? The answer is substantially found in the fact that child abuse/neglect matters usually do not find their way into the criminal

73. See, e.g., Elizabeth Loftus and Katherine Ketcham, *The Myth of Repressed Memory: False Memories and Allegations of Sexual Abuse* (New York: St. Martin's Press, 1994). More recently, the tide seems to have turned in the courts, with people who have borne the brunt of allegations of abuse, supposedly turned up in repressed memory therapy, winning damage judgments after convincing juries that the therapists actually manufactured the "memories" by the suggestive character of their therapy. See *Washington Times*, December 17, 1994, A1, A14.

74. See *Franklin v. Duncan* and *Franklin v. Fox, Murray et al.*, 312 F.3d 423 (1995) and *Friedman v. Rehal*, 618 F.3d 142 (2nd Circuit) (2010).

75. "President Bush Signs Keeping Children and Families Safe Act of 2003," *Home School Court Report* 29, no. 4 (July–August 2003): 38.

76. "Congressional Breakthroughs in CAPTA Reform," *Home School Court Report* 18, no. 5 (September–October 2002): 24.

justice system. They are treated under a state's juvenile law, or in a manner closely connected with it. In other words, they are civil matters but civil matters of a special type. Juvenile court procedures have been set up to be less formal than normal court proceedings, and the usual legal rules and guarantees do not always apply.[77]

American law has adopted what criminal justice professor Philip Jenkins of Baylor University calls "therapeutic values."[78] Such values have their roots in the thinking of the social work, counseling, and other "helping" professions, and of sociologists, psychologists, and other social scientists (social scientists have been increasingly influential in shaping public policy); their assumptions and understanding about human nature and society, however, are problematic.[79] Jenkins says that therapeutic values, as respects the law, hold "that courts are in the business of enforcing social hygiene rather than imposing punishment." The current laws about child abuse and neglect were substantially shaped by categories of people who abide by such therapeutic values: "academics [in the fields mentioned], feminist theorists, therapists, pediatricians, children's rights advocates, and lawyers [who are working especially in this area]." He explains how those holding therapeutic values approach the role of law. Their views are contrary to the assumptions of the adversarial system of justice, which permit the accused to probe and try to disprove the testimony of an accuser in a public setting and hold that witnesses are to be believed about specifics only if they impress a judge and a jury with their credibility. These upholders of therapeutic values believe that the courts really "have no business regulating the actions of objective professionals such as social workers or medical authorities seeking to protect children." They think that *they* can correctly judge, from their professional understanding of the subject, that when a child or someone else has alleged that abuse occurred that it in fact did. To put obstacles—such as legal restraints—

77. Pride, *Child Abuse Industry*, 229.

78. Philip Jenkins, "Believe the Children? Child Abuse and the American Legal System," *Chronicles* (January 1993): 22.

79. On the point about the assumptions and outlook of contemporary social scientists, see Stephen M. Krason, "What the Catholic Finds Wrong about Secular Social Science," *Social Justice Review* 84, no. 1 (January–February 1993): 5–11.

in the path of acting quickly to protect the child is to fail in their task to help him, to alleviate his suffering. One would not demand constitutional rights when visiting his physician, who can only have his interests at heart. How, then, should rights matter in something like child abuse, where the only concern must be therapeutic—to heal the situation, treat the victim, and separate him from the perpetrator until therapy can correct the problems of each?[80]

When we realize the nature of therapeutic values, we can understand why proposals have been made for such things as licensing parents, coercive "child abuse prevention" programs from the time of a child's birth (in which "potentially abusive parents" are identified at that point and placed in "parenting programs"), and the creation of a national corps of "health visitors" to regularly go to each child's home until he starts school to check up on his parents.[81] A scheme like this, extending all the way through childhood and adolescence until age 18, was set to be put in place in Scotland until it was successfully challenged in court as against the European Convention on Human Rights and ultimately scrapped by the Scottish government.[82] It goes without saying that the devoted advocate of therapeutic values has little or no sense of the natural rights of parents.

Does the current system succeed in protecting children? It is worth considering Besharov's comment, that the "high level of state intervention might be acceptable if it were necessary to enable child protective agencies to fulfill their basic mission of protecting endangered children. Unfortunately, it does just the opposite; children in real danger of serious maltreatment get lost in the press of the minor cases flooding the system."[83]

In other words, as Pride puts it, "If *all* parents are guilty, or could be guilty" (which, as we have said, seems to be the upshot of the cur-

80. Jenkins, "Believe the Children?," 22.

81. Pride, *Child Abuse Industry*, 252–53. Programs seeking to identify "potentially abusive parents" when they have babies and force them to undergo parenting training have already been put into effect in different parts of the country (Pride, *Child Abuse Industry*, 253; Scott, *Out of Control*, 175).

82. "Named Person Scheme Scrapped by Scottish Government," BBC News, September 19, 2019, https://www.bbc.com/news/uk-scotland-scotland-politics-49753980.

83. Besharov, "'Doing Something,'" 562.

rent child abuse laws and agency attitudes), "then resources end up spread thinly. There is no way to separate the criminals from the average Joes.... A system that fails to distinguish crimes from unfashionable child-rearing practices cannot protect children."[84] After all, CPAs have only so many personnel—they frequently complain that they are understaffed and overworked, even while justifying more and more intervention into families—and funds do not flow so freely, especially in periods of governmental belt-tightening. The unprecedented high level of intervention into families has not produced particularly impressive results in protecting children. In 2000, Besharov cited studies revealing that in the then roughly twenty-five years since the enactment of CAPTA, 30 to 55 percent of deaths due to abuse or neglect involved children known about by a child protective agency.[85] This seems to be an ongoing reality. In 2012 the annual report on child maltreatment by the Department of Health and Human Services stated that "Some children who died from abuse and neglect were already known to CPS agencies" and that in thirty states, 8.5 percent of such children had received what it called "family preservation services" from state agencies within the past five years.[86]

When children are removed from their families—justifiably or not—they are typically put into foster care (although, in some states, CPAs are supposed to place them with relatives if possible). Surveys conducted in 1986 and 1990 by the National Foster Care Education Project found that foster children were ten times more likely to be abused than children in the general public[87] (the high incidence of

84. Pride, *Child Abuse Industry*, 55. It has *not* been accidental that the child protective system investigates parents for all sorts of actions, so many of which are completely innocuous. Besharov tells us that the experts who pushed for CAPTA and its state legislative progeny wanted "unrestrictive preventive jurisdiction," which would supposedly enable them to identify even *potentially* abusive parents to predict whether parents would become abusive toward their children. They wanted to stop any *possible* abuse. This even though, as Besharov makes clear, no clinician, psychologist, or other expert can predict with certainty that someone will become a child abuser. Besharov, "'Doing Something,'" 574–75.

85. Besharov, "Child Abuse Realities," 192. See the article for his citations.

86. Report cited in Conor Friedersdorf, "In a Year, Child-Protective Services Checked Up on 3.2 Million Children," *The Atlantic*, July 22, 2014, https://www.theatlantic.com/national/archive/2014/07/in-a-year-child-protective-services-conducted-32-million-investigations/374809/.

87. Timothy W. Maier, "Suffer the Children," *Insight on the News*, November 24, 1997, 11,

abuse in foster care was suggested above). Studies cited by the National Coalition for Child Protection Reform, which is headed by Richard Wexler (a former journalist and longtime critic of CPS), give a further disturbing picture about the treatment of children in foster care and institutional care. One in Baltimore showed that the number of "substantiated" cases of sexual abuse of children in foster care was four times higher than in the general population. An Indiana study revealed that there was more than ten times the rate of physical abuse and more than twenty-eight times the rate of sexual abuse of children in group homes than in the general population. A Georgia study found that 34 percent of children in foster care had experienced abuse, neglect, or other harmful conditions.[88] A study in New York State found that 28 percent of children had been abused while in foster care there.[89] There are ongoing accounts of abuse in both the foster care and state group home situations.[90]

Another way that children are harmed by unmerited intervention in their families by the CPS, even if they are not taken away from their parents or are taken away only for a short period of time, is by the psychological and physical effects of the experience and the damage done to their relationship with their parents. This is intensified in the face of their sometimes undergoing long, repeated interrogations by social workers—and the outright intimidation that sometimes accompanies them—forced physical and sexual examinations in some cases to de-

cited in "A Critical Look at the Foster Care System: How Widespread a Problem?," http://www .liftingtheveil.ord/foster04.htm; Internet (accessed 17 March, 2012).

88. See National Coalition for Child Protection Reform, *Foster Care vs. Family Preservation: The Track Record on Safety and Well-Being*, Issue Paper 1 (Alexandria, VA: National Coalition for Child Protection Reform, January 3, 2011). The studies are cited in the paper and are apparently from the 1980s and early 1990s. Chill contends that the number of "emergency removals" of children from families in the United States—i.e., they are removed supposedly because they are threatened with harm from their parents—doubled to 555,000 over the twenty years just prior to when he was writing in 2003. He says that the number of erroneous removals "is alarmingly large"; e.g., in 2001, 100,000 children removed, and more than a third were later determined not to have been maltreated ("Burden of Proof Begone," 458).

89. Susanne Babbel, "The Foster Care System and Its Victims," *Psychology Today*, January 3, 2012, https://www.psychologytoday.com/us/blog/somatic-psychology/201201/the-foster -care-system-and-its-vic- tims-part-2.

90. Even with a staff that is supposedly trained to help children, Babbel tells us that "the occurrence of child abuse in group homes is not uncommon" ("Foster Care System and Its Victims").

termine if they have been sexually abused, and (essentially) forced therapy by psychologists, counselors, and the like.

A CPS investigation of an innocent family—perhaps triggered by an anonymous report—can lead to emotional strain, anxiety, fear, insecurity in children and their parents, and an increasing tendency of children to be out of control. The children can become distrustful of outsiders, neighbors, and those in authority. They can have their ability to form attachments compromised and suffer psychological consequences. Strains can also develop between the parents. Parental anger toward their children can result (the very kind of thing CPS claims it wants to stop). The orderly flow of a family's life can be disrupted, and this is often not easily overcome (especially if it is facing ongoing CPS monitoring). Children are also obviously hurt by the financial harm that can occur to their families from extended legal battles with agencies. Sometimes, the strains on parents by unwarranted, ongoing CPS intrusion into the family lead to marital breakups with the obvious harm that causes to children.[91]

In my first major article about CPS (in 1988), I called for the enactment of several legal reforms that would protect innocent parents from the abuses of CPS. They were as follows. First, the anonymous hotlines, which have been an open door to false reporting, should be eliminated. Second, I said that the laws should be altered so they spell out more specifically what "child abuse" and "child neglect" are. I called for the elimination of legal provisions that infringe or could be interpreted to infringe upon the parent's right to choose the child-rearing practices he or she wishes, including reasonable corporal punishment. Third, child abuse and neglect should be treated as criminal matters to be dealt with in regular courts, where accused persons have the full range of due process and other constitutional rights. I said that due process guarantees should be established by statute for persons involved in any related matters that are indeed more appropriately dealt with in juvenile court. For example, noncriminal neglect should perhaps receive

91. On these points, see Joseph Goldstein, Anna Freud, and Albert Solnit, *Beyond the Best Interests of the Child* (New York: Free Press, 1973), 25, 72–74; Besharov, "'Doing Something,'" 586; Chill, "Burden of Proof Begone," 457, 462.

a hybrid status under the law—not a criminal matter, but no longer treated as a civil matter—but with the accused person's constitutional rights fully protected. I insisted that part of the reform in this area should include permitting accused persons to waive confidentiality in child abuse proceedings; sometimes the very thing needed to protect rights and guard against state abuse is the watchful eye of the public. Also, strict requirements should have to be met before state agencies can remove children from their homes. Children should not be removed, even temporarily, unless authorities can *conclusively* prove in a proceeding before an impartial judge that they are in danger. In the case of emergency removals, authorities should have to supply this proof to a judge within twenty-four hours or automatically be required to return the child. Actually, I said, perhaps Pride made an even more preferable proposal: simply remove the *perpetrator*, as would be done with any criminal offense. I also said that government agencies should not be allowed to retain records of unsubstantiated or false complaints. The statutory changes of recent decades that have permitted the admission into court of hearsay evidence and videotaped testimony (and generally give the child the overwhelming benefit of the doubt against the accused) should be repealed; child abuse should be dealt with like any other crime. Next, I called for safeguards to be put in place to insure against manipulation of children by prosecutorial authorities, psychologists, and other interrogators. I said that perhaps besides providing free legal counsel for needy accused persons in child abuse cases,[92] the state should also provide free psychologists and psychiatrists to counter the ones that CPS brings in.[93]

I also said that the laws should be changed to outright discourage and even make it risky for people to file false and malicious child abuse complaints. The laws should require something like probable cause be established before an agency has the authority *even to commence an investigation*. This seemed reasonable because, after all, we are dealing with the natural rights of parents and with an intrusion into the most

92. This was not meant just to include the poor but many middle-class people who simply cannot bear the massive cost of a legal defense in one of these cases.
93. The proposals recounted in this paragraph were in Krason, "Child Abuse," 192–94.

basic human institution, the family, and one of the most intimate of human relationships, that between parent and child. If someone makes a malicious or intentionally false complaint, I said that he should be liable to suit in tort by the accused party. If a person has to face a trial or other legal proceedings as a result of a knowingly false or malicious charge of child abuse and is exonerated, reimbursement of attorney's fees should be permitted. Generally, American law does not allow for this, but exceptions have been made when a person is the victim of some particularly outrageous conduct.[94]

Finally, I insisted on reversing the "one-sided liability" discussed. Social workers and agencies should not be subject to suit or prosecution for non-removal unless their conduct is clearly outrageous and/or in bad faith. I said that they *should* be subject to suits by parents and legal guardians for wrongful removal, but only if they violate legal provisions—presuming the laws would have been tightened up to prevent the easy removals that are now occurring—or act recklessly or maliciously. Local or state prosecutorial authorities should also be subject to suit if they act in such a manner.[95]

So far, no significant trends have emerged to promote the adoption of any of these changes (I did mention changes regarding probable cause). The increasing search and seizure protections are encouraging, and the 2003 CAPTA amendments helpful but limited. Another positive development in certain states has been the enactment of statutory changes that subject to criminal prosecution anyone who knowingly makes a false child abuse/neglect report.[96] The latter probably resulted from the substantial number of false abuse allegations that were being made in child custody battles connected to divorces.[97]

In Scott's book, she lists the following additional sound proposals

94. Krason, "Child Abuse," 194.

95. Krason, "Child Abuse," 194–95.

96. See, e.g., Ohio Rev. Code Annotated, Sec. 2921.14, enacted in 1991. This makes the knowing filing of a false abuse/neglect report a first-degree misdemeanor. It apparently does not apply to mandated reporters.

97. For a discussion of how serious this problem had become, see Pride, *Child Abuse Industry*, 54, 239; Slicker, 16; *US News and World Report* 98 (April 1, 1985): 66. Prior to the adoption of Sec. 2921.14 , the Ohio courts had held that if an ex-spouse made a false report, even knowingly and in bad faith, there was no legal recourse for the accused (*Hartley v. Hartley*, 537 N.E. 2d 706 [1988]).

for change: the required videotaping of all interrogations of children by authorities and the making of these immediately available to the accused; the presence of a friendly adult advocate to be with the child (presumably someone of the parents' choosing) when being questioned; the setting up of independent review boards to hear complaints of the accused (this in some form was done by the 2003 amendments to CAPTA); ensuring that relatives receive the first consideration in a foster care placement if children have been removed from their home, that parents be allowed daily phone calls and visits to children who have been removed, and that if more than one child is removed from a home, they be kept together; the elimination of the routine practice of some agencies of forcing children in every case taken up by the agency to undergo therapy; and the elimination of intrusive searches and physical examinations of alleged child-victims.[98]

All of the above ideas are worth pursuing; they would certainly go some distance toward ending the grave abuses and injustices of the system. I came to the conclusion, however, after a decade more of observation and reflection after that article (and since then my thinking on this has not waivered), that the best course of action is simply to dismantle the current CPS and scrap CAPTA and state laws passed pursuant to it.

I set out the reasons for this in a lengthy article I wrote in 2013 in the book *Child Abuse, Family Rights, and the Child Protective System* (the book was composed of papers at a conference about CPS that was cosponsored by the Society of Catholic Social Scientists and the Catholic Social Workers National Association). I said that CPS is conceptually and structurally incapable of carrying out its self-proclaimed purpose. Its basic problem is that it is a therapeutic system—although *coercively therapeutic*. Its structuring and the very nature of that kind of system suggests the following drawbacks: (1) it sees true child maltreatment too much as a condition to be remedied by treatment, instead of a moral evil and criminal act to be punished; (2) while it commendably believes in prevention, it wrongly believes that state action can universally bring that about without also creating

---

98. Scott, *Out of Control*, 183–84.

universal regimentation and a monstrous tyranny; (3) it is routinely manned by people whose education and training has not made them particularly sympathetic to the family or aware of its basic, natural, and irreplaceable value; (4) the confusion among CPS operatives about what constitutes child maltreatment also reflects their training in contemporary relativistic social science with its ever-changing notions, theories, and even definitions for words (so, even with more precise legal definitions of abuse and neglect, we could expect CPAs would still find grounds to infringe on legitimate parental actions); (5) it is beleaguered by the rigidities, limitations, self-interestedness/self-protectiveness, and inanities of bureaucratic institutions everywhere; (6) it is beset by the basic contradiction of providing social services and assistance on the one hand and being an enforcement arm on the other—and not only are social workers not trained for the latter, but also help and coercion do not readily go together under the same institutional roof; and (7) a specialized agency, with a particular focus, often goes to an extreme in carrying out its mission. It tends to see problems where they do not exist and overemphasizes the significance of those that it finds. It easily loses its sense of balance, and that tendency is not moderated by additional perspectives or factors that otherwise would come into play.[99]

In short, what I have shown about CPS is that it does not know clearly what it is supposed to stop. A big percentage of what it investigates is nothing that needs to be investigated in the first place. It ends up hurting children with its interventions supposedly on their behalf and even sometimes fails to stop true cases of maltreatment. It is inattentive to parental rights, its failures have been ongoing and consistent, and its attempt to monitor and control vast numbers of people in the minutest of details about how they conduct their lives and raise their children is more than a touch of totalitarianism. It is difficult to conclude that such a system should be continued.

99. See Stephen M. Krason, "The Mondale Act and Its Aftermath: An Overview of Forty Years of American Law, Public Policy, and Governmental Response to Child Abuse and Neglect," in *Child Abuse, Family Rights, and the Child Protective System: A Critical Analysis from Law, Ethics, and Catholic Social Teaching*, ed. Stephen M. Krason (Lanham, MD: Scarecrow Press, 2013), 60–61.

In my judgment, the entire matter simply ought to be turned over to the criminal law and dealt with by current or expanded statutes concerning murder, assault, rape, statutory rape, incest, and the like. Carefully drafted criminal child neglect statutes—spelling out *clearly and unambiguously* what the proscribed offenses are, and not including anything resulting from poverty or disadvantage or concerning reasonable parental educational choices—ought to be added to address this aspect of the problem. It must be remembered that this is the primary way the law dealt with child maltreatment for most of American history, and there has been no evidence proving that it was not adequate. Moreover, besides their stronger investigative skills, law enforcement personnel tend not to have been schooled in the intellectual environment of academic social work and related fields that is laced with an anti-parental authority and anti-traditional family ideology and the ethos of "we 'experts' know better." There have been abuses by law enforcement agencies in this area to be sure, but they would likely be diminished if their personnel were no longer trained in this area by the CPS and if there were not cooperative interagency arrangements such as those seen in the current child advocacy center movement through which the "CPS perspective" is disseminated.[100]

100. Child advocacy centers began in the mid-1980s. What they seek to do is to better coordinate the efforts of the CPS, the law enforcement and criminal justice community, and medical and mental health professionals to deal with child abuse. The National Children's Advocacy Center (NCAC) in Alabama trains professionals from around the United States and other countries to, it says, learn "how to recognize and support endangered children" (see the National Children's Advocacy Center website, accessed March 8, 2012, http://www.nationalcac .org/history/history.html. Various local communities around the country have these centers, which provide such training on a localized level and say they aim to help children who allegedly have been abused to not be also "victimized" by the system investigating and dealing with abuse (e.g., by having children interrogated by a CPA, and then law enforcement, and then health care providers in intimidating surroundings, etc.) and also to ameliorate a coordinated agency response to the alleged abuse and facilitate the provision of various therapeutic and other services to the children. Some of the subjects that the child advocacy centers (CACs) are concerned about—as judged, say, from the NCAC's spring 2012 National Symposium on Child Abuse—indicate a focus on some legitimate traditional moral questions that indeed involve or can lead to child maltreatment, such as child pornography and pornography generally, sex trafficking, sex tourism, sexual experimentation among children, and illicit drug use. The dominance of child welfare professionals and child abuse prosecutors and the absence of parental rights advocates among the speakers and the NCAC's seeming ready acceptance of such problematical legal developments as permitting young child witnesses in cases—which, as noted, contravened traditional criminal law practices—makes one think that the CACs essentially

Ending the current laws and system would also largely overcome the vagueness about what abuse and neglect and all related categories are, and help ensure that the law would only treat as abuse or neglect actions or omissions which the community—and common sense—widely regard as such. It would also, correspondingly, guarantee that families are not targeted for innocent or trivial actions. It would get the state out of the business—for which it has no competency—of dictating to parents preferred methods of child-rearing. Further, all of the usual constitutional protections would also almost automatically attach.

---

espouse the mindset of the CPS. This is further reinforced when one goes to the websites of various local CACs, which feature some of the typical CPS claims that this chapter has shown are questionable or false: intrafamily sexual abuse crosses—and implicitly is equally prevalent within—all socioeconomic groupings; one in three females and one in four males experience sexual abuse before age 18; spanking is bad for children; genuine physical abuse of children is common; children rarely lie about abuse; aggressive or disruptive behavior, or passive, withdrawn, or emotionless behavior, or frequent urinary tract or yeast infections are signs of abuse (of course, they are more typically signs of things that have nothing to do with abuse). See, e.g., the websites of CAC of Springfield, Missouri, http://www.childadvocacycenter.org/about -child-abuse.php; Athens County, Ohio, CAC, http://www.athenscac.org/; Dallas Children's Advocacy Center, http://www.dcac.org/reportingchildabuse.aspx, all accessed March 8, 2012. The website of the National Children's Alliance, which accredits CACs, claims that in 2009, 763,000 American children were determined to be victims of abuse or neglect. That would be a substantiation rate of 23 percent, whereas, as we have seen, HHS data indicate that it is only 14 percent. It correctly says that most of the substantiated cases were for neglect but says nothing about how most of these were actually poverty matters. It also claims that many entirely innocent child behaviors are signs of abuse. See the website of National Children's Alliance, accessed March 8, 2012, http://www.nationalchildrensalliance.org/.

13

Parental Rights in the United States and Internationally

The Right to Determine the Values Taught to One's Child

MICHAEL FARRIS

The natural right of parents to direct the upbringing of their children is universally recognized as a protected interest.[1] Perhaps the best evidence for this proposition comes from the United Nations' nearly unanimous adoption of the Universal Declaration of Human Rights (UDHR),[2] which contains the following provision: "Parents have

1. Both the International Covenant on Civil and Political Rights as well as the International Covenant on Economic, Social and Cultural Rights contain express protections for the protection of parental rights. The ICCPR has been joined by 173 state parties. The ICESCR has 171 state parties. Of the 100 most populous nations (population >8.5 million), only 4 are parties to neither of these treaties: Cuba, Malaysia, Saudi Arabia, and United Arab Emirates.

2. The vote was 48 in favor, 0 opposed; eight nations abstained. The eight included the Soviet Union and five of its satellite nations, South Africa (the racial equality provisions of the UDHR were unacceptable), and Saudi Arabia (objections to the right to change one's religion

a prior right to choose the kind of education that shall be given to their children" (Article 26(3)). Although a general support for parental rights may be legitimately inferred from Article 16(3), "The family is the natural and fundamental group unit of society and is entitled to protection by society and the State," it is the right of parents in education that was singled out for strong protection in the UDHR.

As is often the case, there was a historical reason for the special attention given to the protection of the right of parents to choose a form of education consistent with the values of the family. The UDHR was generally adopted in response to the atrocities committed by the German government under the National Socialist Party of the Third Reich. The provision on parental rights in education was no exception.

Hitler's educational program received considerable emphasis and was integral in his long-range dreams of domination, as his words indicate.

In my great educative work, I am beginning with the young. We older ones are used up. Yes, we are old already. We are rotten to the marrow. We have no un-restrained instincts left. We are bearing the burden of a humiliating past and have in our blood the dull recollection of serfdom and servility. But my magnificent youngsters! Are there finer ones anywhere in the world? Look at these young men and boys! What material! With them I can make a new world.[3]

Racial studies was a "new subject that formed an integral part of the curriculum under National Socialism."[4] In fact, any traditional subject that got in the way of Nazi indoctrination was to be abandoned. A Nazi directive of 1940 explained the approach:

It is *not* the task of the elementary school to impart a multiplicity of knowledge for the personal use of the individual. It has to develop and harness all physical and mental powers of youth for the service of the people and the state. Therefore, the only subject that has any place in the school curriculum is that which is necessary to achieve this aim. All other subjects, springing from obsolete educational ideas, must be discarded.[5]

and to equal rights for women). Honduras and Yemen, member states of the UN, failed to either vote or to abstain.
3. Lisa Pine, *Education in Nazi Germany* (New York: Berg, 2010), 1.
4. Pine, *Education in Nazi Germany*, 57.
5. Quoted in Pine, *Education in Nazi Germany*, 41.

Similarly, the Soviet Union viewed the public schools as a key component of its long-range program. It was clear that "inculcating in children a true sense of collectivism is a major goal of Soviet education [and] second is ensuring that children are brought up with an appropriate set of attitudes about labor."[6] Lisa Pine concludes her seminal work on Nazi education with the following observation: "An understanding of education in the Third Reich illustrates the dangers of political ideology determining which subjects are taught in schools and how they are taught."[7]

Realistically, there are only two possible answers to the question, Who decides how children should be educated? The Nazis and Soviets determined that the state should make that decision. Both regimes used their public education system intentionally with the goal of forming the child's worldview in a manner acceptable to the state. The rest of the world, in reaction to the evils of totalitarianism, strongly endorsed the alternative: Parents should decide the schools for their children and the philosophy that should be taught.

The US Supreme Court had long recognized the rights of parents to direct the upbringing of their children, particularly in the area of education. When Oregon sought to ban private education so that all children would be put in the melting pot of the public schools for the express purpose of molding their values and beliefs to be that of "true Americans," the High Court held such a goal to be contrary to constitutional protections and American values:

The fundamental theory of liberty upon which all governments in this Union repose excludes any general power of the State to standardize its children by forcing them to accept instruction from public teachers only. The child is not the mere creature of the State; those who nurture him and direct his destiny have the right, coupled with the high duty, to recognize and prepare him for additional obligations.[8]

6. Jonathan Tudge, "Education of Young Children in the Soviet Union: Current Practice in Historical Perspective," *Elementary School Journal* 92, no. 1 (1991): 131.

7. Pine, *Education in Nazi Germany*, 140.

8. *Pierce v. Society of Sisters*, 268 U.S. 510, 535 (1925).

The court went further when, in the 1940s, the state of West Virginia sought to expel Jehovah's Witness children from the public school for refusing to recite the pledge of allegiance to the flag.

Of the many important proclamations from the court in *West Virginia v. Barnette*, two stand out as especially relevant for our consideration:

> As governmental pressure toward unity becomes greater, so strife becomes more bitter as to whose unity it shall be. Probably no deeper division of our people could proceed from any provocation than from finding it necessary to choose what doctrine and whose program public educational officials shall compel youth to unite in embracing. Ultimate futility of such attempts to compel coherence is the lesson of every such effort from the Roman drive to stamp out Christianity as a disturber of its pagan unity, the Inquisition, as a means to religious and dynastic unity, the Siberian exiles as a means to Russian unity, down to the fast-failing efforts of our present totalitarian enemies. Those who begin coercive elimination of dissent soon find themselves exterminating dissenters. Compulsory unification of opinion achieves only the unanimity of the graveyard.[9]

The *Barnette* decision was grounded on broad principles that applied to all parents and all children—not merely those with particular religious scruples.[10] And the breadth of the protection was not limited to particular subjects in which the government might seek to coerce uniformity of viewpoint.

> If there is any fixed star in our constitutional constellation, it is that no official, high or petty, can prescribe what shall be orthodox in politics, nationalism, religion, or other matters of opinion, or force citizens to confess by word or act their faith therein. If there are any circumstances which permit an exception, they do not now occur to us.[11]

There are two principles that we can distill from what we have considered to this point. First, any government that seeks to use the public schools to indoctrinate children in its preferred worldview employs the recognized tools and tactics of totalitarian governments. Second,

9. 319 U.S. 624 (1943).
10. 319 U.S. at 634–635.
11. 319 U.S. at 642.

any government engaged in this practice violates universal norms of the right of parents to determine the moral and general worldview of their children's education.

Parental rights deal with a host of substantive issues beyond education—medical care, religious upbringing, disciplinary choices, and much more. And parents have procedural rights for various components of due process if an agency of government seeks to remove custody of a child from a parent. But I would respectfully suggest that the ultimate and most dangerous invasions of parental authority involve government efforts to impose the government's preferred worldview or moral philosophy upon all children. If governments possess the power of coerced indoctrination of children, little is left of the family's true purpose and scope. And little remains of freedom for any citizen of any age. Governments that seek to indoctrinate children are always tyrannical. Even if such governments are not yet tyrannical in every function, coerced indoctrination is the very essence of tyranny and, at the same time, the gateway to an increasing scope of soul-numbing oppression.

Current Conflicts in the United States

The reports coming out of the school systems of Portland, Oregon, and its suburbs are simply terrifying. Children are being taught the narrative that America is fundamentally evil and the rioters who continue to wreak havoc on that once-beautiful, quiet city are held up as heroes. As Christopher Rufo has reported, "the schools have self-consciously adopted the 'pedagogy of the oppressed' as their theoretical orientation, activated through a curriculum of critical race theory and enforced through the appointment of de facto political officers within individual schools." And it is working. The schools have become, Rufo notes, "a school to radicalism pipeline."[12]

But it is not just in radicalized Portland or Seattle where these forces hold sway. In my own home county of Loudoun County, Virginia, the radicals have seized control and have no apparent misgivings as

---

12. Christopher F. Rufo, "The Child Soldiers of Portland," *City Journal* (Spring 2021): https://www.city-journal.org/critical-race-theory-portland-public-schools.

they spin in a radical direction that is leaving a sizeable portion of our community gasping at the sheer audacity of their tactics and shuddering at the implications for the future of our community and our nation should they succeed. The Loudoun County School District suspended teacher Tanner Cross for having the audacity to speak for one minute at a recent school board meeting in opposition to a proposed sexual/political mandate.

One Black mother in Beachwood, Ohio, confronted that district's all-white and all-woke school board with a stinging denouncement of critical race theory. She said to the board concerning an official district policy:

Your stated goal is to make children advocates—I mean activists—in their own home. What does that mean? You are creating an atmosphere trying to create an adversarial relationship between parents and child, when that relationship needs to be strengthened. You're intrinsically advocating the kids to just be adversarial to their parents. It's nuts. This is nuts![13]

The efforts of progressive education advocates to supplant the views of parents is not limited to their control of public schools. Many have taken dead aim at the homeschooling movement.

Catherine Ross teaches constitutional law at George Washington University and is the coauthor of a treatise on family law. Her opinion of parental rights is as follows:

Many liberal political theorists argue ... that there are limits to tolerance. In order for the norm of tolerance to survive across generations, society need not and should not tolerate the inculcation of absolutist views that undermine toleration of difference. Respect for difference should not be confused with approval for approaches that would splinter us into countless warring groups. Hence an argument that tolerance for diverse views and values is a foundational principle does not conflict with the notion that the state can and should limit the ability of intolerant homeschoolers to inculcate hostility to difference in their children—at least during the portion of the day they claim to devote to satisfying the compulsory schooling requirement.[14]

13. Daily Wire, "Must watch: Black mother rips all-white school board," Facebook, May 27, 2021, https://www.facebook.com/DailyWire/videos/must-watch-black-mother-rips-all-white-school-board-for-teaching-critical-race-t/938685763598306/.

14. Catherine Ross, "Fundamentalist Challenges to Core Democratic Values: Exit and Homeschooling," *William and Mary Bill of Rights Journal* 18 (May 2010).

Kimberly Yuracko is the former dean of Northwestern University School of Law. She agrees with Ross:

Virtually absent from the debate has been any discussion of the extent to which a liberal society should condone or constrain homeschooling, particularly as practiced by religious fundamentalist families explicitly seeking to shield their children from liberal values of sex equality, gender role fluidity and critical rationality.[15]

Yuracko further contends that the Constitution requires states to regulate homeschooling to achieve "a minimum education." This constitutional norm imposes a duty on the state "to ensure that children receive a liberal multicultural education that promotes at least minimal autonomy." Her analysis cites neither a constitutional text nor any case law as claimed justification for the existence of this alleged norm.[16]

Martha Albert Fineman, professor of law at Emory University, stakes out an ultimate solution for the problem posed by Christian home education. She wants to ban all private education. "Perhaps the more appropriate suggestion for our current educational dilemma is that public education should be mandatory and universal." She wrote that "parents or private schools unfairly impose hierarchical or oppressive beliefs on their children."[17]

Professor Elizabeth Bartholet of Harvard made national news as the subject of an article in the June edition of the *Harvard* magazine, which featured, ironically, an illustration of a homeschooled child locked in a home with bars. Its exterior walls were constructed of books, one of which, ironically, was a mathematics book (although the Harvard illustrators and editors didn't notice that the artist misspelled "arithmetic").

The article was a summary of a much longer article Bartholet published in the *Arizona Law Review* earlier in 2020. Her article is a fron-

15. Kimberly Yuracko, *Education Off the Grid: Constitutional Constraints on Homeschooling*, Northwestern Public Law Research Paper No. 07 (Evanston, IL: Northwestern University School of Law, 2007), http://dx.doi.org/10.2139/ssrn.1016778.

16. Yuracko, *Education Off the Grid.*

17. Martha Fineman and Karen Worthington, *What Is Right for Children? The Competing Paradigms of Religion and Human Rights* (Burlington, VT: Ashgate, 2009), 237.

tal attack on homeschooling based on a classical straw man argument. Before I dismantle her straw man, let me get to the heart of her motivation. Here is what she says about Christian homeschoolers:

These parents are committed to homeschooling largely because they reject mainstream, democratic culture and values and want to ensure that their children adopt their own particular religious and social views. Many belong to fundamentalist religious groups, [who believe] "that exposing their children to ideas such as secularism, atheism, feminism, and value relativism is inconsistent with the values they espouse anundermines their ability to inculcate in their children their beliefs in the sacred, absolute truth of the Bible." ... many religious homeschoolers object in principle to some core goals of public education.[18]

Apparently, secularism, atheism, feminism, and value relativism are among the core goals of public education. A different phrase from Bartholet deserves further attention. She says that Christian parents "want to ensure that their children adopt their own particular religious and social views."[19] It is highly likely that Bartholet would describe herself as a secularist, atheist, feminist, and believer in value relativism. So, in short, she wants Christian kids to be taught her values in school rather than the values of their parents.

International Efforts to Control the Minds of Children

In England, official inspectors from the state-run British Office for Standards in Education (OFSTED) are reported to have asked intrusive and inappropriate questions of children at schools across the United Kingdom. At Grindon Hall Christian School, inspectors asked young school children "if they knew what lesbians did" and whether "any of their friends felt trapped in the wrong body."[20]

---

18. Elizabeth Bartholet, "Homeschooling: Parent Rights Absolutism vs. Child Rights to Education and Protection," *Arizona Law Review* 62, no. 1 (2020): 11.

19. Bartholet, "Homeschooling."

20. Nicola Woolcock, "Do You Know What Lesbians Do, Ofsted Asked 10 Year Olds," *The Times*, January 14, 2015, https://www.thetimes.co.uk/article/do-you-know-what-lesbians-do-ofsted-asked-10-year-olds-v9zlnqom7xc.

The Scottish government was forced to withdraw its "named person" scheme after the UK Supreme Court ruled that parts of it violated human rights law. The scheme would have required that every child, from birth until age 18, have appointed for him or her an external "named person" other than his or her parents as a clear point of contact responsible for their "wellbeing."[21]

In Germany, Kindergartens (which teach children ages 3 to 6) have faced significant criticism over the past decade regarding the implementation of "naked play."[22] It was originally implemented with the view of encouraging children to become "acquainted and comfortable with their bodies," but soon children began behaving inappropriately, even harassing younger children.[23] There is also a push for a specific type of further education[24] for those who work at Kindergartens to implement teaching on the benefits of "naked play" and "sexual education at a young age."

At the UN level, the International Guidelines on Sexuality Education were published by UNESCO.[25] According to the guidelines, children aged 5 to 8 should be taught that "bodies can feel good when touched" (48) and that "touching and rubbing one's genitals is called masturbation." Updated guidance from 2018 (International Technical Guidance on Sexuality Education)[26] calls on 9- to 12-year-olds to "demonstrate respect for the gender identity of others" (50) and to "identify cultural, religious or social beliefs and practices related to sexuality that have changed over time" (48).

21. "Named Person Scheme Scrapped by Scottish Government," *BBC News*, September 19, 2019, https://www.bbc.com/news/uk-scotland-scotland-politics-49753980.

22. "12 Kinder rausgeworfen: Doktorspiele in Kita laufen aus dem Ruder," *RTL*, February 21, 2019, https://www.rtl.de/cms/12-kinder-rausgeworfen-doktorspiele-in-kita-laufen-aus-dem-ruder-4297391.html.

23. Friederike Steensen and Nicole Demmer, "Sexuelle Übergriffe von Kindern in der Kita: Eine Geschichte von Angst und Vorwürfen," *Hessische Niedersächsische Allgemeine*, February 11, 2017, https://www.hna.de/lokales/witzenhausen/witzenhausen-ort44473/sexuelle-uebergriffe-kindern-kita-eine-geschichte-angst-vorwuerfen-7384060.html.

24. Danilo Ziemen, "Mehr Als Doktorspielchen: Sexualerziehung in der Kita," *Frühe Bildung Online*, July 13, 2018, https://fruehe-bildung.online/kita/paedagogische-praxis/mehr-als-doktorspielchen-sexualerziehung-in-der-kita.

25. UNESCO, *International Guidelines on Sexuality Education* (Paris: UNESCO, 2009), https://reliefweb.int/sites/reliefweb.int/files/resources/8556521DD9D4A9E6492576200024012 0-UNESCO-Aug2009.pdf.

26. UNESCO, *International Technical Guidance on Sexuality Education* (Paris: UNESCO, 2018), https://www.unfpa.org/sites/default/files/pub-pdf/ITGSE.pdf.

In the context of homeschooling, many European nations are in clear violation of the International Covenant on Economic, Social and Cultural Rights (ICESCR), International Covenant on Civil and Political Rights (ICCPR), and the UDHR by their open refusal to permit parents to choose homeschooling in conformity with their religious and moral beliefs. Germany effectively bans homeschooling because of its fear of parallel societies—which really means that they are afraid of people who think and believe differently from government-sanctioned views. It does not appear to be an effective method of combatting Islamic extremism, but it has been effective in making the lives of serious Christian families so untenable that leaving the country is the only viable option for many people.

Much of Europe takes a similar approach to homeschooling. President Macron has threatened to severely limit homeschooling in France.

The relatively recent decision of the European Court of Human Rights in the *Wunderlich*[27] case gives insight into official antipathy toward home education. This case officially involved a challenge to the legitimacy of the removal of the Wunderlich children—as opposed to a more direct consideration of the right to home educate itself. In the end, however, the court's decision contains a blend of the two issues. It begins with the helpful principle that children cannot be removed from parents merely because there might be some improvement in the circumstances of the child. Rather, the government must show that there is some necessity that warrants the removal.

The "necessity" for removing the Wunderlich children, the court believed, arose from the government's interest in compulsory education. The court said that Germany's goal "in introducing such a system, had aimed at ensuring the integration of children into society with a view to avoiding the emergence of parallel societies, considerations that were in line with the court's own case-law on the importance of pluralism for democracy." This reasoning may have a lilting melody and beautiful harmony, but the lyrics of this song simply don't make sense.

Pluralism does not mean homogenization. It means that a soci-

27. *Wunderlich v. Germany* (no. 18925/15).

ety welcomes those who think and act differently. A parallel society is one that does not accept all of the premises of the current mainstream trends, but it is parallel, not perpendicular, to the mainstream of society.

Finding a Remedy

In the 1940 decision of *Cantwell v. Connecticut*,[28] the Supreme Court proclaimed that the Free Exercise Clause "embraces two concepts— freedom to believe and freedom to act. The first is absolute, but in the nature of things, the second cannot be." It is my contention that worldview indoctrination affects the right to believe far more than it affects the freedom to act. This is corroborated, I believe, by the statement in *Barnette*, that the government is prohibited from ever determining what is orthodox in matters of opinion on any subject and forcing conformity to such orthodoxy. Although I would resist ever using international law as a mechanism for interpreting the Constitution, it is instructive to note just how highly parental rights in education are held in international law.

The right of parents to ensure that their children will receive an education in accordance with their own beliefs is found in Article 18(4). Article 4 contains a general rule concerning when rights contained in this treaty may be overridden: "In time of public emergency which threatens the life of the nation and the existence of which is officially proclaimed, the States Parties to the present Covenant may take measures derogating from their obligations under the present Covenant to the extent strictly required by the exigencies of the situation, provided that such measures are not inconsistent with their other obligations under international law and do not involve discrimination solely on the ground of race, colour, sex, language, religion or social origin."

That's a pretty tough standard. Only existential threats to the nation qualify, and there are strict limits. But Article 4(2) says that this exception does not apply to the rights protected in seven different articles. These rights are called non-derogable rights. So, even if the very existence of the nation is at stake—a finding that would seem to al-

---

28. *Cantwell v. Connecticut*, 310 U.S. 296, 60 S. Ct. 900; 84 L. Ed. 1213; 1940 U.S.

ways satisfy the compelling interest standard—then these seven rights may not be violated. One of the articles listing non-derogable rights is Article 18, which contains the section protecting the parental right to choose an education in conformity to their own values and morals. We are in rarified territory when we talk about the right of parents to protect their children from compelled government indoctrination in a contrary worldview.

Potential Solutions

In a recent speech, former U.S. Attorney General William Barr argued that the indoctrination going on in the public schools has gotten so egregious that it possibly violates the Establishment Clause of the First Amendment. Such an argument could be brought along with both free exercise and parental rights claims to argue that a constitutional violation exists and that a remedy must be afforded. One possible remedy would be to require the removal of worldview indoctrination programs from the public school. This is something under active consideration in many state legislatures. And litigation is beginning to percolate in this area seeking this kind of relief.

Perhaps a more likely remedy would be to impose on offending districts a program of educational choice where any parent objecting to such indoctrination could take the full share of public funding for their children and transfer that money to the school of their choice. The educational choice line of cases seems open for this development. But it would be a third stage of litigation that affects this area.

The first stage was securing a ruling from the Supreme Court that including religious schools in a broad, neutral program of educational choice did not violate the Establishment Clause. This rule was first announced in *Mueller v. Allen*[29] and made even more secure by the unanimous victory in *Witters v. Washington Department of Services for the Blind*[30] (which I argued before the Supreme Court). In *Witters*

---

29. *Mueller v. Allen*, 463 U.S. 388, 103 S. Ct. 3062; 77 L. Ed. 2d 721; 1983 U.S.

30. *Witters v. Washington Department of Services for the Blind*, 474 U.S. 481, 106 S. Ct. 748; 88 L. Ed. 2d 846.

the court ruled that even when the educational choice was being exercised to attend a Bible college to study to enter the ministry, there was no Establishment Clause violation so long as the program taken as a whole is neutral toward religion. Thus it is impossible to successfully argue that any future form of educational choice involves schools that are "too religious to qualify."

The next stage was the holding that when states do operate programs with general benefits for schools outside of those operated by the government, it violates the Free Exercise and Equal Protection principles to exclude religious schools from such programs. The first ruling in this regard was *Trinity Lutheran Church of Colombia, Inc. v. Comer*[31] (a case argued by the organization I lead, Alliance Defending Freedom), involving a preschool playground safety program. Following that victory, the Supreme Court applied the *Trinity Lutheran* rule to a broad educational choice program for K–12 education in Montana. In *Espinosa v. Montana*[32] the court held that the Montana constitution's Blaine Amendment, which prohibited funding for religious schools under any circumstances, was likewise a violation of the Free Exercise Clause.

It is a short but important step to extend this line of cases to situations where educational choice is not offered by the legislature. Funding a public school system that violates the Establishment Clause, Free Exercise Clause, or parental rights would seem to be a sufficient basis for the courts to hold that educational choice is a constitutional mandate.

It is my firm belief that we now stand in a moment when parental rights in education will either disappear or be significantly enhanced. The outcome will depend to a considerable degree on the willingness of those who believe in parental rights to stand up and do something about it.

---

31. *Trinity Lutheran Church of Colombia, Inc. v. Comer*, 582 U.S. ___, 137 S. Ct. 2012; 198 L. Ed. 2d 551; 2017 U.S.
32. *Espinosa v. Montana*, 591 U.S. ___, 140 S. Ct. 2246; 207 L. Ed. 2d 679.

Contributors

GEORGE ASH, EDD, is associate professor of graduate education and chairman of the Education Department at Franciscan University of Steubenville.

ALLAN C. CARLSON, PHD, is president emeritus of the Howard Center for Family, Religion, and Society.

MICHELLE CRETELLA, MD, is executive director of the American College of Pediatricians.

MICHAEL P. DONNELLY, ESQ., is senior counsel and director of global outreach at the Home School Legal Defense Association.

PATRICK FAGAN, PHD is director of the Marriage and Family Research Institute at the Catholic University of America.

MICHAEL FARRIS, ESQ., is president of the Alliance Defending Freedom.

ALLISON FOLMAR, ESQ., is a civil rights attorney in Detroit, Michigan.

MARY RICE HASSON, ESQ., is the Kate O'Beirne Fellow in Catholic Studies at the Ethics and Public Policy Center.

ANNE HENDERSHOTT, PHD, is professor of sociology and director of the Veritas Center for Ethics in Public Life at Franciscan University of Steubenville.

CHUCK KOKIKO, EDD is superintendent of the Jefferson County (Ohio) Educational Service Center.

STEPHEN M. KRASON, ESQ., PHD, is professor of political science and legal studies at Franciscan University of Steubenville and president of the Society of Catholic Social Scientists.

PATRICK LEE, PHD, is professor of philosophy and director of the Center for Bioethics, Franciscan University of Steubenville.

JAMES R. MASON, ESQ., is president of the Parental Rights Foundation (ParentalRights.org).

CATHY RUSE, ESQ., is with the Dominion Law Group.

Index